PRAISE

Going through each of the business leaders' sections and seeing their many commonalities, I also discovered nuances and nuggets of guidance in every one that makes this book a very rich read. For people looking for mentoring ideas or just interested in optimizing their business operations, this book is highly recommended.

Helen Feber, CCAP III | managing partner, Referential, Inc.

What a great way to gain some insights into mentoring! Whether a leader is conscious of it or not, they are always serving as mentors to those who work with them and for them. Just as a parent is always setting examples, good or bad, for their children, leaders are doing the same. Formal mentorship programs are, no doubt, of value. But even informal ones, as I've engaged in (usually subconsciously), can prove quite valuable.

David D. Spaulding, DPS, CIPM | The Spaulding Group, Inc.

Do yourself a favor and read this collection of essays on how mentors can change the trajectory of business. This book is an easy yet powerful read that illustrates the practices and mindset people embrace to reach the top. You have probably not heard of these leaders, but it doesn't matter—you'll appreciate their insightful road maps on how to stay successful in business for a quarter of a century. It gave me both hope and push to hang in there and make it happen for myself. The seventy-ish interviewees write in a way that many will find inspirational. Get it now!

Mar Ricketts | principal & founder, GuildWorks

Supreme Leadership Mentors is an excellent book that breaks down the principles of mentorship and applies them to the uniqueness of many different types of businesses. It's insightful about the differences between how leaders seek mentorship and apply it to their different brands. Also, it's organized by sections that indicate how each of these "supreme leaders" leaned on the knowledge and experience of those who can before them. This wide variety of CEOs explain how being mentored by friends, family, community, and other business leaders can vary significantly from organization to organization. I plan to seek mentors in the areas suggested after reading about the impact mentors can have. Thank you!

Kathy Stack | president/CEO, Grafx Design and Digital

I have read the entire *Supreme Leadership* series and couldn't wait to purchase another collection of knowledge—and this book did not disappoint. This is a granular look at how the types of mentors can be different, yet their influence on the authors in this book is inspiring. It addresses how to find mentors and comes to a very practical conclusion: you need to find them and be them! This book has helped my team completely refocus and redefine our organization, and it's paying huge dividends. We've set up an internal mentorship structure, and our leaders have actively sought outside mentorship through more active participation in our local clubs and community. Highly recommended!

Tod Sager | president, AWE Tuning

Alinka Rutkowska nails it once again with another deep dive into what makes leaders successful. The authors in this collection share a lifetime of hard-learned lessons for using mentorship to grow themselves as well as their teams and organizations. They effectively show the tremendous value of seeking the advice of others versus going at it on your own. It gave me great, practical ideas on how to improve myself, my team, and my peers by providing insight on how to find and grow with mentors. A must-read for leaders in any business!

Don Zerivitz | president, Pro Clean

I have read all the *Supreme Leadership* books and was waiting for more books. I didn't think I needed a mentor, but I read this collection of interviews, and it was a pleasant delight! This book expanded my thinking around mentors specific to how to find them, which is pretty much everywhere. Examples include professional organizations,

SUPREME LEADERSHIP MENTORS

TOP ENTREPRENEURS' GREATEST BUSINESS STRATEGIES

ALINKA RUTKOWSKA

Copyright © 2020 Alina A. Rutkowska

All rights reserved. Published in the United States by Leaders Press, www.leaderspress.com

No part of this book may be reproduced or transmitted in any form or by any means, electronic or mechanical, including photocopying, recording, or by an information storage and retrieval system—except by a reviewer who may quote brief passages in a review to be printed in a magazine or newspaper—without permission in writing from the publisher.

1. Leadership. 2. Business communication. I Rutkowska, Alinka. II. Title.
ISBN 978-1-943386-76-5 (pbk)
ISBN 978-1-943386-75-8 (ebook)
Library of Congress Control Number: 2020932527

family members, religious organizations, local groups, and leaders from previous places of employment. The anecdotes in the book are helpful and practical. I would recommend this book to anyone who want to discover how mentorship can improve their organization.

Tom Fedro | co-founder, Paragon Software Corp.

We used *Supreme Leadership Mentors* as a precursor to our strategic planning process. It was very helpful in generating ideas for mentorship for the planning process. Our team members were instructed to read the book and come prepared with their preferred avenue to find mentors: internally, externally, family, friends, or community. From that planning process, we put in place several new concepts to help our team grow and have achieved phenomenal success. Although reading all the *Supreme Leadership* books is the best way to get the most out of learning from peers, this book is a great tool to lead us in a journey with mentorship.

Ali Razi | founder & CEO, Banc Certified Merchant Services

A great read for those wondering how, or perhaps whom, to leverage for results. As a new company leader, I have often wondered how best to tap the knowledge and experience of those who know more than I do. In my short career, I can now see clearly the many connections in the business world I can utilize to take advice instead of learning the hard lessons. A great book written by leaders to shine the light for the rest of us.

Tony White | president, enChoice

I used this book for a staff retreat discussion to inspire our employees on how to reach out for assistance. This book works well as a basis for discussion, analysis of your organization, and a personal challenge to explore organizational change. You will be inspired to make changes in your organization as it makes for excellent reading and discussion. When seeking ways to maximize your team's potential, this book is a great discussion starter.

Mark Nureddine | CEO, Bull Outdoor Products; best-selling author of *Pocket Mentor*

I have purchased several copies of this book to give out to staff and others I feel will benefit from learning more about mentorship. I am doing this with all the other *Supreme Leadership* books I have purchased. As CEO of my organization, I am always seeking ways to educate my teams. This book has a firm place on my desk now, and I use frequently it as reference on whom I could tap for advice. One side benefit is that this book has inspired my teams to seek guidance from people in their network, which has released the pressure from our internal leaders.

Chris Catranis | CEO, Babylon Telecommunications

This is an excellent primer to give board members and leaders in strategic planning sessions on how to incorporate mentorship into their company structure. Many leaders and board volunteers could benefit from guidance. So this is an inexpensive and fast tutorial that can bring them up to speed prior to a strategic planning program. Several people I've given this book to have been so impressed with the mentorship approach that they've sought assistance from the areas recommended in this book. I greatly enjoyed learning from the peers in this book and look forward to reaching out to a few of them to see if they would be willing to mentor me.

Mary Feury | president, Altec Systems.

ARE YOU A LEADER WITHOUT A BOOK?

Nothing increases your authority and visibility as powerfully as a book.

It's a cash-generating asset that funnels in clients for your business and allows you to tell your story the way you want it to be told.

At Leaders Press (a *Wall Street Journal* bestselling press), we've developed a process that allows you to get your book out without you ever having to write a word.

It's featured in *Entrepreneur* magazine and all our books produced this way are bestsellers!

Discover how you can quickly and painlessly get your book out and put together an extra revenue stream!

Download your free copy of *Outsource Your Book* at www.leaderspress.com now!

Download it for free at www.leaderspress.com

CONTENTS

Introduction xiii

Chapter 1 Family 1
  AiVita Biomedical, Inc., Hans Keirstead.................................. 3
  On Safari Foods, Teresa Carew 15
  Wodify, Ameet Shah 20
  Aurora Fine Chemicals, Alexander Kutyrev...............................26
  Discover Publications, Catherine and Leo Zupan 29
  Infomedia, Jonathan Rubinsztein..36
  Chicwrap, Ian Kaiser 43
  Ingenius Prep, Joel Butterly..49
  Trepwise, Kevin Wilkins..55
  KG+D Architects, PC, Erik Kaeyer 60
  Forward Financing, Justin Bakes 70
  American Business Systems, Adam Phillips 73

Chapter 2 Community 79
  Impact Personnel, Inc., Maryann Donovan.............................81
  CG Environmental Cleaning Guys, Erick McCallum...................87
  AATA International, Inc., John Aronson 94
  Altec Systems, Inc., Mary Feury 103
  Pro Clean Building Maintenance, Inc., Don Zerivitz 109
  Barkhouse, Chris McCurry 114
  Tenon Tours, Katie Fleming.. 122
  OnCourt OffCourt, Joe Dinoffer... 126
  Great Dane Pub & Brewing, Rob Lobreglio 130
  Japan Intercultural Consulting, Rochelle Kopp 134
  Contacts Count, Lynne Waymon.. 140

AOO, David Merrell 144
CEO Coaching International, Mark Moses............................ 148
Scale Capital, Jacopo Bracco.. 152
Oh My Green, Michael Heinrich 156
Aviv Service Today, Ofer Hubar 162
Womply, Cory Capoccia.. 166
Magellan Jets, Joshua Hebert.. 174
Scentered, Sherry Orel 180
Lead Wingman, Tyson McDowell 191

Chapter 3 Coworker 199
Joan Rivers, David Dangle 201
Grafx Design of Tampa, Kathy Stack 207
Alderson Loop, Lauren Asghari 209
G&G Fitness Equipment, Gordon Gronkowski 216
Crofton Bike Doctor, Ernest Freeland 221
Resodyn, Lawrence Farrar 225
KDuncan & Company, Kevin Duncan................................... 229
Lanson B Jones & CO, Michael Allen.................................... 231
Tethers Unlimited, Rob Hoyt 239
Diversified, Kevin Collins 245
Nexceris, Scott Swartz 250
Hawkins Point Partners, Steve Mersky 256
Spain Commercial, Inc., Steve Spain 263
Barlis Wedlick Architects, Alan Barlis 267
Lewis & Clark Ventures, Tom Hillman 271

Chapter 4 Clients 277
Iuvo Technologies, Bryon Beilman 279
Referential, Helen Feber 284
4490 Ventures, Dan Malven.. 289
Lion'esque Group, Melissa Gonzalez..................................... 293
Akendi, Tedde Van Gelderen 300

Chapter 5 Books 307
COO Alliance, Cameron Herold... 309
Hireclout, Avetis Antaplyan 318
Diplomatic Language Services, Jim Bellas.............................. 324
EVR Advertising, Jeff Eisenberg.. 332

Veracity, Angela Hurt 340
The Spaulding Group, David Spaulding 347
Mora Communications Inc., Anthony Mora 353
Addteq, Sukhbir Dhillon 359
Awe Turning, Todd Sager 364

Chapter 6 Reverse Mentoring 373
Passageways, Paroon Chadha 375
Meeting the Challenge, Inc., Kent Kelley 385
Kaleidoscope® Innovation, Matthew Kornau 390
GuildWorks, Mar Ricketts 394
Madison Logic, Tom O'regan 399
Millennium Marketing Solutions, Janice Tippett 403

Conclusion 409

INTRODUCTION

Leadership is never a solo endeavor. (You know, that whole "no human is an island" thing.)

All successful entrepreneurs have advisors who—purposely or inadvertently—influence their habits and path to success.

In fact, mentors can be the most critical asset a top leader can engage to help them navigate the twists and turns of their entrepreneurial journey.

In our bestseller *Supreme Leadership*, we explored the common traits among thirty-four entrepreneurs with more than twenty-five years in business, and we uncovered that our leaders were *like-minded* in the following areas:

- Passion
- Vision
- Adaptability
- Persistence
- Customer-centeredness
- Relationships

But our readers were curious and wanted to know more. Specifically, they wanted to know what to do daily to obtain the kind of success these thirty-four leaders achieved. So *Supreme Leadership Habits* was born when we interviewed another seventy business leaders and explored their daily habits. Remarkably, we found similarities in their *practices* that included the following:

- Childhood entrepreneurship
- Giving versus taking
- Positive habits
- Negative habits
- Morning routine
- Reading and writing

Next, we became curious as to who and what *influences* top leaders. So we spent a year interviewing another batch of seventy entrepreneurs, CEOs, founders, and company presidents, diving deep into their significant influences.

Not surprisingly, we found another pattern and an absolute gem of knowledge—that entrepreneurs know when to ask for help.

So where do they find guidance?

Here are the top six mentor groups that our leaders went to for mentoring:

- Family
- Clients
- Books
- Community
- Coworkers
- Their own mentees

Are you curious to discover how you could be tapping the abundant resources from those around you for information, knowledge, improvement, encouragement, and valuable advice?

Please keep reading to avail yourself of help from short chapters from our next group of seventy seasoned entrepreneurs—that's a whole lot of wisdom!

FAMILY

Our earliest experiences with those around us can have the most profound influence on our careers. We learned from this first group of leaders that it's often our family members that can help us set the stage for our future success. Mothers, fathers, siblings, aunts, uncles, and grandparents can be the guides holding the torch that lights our way.

Perhaps the boundaries set by loved ones are the most influential in helping us develop good habits and wisdom of learning what works and what doesn't. Relatives can offer encouragement and hope as we thread our way through our business lives. Family members can act as trusted advisors and sounding boards, and their guidance was invaluable to the following group of entrepreneurs.

Hans Keirstead
AiVita Biomedical, Inc.
Aivitabiomedical.com

I think that it's fair to say I have made good use of being a leader of a company and made good use of mentors. I learned early on that you need to know thyself—meaning knowing what you don't know and finding mentors who can fill those deficits and gaps.

One thing I've learned from my mentors is that anything is possible. I've had the pleasure of seeing mentors and people around me do the most amazing things—things I thought impossible growing up or even as an adult. It's wonderful that I've had the benefit of knowing their experiences, which seeped into me. My mentors told me what they've done and how they've done it, and what I take from their stories is that you can do anything.

The most significant barrier to doing anything is self-doubt. When you see other people do it, such as your mentors, you know that you can jump on that train and go. In the mentor-mentee relationship, humility is a vital component. As a mentee, you've got to be open to being taught as well as being humbled.

I am a professor with a PhD in neuroscience, and I have to tell you that from hanging out with a lot of professors and medical doctors during my whole career, humility is not a common trait amongst our lot. But I've always had that, and I have to say it's one of the reasons why mentors will teach you. Because if they see you being recalcitrant to their inputs, and if they see a great big wall in front of them, they're not going to bash it down. They've got their battles to fight; they don't need to fight your ego.

At AiVita Biomedical, I have found that mentors have been so impactful on my career that I have decided to become mentor in return. Every year, I have somewhere around eight to fifteen mentees, and the youngest I have now is eleven years old, the oldest being forty.

I have a broad range of individuals, and of course, in the young group, what you're showing them is *what is possible*. You're showing them things like culture. You're showing them something like the type of person that gets into this field.

Scientists can be cool too, and it's great for young people to see that. They think PhDs and MDs are on what I call the pedestal effect: someone out there that you can't even touch. They come in here, and they see in my company that I've got a majority of PhDs and MDs amongst the employees, and they're all ordinary, wacky-quacky people that are driven and silly like everyone else.

When you give them a culture to perform in, like a sandbox to play in where they feel respected and relaxed, they not only become extraordinarily brilliant but also extraordinarily approachable. I love showing that to young people because it completely changes their access. It gets rid of the barrier, and they think, "You know, I can relate to these people. This is nothing special."

Like I was saying with mentors, anything is possible. It shows you that the people doing the big stuff are people too. The only difference is that they think the task is attainable, and most people don't.

A month from now, I've got a group of fifteen high-school students coming in, and some junior-high-school students with whom I'm going to spend a few hours. Often, it's individual, so this past weekend, I was with a woman who has a daughter that blew her away. Her daughter made the top of her class in science but knew nothing about the real world of science. So I said, "Bring her in. Why doesn't she come in for the summer, and I'll have her doing something, even if it's washing dishes in the laboratories? But at least she can hang out with everybody, and then I'll pull her into various activities."

I have a program with my interns where I ship them around from thing to thing, from skill to skill, and then they can learn what they like; and often, perhaps a good third of the time, the interns will find that they don't like it at all. They don't like biotechnology in practice. They don't feel it, and I can relate to that.

I started as a premed in medical school, and I left and did a PhD instead because I didn't like the practical environment of a hospital. It has a lot of negatives for me, and I'm more visionary and hypomanic. I need an environment around me that's breeding positivity, and I found that a hospital, with a lot of sick people in it, weighed me down. It doesn't weigh other people down, but it did me, so I think that there's something to be said for simple exposure.

Let a student of life, or college, be exposed to various things, and they can see that it fits or doesn't. And if it doesn't, well, that's as important as finding something that works. Otherwise, you become an alcoholic professional, and who wants that? So, on the giving side, I make space for interns.

On the taking side, I've joined a CEO self-help group called Young Presidents Organization, and there are a few such organizations, and I think it's essential for people to do that, particularly entrepreneurs.

YPO is a group of individuals that meet for four hours every month, physically, facing one another. Additionally, we hold an event every month with all forty-four of us in this chapter, which gives us time to be around one another. We adopt a code of absolute confidentiality where we can tell each other anything and everything, and there's no advice giving. You have to listen to the speaker and only speak if you have a story or an experience similar or directly bears on theirs.

If somebody's telling the group about a pending divorce, the only people that speak up are people who've been through divorces. If someone's telling the group about a forthcoming bankruptcy, or an IPO, you only speak if you have a story to tell that might benefit the speaker. There's no advice giving such as, "I think you should do this. I think you should do that." It's an excellent forum where you can share everything and get real-life experiences back.

I use YPO a great deal, and it's something I have cherished and to which I have credited a great deal. When joining such organizations, you get to see real-life experiences and get to have, in effect, your board of directors, a group that knows you as an individual but also understands your business.

And you can't tell your senior employees some things. You can't tell them if you're entertaining the thought of selling the company when they're all going to lose their job. You can't tell them that you're thinking of leaving, or you're gone as the founder, originator, CEO, cultural leader.

You can't tell your employees about the money side of it where your compensation may be entirely out of league with theirs, as they may have difficulty with that. So it's nice to have a group of equal professionals with confidentiality that encourages you to share, and you end up realizing that everyone's experiences are similar.

There are a lot of people who have been through IPOs. There's a lot of people who have been through bankruptcies. There's a lot of people who have had problems with their board of directors. They've gone through everything you can imagine. You get a group of ten skilled CEOs around you, and someone there is going to have two or three experiences that directly bear on yours.

The last thing I wanted to say on the mentoring side is to step up. Do a little work. Being an ex-professor at the University of California, Irvine, I did a lot of work with the law school, although I was a professor of neuroscience. I helped entrepreneurs get access to law and legal services. They asked me onto their advisory board, and I ended up setting up an internship program for second and third-year law school students to get out into the community.

I have one in my company, and I told my YPO buddies about this, and a dozen or so have accepted students. The student gets paid, which is wonderful, and they gain experience. Of course, we match them up to the type of industry they think they might like, and they either make a relationship that turns into a job or make a decision that could be, "Oops. I screwed up. I don't want to do the entertainment business," or "I don't want to do neuroscience." It gives them a chance early on to get their feet wet and decide whether they like that area or not. They can go somewhere else. So that type of work is essential, and something that I feel obligated to do as having mentors during my journey was so impactful for me.

The mentor who has had the singularly most significant impact on my life has been my father. He was a senior executive, an executive vice president, of three of the world's top ten big pharmas when I was growing up and didn't know anything about his world. I think he was terribly disappointed that I went to get a PhD in neuroscience rather than become a businessman or a thief. But it turns out my father wasn't successful at business. He went bankrupt. He started, I believe, seven companies that didn't work.

You'd think, Oh, that's a bad mentor. Quite the contrary, as he was a fantastic mentor. He gave me a lot of nuts and bolts on how to get started. What is a board meeting? What are minutes? Why do you need governance? Why do you need this and that and the other thing? He taught me a lot of the structural ABCs of running a business.

Now, why does someone go bankrupt? They make wrong decisions and spend money in the wrong way, perhaps. Maybe back the wrong horse, but it's all about decision making. And so I had the privilege of seeing him and being close to him, as he made both good and bad decisions. It gave me a chance to learn in a way that I think was far superior to merely learning from someone who always made all the right decisions because every single business is different.

There's no common path. There are no two businesses that follow the same trajectory, and that's certainly the case with entrepreneurs. It may be the case with some service industries that you, as a hired-gun CEO, jump into and run them one way, and you'll be successful. But entrepreneurial endeavors are not like that.

I've never seen two stories that are the same, so it's terrific to have the experiences that tell you to think on your feet. It's all about your judgments, and you gain so much value from hearing stories, seeing live the failures and the successes.

Being close to my father and watching a couple of his failures along the way taught me fundamental lessons about decision making and how to preserve wealth within the company and keep the doors open and the lights on a little longer than most. And also about culture, such as how to treat people.

I saw him run companies where the employees had a mission and others where the employees didn't have any. The former proved to be tightly bound as if glued while the latter fled as soon as they had a larger paycheck coming from other competitors. My father taught me to marry culture and mission extraordinarily tightly.

I never read self-help books, and there's one reason for that: I'm a PhD academic. I was an assistant, associate, and then a full professor. In that line of scientific endeavor, you don't have time for anything but the scientific literature. Every day you leave your workplace, you are terribly, terribly behind and bordering on irresponsible for not sticking around for another ten hours to continue reading the literature.

The literature is far greater than any human can ever take in, even in a subspecialty area, so I've dedicated my time to learning the science, and I think that that has made me a better CEO of biotechs that are under $500 million. Over $500 million, I think you do need an administrative CEO, and it's less critical that they know the depths of the science. In biotechs under half of a billion, I feel it's vital that the leader of the company has a profound understanding of the science.

As a scientist, I can tell you that even the technologies and science that I invented, and discovered, hypothesized, and proved can be wrong. Even the closest person to it can be way wrong, and that means your product is dead; or more commonly, that it's going to take longer to work than you thought. And if the CEO doesn't know that it's going to take two years instead of one year, that CEO will kill the company working on a burn rate preparing things for one year to hit a milestone when, in fact, you need two. And that is the most common downfall of biotechnology.

To keep up with all the literature, I have good PhDs under me that I hired specifically for this reason, and I will task them with doing vast amounts of early reading, and then I get updated from them piecemeal. I'll allow them to do a week of reading and then pop in for one hour of my time and have them run me through that week of reading in a short period, like an hour out of forty or fifty hours.

Then I get it compacted, and I discard, discard, discard and keep what I need. I have them do the initial broad scope of the sequence work, and then once I have honed in on the pertinent material, I'll download it myself and get deep on the particular readings.

I've made a good number of mistakes, and you're truly an idiot if you don't learn from your mistakes. The smartest people in the world make mistakes. All you have to do is sit around with a bunch of leaders—like this YPO group I belong to—and listen to stories for a little while, and you'll realize that the success is attributed as often to mistakes as it is to luck, blood, sweat, or tears.

I call it my dark shroud. I tell my senior staff, "Okay, I'm putting on my dark shroud right now," where I'm looking for the death of the company, looking for something that's going to come out of the left field and destroy us. One of the best bits of advice I ever received was from a venture capitalist when he said a straightforward thing, "Raise more money than you need." You hear that all the time, and it's water off a duck's back for an entrepreneur.

He said, "Listen, I've been in this business for thirty-five years, and I've had success with investing, and I've got to tell you that even my best stories, the ones that I made the most money from, the ones that did the most in the world, had the greatest impact on the world, at some point or another, ran out of money. And the difference between the ones that survived and the ones that died was not the leadership. It was not technology. It was having a little bit of money in the bank to weather a storm that you don't see coming."

When I heard that, I thought, "Ah. That, I relate to." Doubt yourself. Put on that dark shroud for a little bit and wonder, "What could take this ship down?" It could be litigation from some other company that you couldn't foresee in a million years. It could be malicious litigation, completely ridiculous, but it's enough to drain your coffers, and then suddenly, you can't make payroll, and your five top people leave. But that dark-shroud type of thinking, understanding why it's essential to raise more money than you need, is crucial. You need to weather the storm sometime, and that's going to protect the best companies—even the ones that are still trying to figure it out—from premature death.

I would say most entrepreneurs have more than they need. So we don't need to give them more ambition. Because they're entrepreneurs, we don't need to provide them with more smarts. That's generally self-selecting for a bunch of bright people. So there's a whole bunch of things I have found: one of the reasons I haven't read a lot of self-help books is that I find so much of it so darn obvious. They're telling a CEO to do things that are just so darn obvious.

I don't have time for the basics. I'm very busy (all entrepreneurs are). But I find that the one thing that most entrepreneurs need is innocent intrigue. They need to maintain that spark that caused them to want to create or build in the first place. They need to keep that spark that moved them away from the security of a nine-to-five paycheck and into completely trepidatious, rocky seas, where your paycheck could disappear at any time. All that you've done could topple over when a bad wave comes along. It's the innocent intrigue that CEOs are born with that brings them to that entrepreneurial journey. But when they lose that innocent intrigue, usually when they start to get good, they get technical and think, "I need to know everything."

And it's true. The CEO does need to know everything. But the trick is knowing how deeply you need to know everything. I, of course, pay a lot of attention to finances, but a CFO for me is my right-hand guy because I get to dump it all and not worry about it. When we meet for our regular finance meeting, I will often go in there and say, "Don't tell me the details. I don't want to know because it's going to bring me down. I want to know how many months of life we have?"

And if he says, "We've got fourteen months," I'm ecstatic. I can do a lot in that period. When does D-Day come along? When do we run out of money? What are our major milestone events with cash coming in or going out? And frequently, that's all I need to know because I am forever nursing my sense of innocent intrigue.

I need to keep it light and exciting because that's where I work best, so I'm always constructing situations around me and sheltering myself from things that bore me. Don't get me wrong—I don't mean that I live in a world of naivete. I will go through finances in excruciating detail, but not all the time.

My advice to new entrepreneurs is to do whatever it takes to keep that innocent intrigue about you. You want to wake up so excited in the middle of the night or close your door and do a silent scream of victory every once in a while. You need to do those things. Otherwise, you're going to become that boring old fart who doesn't go anywhere anymore, the one who doesn't have the push and drive.

There are no outward influences on these things. If you lack your innocent intrigue, nobody wants to be with you. They don't see the energy anymore. They neither see the vibrancy nor the vision.

You've got to protect your time so you can dream and think of the next big thing. You've got to protect your sense of childish wonder. You've got to give yourself the time to do the reading or talking, where nine out of ten of these things is going to be useless, but one is going to be that thing that sparks in you some type of extraordinary endeavor, desire, or push to build the next thing.

You want to deliberately build this fortress of positive energy around yourself. The tricks and tools to do so are that you have to take it lightly. You've got to do it in a way that is structured, and I have a list of them.

I'm amazed that more people don't run their own businesses and become entrepreneurs. It's been a puzzling thing I've experienced all my life with all these people who have worked for me. Why don't they do what I do? Why are they working for me? What's the difference, and what would I tell them?

If I were to write a book, I think my main message would be to tell people to just try. In my career, I've always bitten off the big things. I never could determine whether something is an outrageously big, moderate, or small bite. I see a task in front of me, and I say, "That's cool, let's do it." I have found out over the years, trying as a game to figure out, why I am different and why everybody doesn't want to be an entrepreneur.

I think it's because I believe an entrepreneur can't assess the level of difficulty, and therefore, they jump straight in. When I started developing a company to treat spinal cord injury, there wasn't any sense of "this is an impossible task." Perhaps all the rational people around me were thinking, "Well, that's an impossible task," but because I couldn't see it as impossible, I tried.

Well, the project got underway, and suddenly, I'd developed a treatment for spinal cord injury, and that became Geron Corporation. Then it became Asterias Corporation, and now we have humans that have regained arm and hand movement from receiving my treatment.

Cancer is another thing. I was being interviewed a little while back, and someone asked, "How can you be so brazen? How can you be so egotistical to think that you can do something about cancer?" I don't get angry, but I almost dismissed him and walked out. I thought, "You're an idiot." What if everybody thought, "Oh, that's too big of a thing, and it's egotistical of me to try"? Just shut up and try.

I grew up very poor, and one of the first jobs I made for myself was to run a painting company, Exterior Residential. Of course, I made the largest one of the student things and received an award for North America because I ran the biggest thing and didn't even know it. When you're on the side of a house that's three stories high, facing thousands and thousands of square feet of rough siding, and you've got to sit there with a brush and paint it all, that's something.

What you realize is that it's the drama in your head that stops you from doing the big things. It stops you from asking that person that you're attracted to if they'll have a drink with you and talk to you. It's the drama in your head that stops you from reaching to where your will wants to go.

I had found out that during my painting experience, I was always coaching my painters, "Just shut up and do it. Don't let the drama get in your head and feel like, 'Oh my god, I have five thousand square feet ahead of me!' You're still going to have it whether you fret about it or not."

If you whistle and think of something else, then without noticing it, you would have three thousand feet left, then two thousand feet. It's the same thing with the big stuff around which companies are built, yet at some point, you have to shut up and do it. It doesn't matter if there are tons of competition. It doesn't matter if only the big pharmas are doing it. It doesn't matter if everyone around you tells you it's impossible.

Just try, and in the trying, you can't go wrong. You're either going to succeed or not. I'm fortunate and lucky and a hard worker, and I've succeeded at all the things that I tried. I didn't expect to, though, and it's not bad if you don't. You'll find out why, and then everyone around you gets to see that barrier because no one ever uncovered it before. Now it's a definite barrier that got in the way of Keirstead, and so everybody starts avoiding that barrier, but at least now, they know what to avoid because they never knew it before.

If you try, nothing can go wrong. You're always going to learn from the mistake. You also have to be a realist and realize that nine out of ten businesses don't end, if they're successful, with what they began with. If you try on spinal cord injury, and then it becomes another spinal cord disease, and then it becomes cancer. That's okay. That's a long-winded way to say I think my primary book theme would be try. What I want to say is, "Shut the fuck up and try."

The person who tries is saying, "I have no idea. Let's try. I don't see any barriers. I don't see any parameters here that can restrict me. Let's go." Humans have done lots of incredible things, such as putting a man on the moon and developing treatments for various diseases that have changed our lives and the way we live. There's no reason why you can't be the disruptor. You've got to try.

During a recent interview, this person said, "I'd like to study the development of your company so I can understand how to develop mine."

I said, "Well, that's a completely useless exercise because I have never seen two builds in my sector that are the same." There just aren't. It's the nemesis of the entire field, and I think what breeds middlemen is the training.

Humans have this desire, this natural tendency, to normalize things and make a story out of something. By making a story out of it, you're taking the conventional path. You go to school for an MBA, you do case studies. This is how it's done, and this is how it's done, and this is how it's done. Instead, you should be trained on another way to do it. It's hard to do that, and it still hasn't been done yet. It's an interesting thing when the entire system breeds the average in business development.

I always think to myself, "What the heck would I do next? I'm not trained for anything." I'm the guy who has built four companies, exited well in all of them, a professor, and a PhD in various things, but I still think to myself, "I don't know what I'm trained to do. I'm trained to do this. I'm a good fit for what I'm doing because, of course, I built it around myself, but my goodness, if this ever ended, what could I possibly do?"

I'm so immersed in this particular mission that I forget about all the other stuff, and so I try and keep pushing, leverage everything I can, and build what I have. That's a beautiful journey. It's all about doing what makes you happy.

Teresa Carew
On Safari Foods
Onsafarifood.com

How our company has been affected by mentoring is a two-way question because there are mentors, and then there are mentees. We both mentor each other, but we must put this in context.

I own a catering company, so it's hands-on and people oriented. I had one particular chef who taught me all about excellence in cooking, and we pride ourselves on making the most delicious quality food in the city. That was huge because that led to establishing a mission statement, which was to "be kind to Earth, our employees, and our clients." That may sound flippant, but being kind to Earth meant that we would only buy sustainably sourced food, use only humanely raised proteins, be kind to our employees and clients by treating them like human beings on a case-by-case basis.

The biggest mistake I made was to hang onto certain employees for too long. But what I learned through this mistake was utterly valuable: personality trumps excellence. It doesn't matter how good your employee is at whatever they do; if they create mayhem in the workplace, it's not worth it. So I learned from that mistake and fixed that first.

You have to know your employees to teach, mentor, and understand what it is that they're looking for, as well as have them understand what we're looking for. The only way you can do that is if you read about how the mind works. Jonathan Haidt wrote a brilliant book called *The Happiness Hypothesis*, where he describes how the mind works and what motivates us and how we behave. I've drawn a lot of inspiration from that book.

I've had various mentors throughout my life, starting with my mother, who taught me never to give up. I have a friend who became an incredibly successful businessman who taught me all about risk management and risk assessment, which is vital when running a company. My third mentor is a brilliant professor (not in my occupation) who taught me how to think through, look differently at, and solve problems. He taught me to look at the big picture in a kind fashion. My fourth mentor is my accountant. Every single business needs a great accountant, as accounting is the backbone of any business, and the employees are the muscle that supports the backbone.

My hardest lesson to learn—and I'm still trying to work on it—is to figure out how to teach people how to care. That's not a lesson I've learned yet. I think the hardest experience of all was understanding that while one should value employees as the essential assets in the company, the biggest mistake I have made is thinking that they're so valuable that I can't live without them. That is so wrong, just downright wrong. I learned that lesson, and now I'm a much happier person.

I have had problem employees that I realized were not worth the chaos. I had one brilliant head chef, probably the most gifted cook I've ever had, who was prone to ruling my kitchen through fear and was just like a naughty elephant in the room.

I'm from South Africa. Baby elephants are playful but can be naughty when they're growing up and not quite fully formed. They can create an enormous amount of destruction as they're quite big, and sometimes we tend to behave like naughty elephants in the room without even knowing it. So being self-aware is critical.

And then I had another brilliant cook who had a horrible mental disorder. We make it dirt cheap for our employees to get health insurance, and so we made sure that she found herself a counselor. We spent a year and a half working with this woman, and it just didn't work out. It couldn't work, and that's when we had to cut our losses. When an employee is underperforming, what you need to do is get into them and find out what makes them tick. You have lots of conversations about valuing oneself, and when you value yourself enough, you tend to care about what you do.

We speak with pride about how we make a difference in the world and how every one of us can make a difference in the world, and employees have been with me for a long time, so something is clearly working. They've been with me from four to eighteen years (my longest-tenured employee).

We pride ourselves on being a different catering company. We don't corporately run our company, and that is something that I'm going to stick to. With a mission like ours, the focus is on what your intention is to bring good into the world versus how much money you're going to make.

What's interesting about my approach is that I make plenty of money, but I come at it from a completely different way. I don't spend my life obsessing about the bottom line. I spend my life obsessing about the quality of the food, how my employees are doing (whether they're optimizing their jobs), and what tools they have to succeed. If you don't look at the bottom line, things flow from there. It's a different way of approaching the idea of capitalism.

I've served as a mentor, personally, in the cooking arena as I've taught people how to cook. I've also done problem-solving with employees. But one doesn't know how to analyze oneself thoroughly. I can analyze other people, but when it comes to analyzing myself, I'm clueless. So I asked one of my employees how she thought I mentored people.

She said it was by lending an ear and providing the tools that people need to grow and believing in what they do. Another huge thing in the workplace is an attitude of gratitude for everything that our employees do. They are the most wonderful human beings, and that's how we like to treat them.

The area that most entrepreneurs need mentoring is in the development of social contracts. I don't think entrepreneurs or corporations value their employees enough. The employees are what make the world go round. Having an open relationship with employees and getting the ego out the way ensures an honest flow of conversation and perspective. Having an open door is huge, as it's important to get honest feedback from one's employees.

When you're the CEO of the company, and you can't do this, you have to go outside to some consulting company and ask them to show you what the log is in your eye. But if you've got employees who will be honest with you about how you're behaving and what you're doing or whether you're a naughty elephant in the room, it makes it collaborative in the workplace. There's not much hierarchy in my company. Everyone has a say, and everyone's opinion is valuable.

Probably the most critical thing depends on what kind of entrepreneur you are. Some entrepreneurs think you can start a business just because you're a good planner or a good cook—or a good this or a good that. You need to have some business sense; you need to know how to put it all together.

Anyone thinking about becoming an entrepreneur probably needs to be mentored in financial management and HR and all the tools that you need to create a good business.

If I were to write a book, my key message to entrepreneurs would be to know both your strengths and weaknesses. Always hire people who know more than you do. If you're an entrepreneur who's good at making widgets, you might not necessarily be a good bookkeeper, communicator, salesperson, or HR person. It's good to hire people who know and understand more than you do.

My other message would be to be kind to your employees and educate them so that they have opportunities to advance. The third and most important thing about running a business through one recession after the next (and we know as we've been doing this for twenty-seven years) is to understand how to assess and manage risk. That's a huge component.

It's different in the catering business from other non-hospitality industries. In the catering industry, we are a slightly different catering company in that we're more food service oriented, and so we've learned from some huge mistakes. We had a massive account with a *Fortune 100* company. We were the smallest company in the world to service these guys, but we were fifth in the world for the quality of food and service. We were little rock stars, but we carried all our eggs in one basket. When they decided they could get a much cheaper product through the world's largest food service management company, they dropped us, leaving us scrambling.

I had a two-week think tank with myself, where I decided to develop a business plan to make my company much more reliable and safer to run. I would not play with any of the big players; I would focus on a certain number of people and a particular demographic. Additionally, I would control my risk that way so that if one account left, it wouldn't be absolute devastation the way it was the first time it happened to me.

We have about ten accounts around town, and we've got a couple that are falling off. They tend to fall off whenever they grow too big, and they move on, but it's not devastation for us. I think that this applies across all sectors of the market. You should never carry all your eggs in one basket. One client should not make up any more than 10 percent of your business.

We get some clients who grow incredibly fast. I had a CEO who sat down in my testing room and said, "Well, can you cater for one thousand people?" They had like three hundred at the time, and they were going to grow to a thousand in a year, and I said, "No problem. We can do that." We do stand that risk when we keep on those clients, but we bring more clients on to spread the risk.

A few years ago, I thought it would be a great idea to give these new guys some tips because I belong to an organization here in Seattle called Cater Round. It's a group of caterers who get together and discuss all kinds of things from employees to policies to legislation that's coming down. I look at some of the newer ones, and I know there's so much to learn.

Ameet Shah
Wodify
Wodify.com

We have been favorably affected by mentoring in reshaping our culture. Today, we're seven years into Wodify, and about a year ago, we were bootstrap profitable. But then something changed, and I just stopped wanting to come to work, which was in stark contrast to the way I used to be. I used to jump out of bed at four in the morning and couldn't wait to go to work because I loved working with the business.

I didn't necessarily go out seeking a mentor, but I sought a solution. I heard about Zappos and their amazing culture, so I decided to take a one-day boot camp and learn about their culture. I purposely went alone so I wouldn't be affected by any outside influences; I wanted to go with a clear mind and learn what I could. My conversations there inspired me, and a few weeks later, I shut down the company for an entire week and flew all our people to the US.

We spent a week collectively defining our purpose and core values, what we stood for, and what our culture was all about. The outcome has been tremendous and remarkable, as we now have measurably happier employees, and we do value specific interviewing.

Now we're mentoring others in our little Philadelphia community. People come to our office, and the phrase they use to describe us is "amazing culture," which they can feel and want to learn more about. So we've been able to share our experience over the last year with others.

I'm an engineer, and I'm male, so I gravitate to objects more than people. I like to have fun, and I'm personable but not necessarily that touchy-feely. Outwardly, I keep it private. When someone asked me a year ago, "How would you define your culture?" I almost laughed.

Our culture was great, but we never defined it because, in the early days, we were a group of eight or nine people. We were like-minded friends, but we never thought to articulate our goal—we just knew it.

But as the company scaled, that fell apart.

One of the things we did as a group was to define our purpose and core values. Now we have value ambassadors in each one of our offices. Each month, we focus on a specific value, and we hold workshops and do activities. This month, we are focusing on integrity and doing the right thing, so we watched the movie about the Theranos scandal in both countries where we operate, Portugal and the US.

Another thing we now do is logistically, or operationally, we have our hiring manager interview for skills, then we conduct another team interview for values. We allow the values interview to trump the skills interview. Someone could successfully fly through our interviewing process, but if they don't pass the values interview, we pass on them. And that has happened already in the last twelve months. I was favorably surprised that there wasn't a big deal made of it. Our people felt it made sense to pass on certain candidates, as we need to make sure that our values are aligned.

Having mentors is essential because they can save you from making a mistake. One of my biggest mentors was my mother. From an early age, she taught me the importance of learning new things, being humble, and having a strong work ethic. To this day, I think I can work hard, but not compared to my mother. My mother can outwork me any day of the week. She got me my first real job at M&M Mars in Elizabethtown, Pennsylvania, as a janitor.

At first, I said, "As a what? I'm not interested in cleaning toilets." She taught me to focus on the idea that I might be cleaning toilets, but there was an opportunity to work for a world-class manufacturing company where I could learn so many other things about manufacturing, best practices, and inventory control. Sure enough, she was right.

I cleaned a lot of toilets and mopped a lot of floors and took a lot of trash cans out. But I had the opportunity to work on the manufacturing lines and work in inventory and learn about manufacturing and distribution. The experience paid dividends later in my career because I graduated, and I went to work for General Motors, and I think my experience at M&M Mars helped me get that opportunity.

Before Wodify, I had a consulting services business called Conigent, where I had the opportunity to work with a $13-billion US company called Old Castle. I implemented ERP and CRM systems, working directly with the CIO, Frank Murtag, who continues to be a mentor to me.

He taught me how to run large projects with large budgets, how to focus on what's important, and how to keep your eyes on the prize. I think a lot of young people (and I fell victim to this) get lost in the details that don't matter in the grand scheme of things. Probably, that was the biggest lesson he taught me.

A book I recently read had a significant impact on me, personally and professionally, is called *Faster Than Normal: Turbocharge Your Focus, Productivity, and Success with the Secrets of the ADHD Brain* by Peter Shankman. The author has ADHD, so he talks about not looking at ADHD as a handicap but as an opportunity and superpower to harness. I could be this author's twin brother and felt like he wrote the book about me. Little tactics that I learned and used in the past six months have made a significant improvement in me, both personally and professionally.

The author talks about how folks with ADHD do not naturally create dopamine as often or as easily as others. Those of us with ADHD have to do thrill-seeking things. For example, he's a skydiver—and I'm a skydiver too—because it provides a dopamine rush. Working out gives us a dopamine rush, such as going for a run. The author has a little tactic where he knows that to be focused, such as when doing presentations. He's got to do a workout before the presentation. If he doesn't, at the presentation venue, he will walk up and down the stairs, do push-ups and jumping jacks in the parking lot, to get that dopamine rush which allows him to focus on his presentation.

I have been following his advice, and I see huge benefits. I'm back to getting up in the morning before the crack of dawn and getting a workout in, and I find that I am way more focused. The closer I am to that workout, the more focused I am. When I have to do detailed work, I now schedule that immediately following the exercise, and then I plan any of those "Hey, do you have fifteen minutes to chat" calls for the afternoon. It helped me organize my day to be way more productive and efficient. Anybody I work with directly, I have them read that book so they can get insight into why I am the way I am.

I've served as a mentor to some of the younger folks in our organization, but recently, we moved our offices to Center City, Philadelphia, and gotten more exposure to the aspiring entrepreneur tech community in Philly.

Lately, I've been spending quite a bit of time with early-stage entrepreneurs who I've met through networking. I enjoy helping people, but I also enjoy learning about other business ideas, even if they're not related to what we do. I feel like it's a valuable data point you tuck away, which you might use some other day.

What I do that may be different from other coaches or mentors is that I try to be brutally honest, because I think it's the best way I can provide value to founders. The truth is not necessarily what they want to hear, so I preface it with, "Look, I'm just going to tell you what I think. You may not like it. So are you sure you want my counsel?"

As an example, I recently was talking to a founder who was working on this app that's related to a niche market. Her understanding of the market was cursory, so I said, "You need to know this forward and backward, so I suggest you go get a job in that industry. Work for free, work for nothing, whatever. But get the experience so that you can speak the speak."

She did not follow my advice, and most people I talk to don't follow my advice because oftentimes, I'm telling them what they don't want to hear. Typically, I recommend hard work. There's no secret formula you're going to learn from me or some other entrepreneur. It's the hard work that counts: you've got to dig in and get it done. You've got to put the time in. There are no shortcuts.

There are areas where most entrepreneurs seem to need mentoring, and one is that there are no shortcuts to starting a business. The other point I would argue is that raising capital is not the end goal. Entrepreneurs hope that I'm going to give them some secret trick to hacking or launching their business, but I recommend hard work:

Talk to customers. Build that product. Get it in the hands of users so you can get real feedback. Then validate or invalidate your assumptions and adjust accordingly.

In terms of raising capital not being the end goal, I might be a little bit biased, because I'm the founder of a bootstrap company. I feel like there's this culture in the startup world where success is measured by the raised capital rather than actual value creation or revenue or profits. Some businesses are structured in a way where you need early-stage investment for the long-term vision, but in most cases, entrepreneurs should look at the finances as a means to an end, not the finish line. Call me old-fashioned, but I love reaching into my pocket and feeling money jingle around.

If I were to write a book, it would be called *Bootstrap or Bust*. I have built companies so that I don't have to answer to anybody. I don't want a boss, a partner, or an investment group. And that has been the driving force around building my businesses the way I want to. I think the only way to do that is to bootstrap your own business, and it takes longer. It means putting in more hours and being more frugal and more effective with your dollars and your resources. For me, and for those who are driven the same way, it's worth it.

It gives me a sense of accomplishment and pride. I don't play the lottery because there's no pride associated with winning the lottery. If I own the lottery and won a million dollars, okay, but I wouldn't necessarily feel proud about that. If I built a company that made a million dollars in cash, and I did it on my own, I'd be pleased. It sounds so cliché, but it's about the journey.

I've met other people at networking dinners who say, "I want to be a billionaire." Those words have never left my lips. I suppose that's okay, but we're on two different paths because that's not why I do what I do. Money is a byproduct of what I am doing.

I've talked to a lot of people where I look at their business and say, "You've created something cool. I love what you've done." And then they say they're going to spend six months in Thailand working remotely and hope to flip the business three months later. I suppose there's nothing wrong with it, but I look at that scenario as a missed opportunity. I say, "I love your product. You're doing so many great things. Don't you want to see what you could do next?" And they're like, "No, no. I want to surf and then sell it so that I don't have to work anymore."

I don't get that because I love working.

Alexander Kutyrev
Aurora Fine Chemicals
Aurorafinechemicals.com

Before I started my company, I worked for a small chemical company in Graz, Austria. I saw how the company operated from marketing and production to logistics and accounting, and later, we built our business, guided by our gained experience. We tried to repeat successful steps and avoid gross blunders.

I remember one case back when companies often sold their products cheaper than the raw materials from which they were made. The executives hoped that the clients would order larger volumes in the future and thus recover their losses, but this didn't happen—the customer never ordered again.

We didn't make such bad deals with our company, and I think we were lucky we were mentoring companies this way. We learned much from negative experiences. When we started our company, we didn't make any of those mistakes.

When new employees start at our company, either on the administrative side or on the chemistry side, we do some one-on-one kind of nurturing and mentoring. I appreciate the achievements of our staff, and I never delay salaries and rewards. On the other hand, I like to see my words match my actions. I demand the same from my colleagues and partners. In my opinion, order, discipline, multitasking, and, of course, hard work are the keys to success, and I always strive to be an example in this regard.

My eldest brother was my role model, and he had the most significant influence on me. Like him, I received a chemical degree at the university, and like him, I became a chemist. At school, I liked many subjects other than chemistry. I was a lucky guy who made the right choice and followed my brother's profession. To some degree, my brother helped me in college when I was studying chemistry, but somewhat less, I would say, because I was too independent for this.

I respected him and followed his example—he was like a father to me. My father died when I was very young. My decision to be chemist was inspired by my brother, by what he did and how he behaved and how he was at that time.

I have always tried to be objective, keep order and discipline, and do multitasking. I don't know if it went through to the staff and my colleagues and partners, but I always try to be an example in this regard.

I made a lot of mistakes. I think the largest one was going into a partnership, and I wouldn't recommend anyone to do so. When you start a company and do all the work, the other side could relax, and if you didn't do work, the company could die. That was my biggest mistake when I tried to find the partners. It didn't work at all.

I think many of us need an objective assessment of our business, and such unbiased expertise could be provided by a real business professional, e.g., a CEO executive. Impartial third-party conclusions would be invaluable. They help to avoid fatal mistakes in the lives of many, many entrepreneurs.

We need help to look clearly at our business and make decisions around what *is* instead of what they *wish* they could see. We need the objective assessment of real business professionals in the specific area.

Most people overestimate their skills. That's the problem with all of us, I believe.

The assessment doesn't need to be positive. Objectivity being both positive and negative. It's like a doctor telling the truth about one's illness. It goes the same way for entrepreneurs. They should improve their skills and know their weaknesses to work on them. I think it should be objective.

What a person objectively says can either break you down or build you up. So it's better to build up so that you have more confidence and can look at your business objectively. If you want to look at it this way, you should probably choose the real professional, not just some unsuccessful businessperson who worked in this specific area. Pick the real successful people who work with a lot of stuff and employees and will ideally have both psychological skills and business skills. They're the people you would need to get an objective assessment of your business.

If I were to write a book, my key message to entrepreneurs to replicate my success would contain just three questions.

First, is your product or service needed by people or organizations? Second, can you deliver your products and services in quality time? Third, would you purchase your product or service?

If your answer is yes to all three questions, you're going to be a successful entrepreneur. I believe that's the most important evaluation for everyone.

Catherine and Leo Zupan
Discover Publications
Discoverpubs.com

Catherine

In 2015, my father, Leo, wanted to retire. We since found out that his retirement was impossible. So he's around the office now more than he ever was—he'll never retire at this rate.

I was a business banker doing commercial loans when my father was looking to sell the business. My husband and I thought it had been a good business for a while, and we wanted to keep it in the family, so we put our hat in the ring. Of course, we're family, so we flipped it over.

The debt structure was complicated, so we've had to do a gradual buy-in. It hasn't been an overnight process, and we're still working on finalizing it, which won't happen until 2020, as there are a lot of little moving parts with a purchase of this size.

In the meantime, Leo spent two years completely stepping out of it, then came back out of boredom. He's got a fire in his belly like he's twenty-five years old, and he won't ever stop. He's been working on a nonprofit for some time now and hasn't quite gotten off the ground, but he does a lot with the church. He never stays still.

We're in Columbus, Ohio, right next to the Busch beer factory on Busch Boulevard, the Budweiser plant. Cleveland is our neighbor, and our entire family grew up in Cleveland.

Quick backstory: my father's father is from Cleveland, and he started a metal company a long time ago. He ended up being hugely successful. Although having only an eighth-grade education, he grew a multimillion-dollar business.

Growing up poor and watching his father build a machine tool and starting a metal business from the ground inspired my father,

Leo. Whirlaway was the name, and a conglomerate from Phoenix bought it for $40 million in 2013. My grandfather had passed, and my brother took it over, then sold it. Anyway, that's a quick background about him to give you a little insight into what drove him to be successful.

Leo

Mentoring is a flattering term, but I guess it's the one thing that would be necessary to innovate. We were in the direct-mail custom newspaper business for 150 years. I started it back in the '90s, and when the crash came in 2008, direct mail became expensive compared to social media, which a lot of people started using.

Our primary market niche was real estate. We also did other small businesses, such as doctors, dentists, car dealers, different things like that, but real estate was our bread and butter. So they took to social media, which had a huge learning curve. It didn't work at all for a few years, but anyway, they stuck with it.

Direct mail suffered. So Cathy came around, and we discussed things over. She was quite a successful business banker with US Bank, and we agreed she was going to come to do this instead. I talked to her about the necessity of changing the mission of the company from total print and other media, and she did that beautifully.

Cathy did a lot of research, and she had used a lot of alternate media at US Bank from their marketing department, though she was in business banking and had outside clients. She took us into the digital area, and that has proven to be quite successful.

Mentoring is a significant thing. But there are a lot of little things—parental advice and business advice and keeping an eye on things with the finances. Cathy has already had to make some tough decisions with personnel, but when you change direction as we did—which was not radical, but quite significant—there were a lot of changes to be done, and she did it quite skillfully.

So those were a lot of fun discussions too. To discuss how we go about it because, in 2008, I had the sad duty of having to let a lot of people go because first, the banks failed, and then about five minutes later, the real estate market collapsed. Without banking, you can't mortgage houses. So we went through a tough period, and I had to let many people go. Everything is built back up now, and Cathy's been doing a splendid job. Those are the salient areas of mentoring.

The man who loomed largest in my life was my father, who was one of the most amazing people I've ever known—not because he was my dad, but because his accomplishments were incredible.

A son of a coal miner in West Virginia, he quit school when he was fifteen years old. He was born in Pennsylvania, and when he died, he had five hundred employees. He was in several different industries. He had a two-thousand-acre farm in Ashland County, where he raised horses and cattle. Talk about an entrepreneur's entrepreneur! I was by his side for many years, and I owe everything to him.

Aside from my father, Jim Collins's *Good to Great* was an essential book in my life. Before that, *In Search of Excellence* by Robert H. Waterman Jr. and Tom Peters was an impactful book. I've read many books as I took an executive MBA course, and my undergraduate background is in English history. I went to Marquette and took philosophy. All three courses will not get you a job.

But it was sure a lot of fun. I use it every day of my life in dealing with people and building things in my dad's way, which is by the seat of the pants in personal relationships. I don't want to call it an empire, but he had quite a sprawling number of business endeavors that were all successful, and they were all based on relationships.

I know that might be passé in light of the mega companies, but that's the way I am, that's the way he is, and that's the way my daughter Cathy is. She becomes friends, as I did, with our clients, and we're sincerely concerned about them. It's not dollars and cents that matter, which fade fast. We try to do a good job and help their businesses, which, of course, then helps ours.

I took an executive MBA at Ohio State, which was about a four-month course, one three-hour night a week. It was abbreviated. But through the course, there were many excellent bibliographies passed along of which I availed myself.

I like Collins because of the methodology. It stands apart from other books in that genre because he got a huge grant from somewhere, big staff, and they examined a lengthy period of historical activity. They were all public companies, so they could get their annual reports, et cetera, quarterly reports, and they analyzed what made the companies go from an excellent company to a great company, and he ended up publishing about fifteen examples.

Walgreens was one of them, and he also discussed the common personalities of the key people. For example, the CEOs were not flamboyant Donald Trump types, but they were more reserved, thoughtful, reflective. There were things like that that I thought was quite instructive, and the way they led the companies was logical and prodigious. So I learned a lot from that about how super successful people measure success. I don't read excessive amounts of business books. Being in the publishing business, I have to read a lot, but those are some of the standouts.

I had custody of my four children after a sad divorce, and as a father, I think that qualifies for mentoring. I think of *mentoring* as an inspirational word, or it has an inspirational connotation. I don't know if it's fair to say I have inspired, but I have tried to do so.

Catherine

My father has done a lot of work with the church and led by example. He's a leader in the community. He's on the board at a local charity, and he's founding a new charity, and all these people are coming to the office to get advice.

A young refugee trying to start a daycare center keeps coming in to have meetings, talking about his next steps. My father helped another refugee get on her feet after her entire family was murdered, and he got her daughter in school, and he helped by working with other programs and initiatives. He's an inspirational man to many people here in Columbus.

Leo

My niece worked for a refugee resettlement company here in Columbus called US Together. I have a big house, and she called me and said, "Now that you're an empty nester, would you like to take in a couple of refugees for a couple of days?"

Well, that turned into five years, and I think there were seventeen babies born at our house. These were all single mothers who were ostracized by the Rwandans and the Congolese because they were raped by soldiers, which you probably know is their favorite way of getting power over villages. It's obscene. Then their communities won't let them live with them.

So anyway, I did that for a while, and that was quite inspiring, and I saw the need to get into people's hearts one way or the other.

I'm currently involved with St. Vincent de Paul, which is a national organization, but I'm on the board at one of the local chapters. We run a grassroots food pantry. About every parish in the world has a branch of St. Vincent de Paul.

Catherine

My father has also done a ton of work with the Ohio Right to Life and was good friends with the founder, Janet Folger (that's her maiden name). But when I was young, nine or ten years old, I remember going to conferences and learning about how important it is to stand up for what you believe in and to make an impact in your community. I got to see him do that at the leadership level—not volunteering on the street, but rather helping to get it off the ground.

Leo

Taking people into your home and guiding them and things like that are not always about business. But it's rewarding. I don't want to overplay it because it's a cliché, but it's true. They give more to you than you give to them.

I was in the construction business. I did architectural glasswork. We did the curtain wall work on high-rise office buildings all over

Ohio and several signature jobs in Chicago, and Washington, DC. Then we had some domestic problems when my wife and I sadly divorced, and that's when I jettisoned that at a bargain price and started the publishing business because that's where my heart is anyway.

The area most entrepreneurs need mentoring in is probably in financial discipline, and the best advice I ever got from my dad is this:

With every business you start, the first two things you do is get a good CPA and a good lawyer. And not that they're at your side all the time, but you have to be able to access them and get their advice and listen to it and follow it within reason. So that, along with the discipline of the checkbook, is critical because it's really easy to spend and real hard to earn sometimes. That's easy to overlook, especially if you start with steep money. There are many various ways of starting a business, but if you do that, sometimes you can get a little careless.

Entrepreneurs need an affinity for people because sooner or later, you're going to be managing people and hiring them and recruiting them, and you need some people skills. I think you're born with that, and I don't know if you can acquire it through HR training or anything. But hire right. That's another cliché. Take your time to hire, and when it's time to fire, do that more quickly. Keep an eye on the books every month. Get good advice, so at month's end, an accountant can come in, look at you, and be able to advise that you're headed for this problem or that problem. Deal with the finances of your business.

If you're talking about an entrepreneur starting from scratch, they need to truly analyze the market, which is a fundamental business plan line item, but a critical one if you don't have a future. My criterion is this: I wanted to be in a business that could not be imported—say, a commercial construction—and what I'm doing now can't be imported easily, although with the internet, there can be some competition now.

If you're serving a large industry or a large population, pick out a niche and exploit them in a good sense. Also, business plans are tedious, and everyone hates doing them, but they're an excellent roadmap to success. I've used them all my life—a good thing to check back on.

I've published a few books here with our imprint of Custom House Press. But that's been over the years, and it was not traditional publishing in the sense of Barnes & Noble or Amazon. What I did was publish books that we sold to our patriotic client base. One was called *They Dreamed Freedom*. It was a collection of primary source material about the founding period of the country, which has now been beaten to death, but back then, it was novel. And then the client would sponsor the book, and we'd design a cover with them on it and say that they are sponsoring this because of their own beliefs. I sold thousands and thousands of copies. They'd buy a thousand books and hand them out as expensive business cards.

I've written lots of essays, primarily in the religious and political areas. I'm active politically, but my interest is mostly in the moral aspect of politics. There's such a vast chasm between the two parties that I'm pretty obsessed with trying to do my little part through essays and letters to editors and things like that.

Jonathan Rubinsztein
Infomedia
Infomedia.com

Quite recently, we identified eight key leaders in our organization, which is going through relatively rapid change. Both our industry and ours actual organization have been changing quickly. We've been on a journey to drive agility in the market and innovate faster than our competitors.

One of the areas that we looked at was identifying key leaders and giving them a process. We engage specific business leaders who had skills not only in mentoring but also in understanding a business environment.

We provide those leaders in the organization with a mirror to get a view on their style to reflect on what they're doing well: how they impacted the organization and how that style was the real disruption happening in the automotive industry. Then we cascade into improving their technique and driving that agility and innovation.

We set up a formal program almost two years ago, and that was in combination with what we call our Infomedia University. We had eight leaders go through their program. I believe it was successful in terms of being on a journey, and there's no end in any of this. So it's the journey that's important, and therefore, I'm thinking about what our success looks like. I think it's the function of improving the individual and them being happier. But I do believe that from my perspective, it appeared to be successful.

With our new hires, we have a reasonably standardized induction process. However, in terms of mentoring, I think the first six to twelve months is about trying to understand the culture and the environment first. We do buddying across some of the senior staff supporting the new hires. Still, typically, as a formal mentoring program, we would probably wait twelve months before engaging.

For the first ninety days, a senior person will support the new hire in terms of understanding the organization and how it works—which is less about mentoring and more around buddying. In terms of mentoring, typically, we wait twelve months before we do the formal program. That's more around them having enough time to explore and understand the environment that they're in.

I read a lot, and I engage in various activities that I hope will give me a perspective on my style and approach in leadership. The one author that stands out for me would be Daniel Pink, as he speaks a lot about motivation in *Motivation 2.0* or *Drive*.

Daniel Pink talks about what motivates people, and he breaks it down and defines how the old models of motivation were around a carrot-and-a-stick approach. His view is that those models don't work.

Academically, they've proven that in a routine-based process, you might find that a carrot-and-stick approach does work. If you're screwing caps onto a toothpaste tube, you might find that there is a way to incentivize the caps per minute when manually doing a tedious task.

However, in terms of what most of us do in a knowledge economy, the current research shows that there seem to be three critical drivers for motivation: autonomy, mastery, and purpose. Those three drive better outcomes than if you want a carrot-and-a-stick end.

One needs to consider how to motivate salespeople, where typically commission is a key driver. While his view is paying them fairly, giving them autonomy, giving them the ability to master a skill or technique or capability, and aligning them to their purpose and the organization's purpose is more powerful than something like a commission. That certainly gave me a structure to think through motivation, which, I believe, is a crucial part of leadership.

We all make mistakes. My father always used to talk to me about the rule of the second mistake. The rule of the second mistake is that often, the first mistake isn't the one that kills you; it's the second mistake. He spoke about, for example, a small car accident. You're flustered, and you're on a highway. You open the door and get out the car, and the car then runs you over. That's a simplistic version, but I think I can use that as a metaphor. It's been a good learning for me, which I always describe as the rule of the second mistake. We all make mistakes, and we live in a world where knowledge is about making mistakes.

I can think of many scenarios where the way we deliver and test business outcomes, and another great book I've used in the mentoring for myself is *The Lean Startup*. We use a process of testing new markets and understanding how a minimum viable product operates in the world. Then we iterate, change, and pivot if that offering doesn't work versus building a whole new product and investing money in a product that might not succeed. I live my life by that iterative process: test things and try and make smaller mistakes early and learn from those.

I make mistakes all the time, whether they're investment mistakes from a business perspective, such as when you think a particular market makes sense. However, in the last ten years, I almost describe those mistakes as the further out they are from your horizon one offering, the smaller the bets need to be made. Therefore, the faster you can identify if you double down, or if you end that bet because it doesn't make sense.

Based on my perspective of mistakes, the worse one I've made is hiring the wrong staff. I can give examples where under pressure, from a shortlist of candidates on which we urgently need to decide, I happened to hire the wrong staff due to supply and time constraints.

That has had a significant impact on the business because your business is all about your team. It's all about your people, and if you employ the wrong people with the wrong cultural set or the wrong capability, that's a mistake. It's less about ability and more about reality. I think they always describe you need to hire for the future potential rather than the skill set, and I genuinely believe that.

I've been fortunate as I've both my parents as mentors. My father was an academic who ran a business, but he was a philosopher. He lived in his own world, but he was the greatest, kindest person I know. People loved working with him. I'm not sure if he had made too much money in that process, but people loved working with him. My mother was probably more of the driver behind me. She used to see and convince me that I could do whatever I wanted to do. From an early age, she used to support me in love by being the Jewish mother, running behind me, making sure that I did stuff, and motivate me. That was very useful in my early years.

Some of my friends and colleagues that I worked with during the early days at Anderson Consulting and Atikani were mentors. Those partners are still good friends and colleagues of mine, formally and informally. There seems to be a two-way mentoring relationship that we have. I'm fortunate to have those relationships twenty-five years through my career. I've had lots of supportive people. I've trusted their opinions, and as there's never been an agenda, I could sit down and reflect on myself. Mentoring is often about putting a mirror before yourself, something we don't always like to do.

If you've got an honest mentor who gives you feedback with no agenda, it allows you to unpack some of those behaviors and reflect on why those things appear. They don't always appear. They might appear under pressure, or they might appear in strange situations. So I feel fortunate and lucky. Certainly, from my perspective, I have made a concerted effort to pay that forward to other people.

I have a fantastic wife, who, typically for a birthday present, gives me an annuity contribution to a charity of her choice. Her view is that if there is a God or a religion that might help me get into heaven, she's managing my future risk. So one of my desires was to support two people who were not explicitly and directly related and were strangers.

Every year, I make a change to people who were not in my sphere of direct influence. Obviously, within the business, it's easier to do that. Still, I thought of it as a way of improving the world and in a pay-it-forward mechanism.

But I did identify two people. One was at a local café who needed help in getting a job. I sat down and did his graphic design CV with him. We sent off his CV to a couple of people I knew, and then I hadn't heard from him for 12 months. Then one of the most gratifying things happened.

Twelve months later, when I was walking around the beach where I live, I saw him, and he ran up to me and hugged me and asked if I knew how much I had changed his life. That was so gratifying for me, yet so easy for me to be able to do that.

I worked with the University of Sydney in their business school, where I formally mentored MBA students for two and a half years. From my perspective, that was an incredible experience. I always say that it was a selfish experience because I think I got more out of that mentoring experience than the mentees did. They were smart young kids, and that feedback gave me great insight, and I'd love to do more of that.

My experience is that often, entrepreneurs don't know they're entrepreneurs, especially when they're in the technology field. So they're smart people who have an idea and desire to do something and build something. But they're technologists, not necessarily entrepreneurs. They are prepared to take the risk, but they often don't understand an entrepreneur or necessarily want to be one. It's a calling, a drive, a desire to build something.

I've typically been working in the field of technology in various areas, and I have stumbled across lots of people who are super smart technologists. Still, their ability to relate to human beings is probably not their strength; however, their ability to build and design great technology is.

My view is that there are lots of opportunities for people to translate their vision and get help in managing their organization and working on how to execute a growth plan. That's often the gap I've seen in the technology field. While the super smart outliers who are incredibly visionary, their blind spot might be that they are wired for strength around the engineering side.

Simplistically, if I can break it down, they probably have a stronger left-brain focus than the right-brain focus. Therefore, getting them to be more rounded and to think through and support the people and the growth side of things and translating a technology vision into a business vision is where I've seen the most significant gap in this space.

There's so much about contextual success. There's so much luck and opportunity that I've had that's made it not necessarily easy to replicate it. Because there's a bunch of luck, and the context often helps.

I am halfway through writing a book, which I stopped about four years ago. The title of the book was *Zing Intuition: What they Don't Teach You in Business School*. The concept was not a mystical concept of intuition where you hear a voice. Still, it was the concept of the reality that we are taught to be so left brain and so formulaic and so rational that often we don't hear our inner voice which says, "You know, I've experienced something similar to this before. I can't quite put my finger on it, but something doesn't feel right."

I provided examples of that within a business environment, where you're interviewing someone for a role, and something doesn't quite feel right. Also, there's a great book called *Thinking Fast and Slow* by Daniel Kahneman. The author is cautious about using the thinking fast process to make decisions, because of the risk of bias, and one has a whole lot of prejudices. My view around intuition is that we have so much data. Our brain operates so much faster than we realize that there's this concurrent process in which your brain is sifting through billions of data points and memories. You can't necessarily identify where that emotion, that *zing*, and thought that come out and go, "Oh my goodness, I'm worried. Something does not make sense."

My strategy is to park that feeling but take notice of it and then try and get the data to unpack what it is. Is it something they said? I think that those feelings are powerful and that they can help. I believe that it's a massive part of your being, and I think we're taught not to feel in this world often. It's always "think, don't feel." I believe that the feeling part is essential. I'm not saying it's right or wrong, but I do think it's necessary to take notice of that intuition, that concurrent process, and try to figure it out.

The more you do it, the better you get. You walk into someone's room, and you get a good or bad feeling—well, that might be because they've got photographs of their kids. Maybe there are books that you pick up, and you don't consciously realize that you've made that decision. But try and work it out, because I think that we're not to feel things; we're taught to believe something.

When we did our MBA, there's undoubtedly no class on intuition I've ever seen in a class.

Ian Kaiser
Chicwrap
Chicwrap.com

I grew up with a lot of creative people. Everyone in my family has been creative, from photographers to painters, so I've always looked up to people who have vast experience in design. Since I was a little kid, I've been inventing products. Mentors matter. You can categorize it in different ways, but being around business people, and watching them do their job and being able to pick their brains and not be afraid to ask questions is how I've done it. I listen, put the phone down, watch, and observe.

One of my significant mentors is my father. I had an idea for something, and he believed in it, so he took my business partner and me under his wing and helped us out. When someone is in business and successful, and someone comes to you and asks for help, it's like passing the torch. It's almost like you're obligated, in a sense, to help someone else out and to pass on your knowledge.

All that knowledge that I've absorbed for the last twenty-six years has evolved into what I'm doing now. I think Malcolm Gladwell said you have to put in ten thousand hours of work before you're great, and that is so true. We also have to have good people that are motivating you, giving you direction, have ideas, and are willing to listen. But the key is you have to listen and observe and not come in thinking you have it all figured out. Put down your wall and be open-minded, and do not be afraid to fail.

My father had an advertising agency, so he had a lot of creative people around. I was around a lot of graphic designers, and then the Mac computer showed up. I got to learn how to do everything from typography to photography. From the financial side, I learned to understand the balance sheet, profit, and loss. My father is a creative person as well, so it's nice to have that.

Maybe it's not your father but a business owner of a small company that you latch onto and pick their brains. But I'm surprised that I offer to help people all the time, but I hardly get anybody wanting help. I'm an inventor, so a lot of people pop in and out like they got it all figured out, and I'm always surprised by that. I think maybe one day when I'm old and crusty, someone will reach out to me, and I'll be more than happy to help them.

The Internet is instant, and you can find anything you want on the Internet. But sometimes by having a face-to-face talk with somebody, you can get so much more out of it. When I have a new idea, it brews in my brain for a while, but the best thing I can do is build a quick, fast prototype to get it out of my mind and into your hands.

It's the same thing when talking to somebody—digging, then acting on it. There's something about meeting face-to-face, which is a lost art. I think that'd be my one piece of advice: have more face-to-face meetings with people.

They can show you the ropes, but they're the things of which you're not necessarily aware. Things always happen, people always say stuff that you're not even expecting, and that's what you want.

When I present something to somebody, I put it in front of them, and I always ask for their initial instinct. What does your instinct tell you? Usually, that first fifteen seconds is golden as they give you that pure impression. Then they start thinking about it. So you never know what someone's going to say when you ask them a question, and it doesn't hurt to get surprised now and again, and then you can act on it.

Mentorship can be a cumulation of many different people in your lives. Tap into it. If someone's making money, perhaps they have a shop or own a business, you have to respect that person. I don't care if that person is driving a Porsche or a Toyota. It doesn't matter. The person went through all the rigors to start a company, and they're making money, which is not easy. You see all these people making millions and millions of dollars, that's great, and they're instant sensations. But many people work their butt off every day to make a living. And those people have valuable information to share.

I grew up respecting Steve Jobs—not the way he treated people, though—but I respect what he did and his passion for excellence. I've read a ton of books, but like everyone else, the one that moved me was Malcolm Gladwell's *Outliers* and how he described doing your ten thousand hours to be great. It hit home.

Mistakes are the best thing. When I make a prototype, sometimes it goes well. But the errors are where the innovation is. If I were to build it on the computer, I'd design it, and it would look great. But when you create a physical prototype, and you make a mistake, I can't tell you how many times that mistake turned out to be the innovation that made it that much better because I wasn't trying to do that.

The more mistakes I make, the more I learn. You have to make mistakes and be excited about them. As silly as that is, but in my life, what I do, it's like boom. But from a product standpoint, you want to limit your exposure to mistakes where it financially exposes you.

I pitched a product to Nike: a basketball net that made out of their regrind. When people return shoes, or when they manufacture, they grind up all that rubber and incinerate it or put it into tracks. So I created this basketball net out of that, and it was great. I pitched it to them, and it went great, and I put a lot of money and time into that. Then, for one reason or another, they declined it. It was probably my biggest failure. It is in my core. I specialize in dispensing and cutting things, so this was something different.

You have to limit your exposure. Do as much research and as many things as you can do without spending cash. If you do launch something, you make a conservative approach. The last thing you want to do is believe in your idea so much that it bankrupts you in the process. Everybody wants to go big, but be conservative and smart. A product evolves. Everything evolves, and you get better and better.

I haven't served as a mentor in an official capacity. I'll help people all the time, like design stuff. But no one's ever come to me and said, "Hey, I want to learn." I'm in Malibu, and I'm with some pretty affluent people. I'm open to it, but it's one of those things where someone has to come knocking on your door. But I would do it because I think it's critical.

If someone had an idea, I could vet it and guide them. I would say, "Continue to do like my dad always said, research, research, and research. With our first idea, my partner and I pitched my dad. He said, 'Your idea and a Starbucks cup of coffee is worth about $2.25. That's how much it's worth. It doesn't mean anything. You have to go out and prove that it's needed, do your research, go out, and do questionnaires."

We went out and did all that, came back with all the data, then he was serious. That is one of the best things a mentor could tell you: "Go back, do your research, and then come back to me." They keep pushing you away until they can't push you away anymore because you have all the facts.

A mentor has to make sure they have all their ducks in a row before they take the plunge. I have a product distribution channel, which is the key to any product. You want to be able to sell it through a channel of distribution. So if someone came to me and needed help, and it was an excellent product, I would jump all over it.

The area most entrepreneurs need mentoring in is probably financials. It depends on what category you are, but must have business sense. You might have the manufacturing side of things. How are things made? How can you make it efficiently? But if you're a painter who only knows how to paint, how do you market yourself? What are the best ways to get your name out there? Those are the big deals. The fun part of creating any business is the creation of the idea, getting it ready, and doing all the stuff.

Say, you're designing a product, including the industrial design, packaging—all that stuff. The hard part is when you have to go out and sell it. You market it, pitch it, do trade shows, and travel. Marketing is vital, the financial second, and then understanding how things are produced. There are so many variables. That's one thing

I've learned over the years. From A to Z, anything and everything, how things are made, and where to make them.

If I were to write a book, my key messages would be never to give up and fail a lot. Have the dream, the vision in your mind that you want, and don't stop. Always believe you're going to get what you want. That's the key.

You're going to hit bumps in the road. That's inevitable. Things are going to happen. I had the whole market for one product, and a competitor stole it, and I lost it all. You're riding high one day, and you're down the next. But you have to pick yourself up and continue to believe that you will succeed, and you'll get through.

You see it all the time, like on *Shark Tank*. I feel like these people are driven. They've given up all their retirement money because they believe so much. But that's what it is—the belief. If you believe, you won't quit. But you have to work your butt off too. And then, it's silly, and I keep saying it, but it's okay to fail. You will be better for it in a lot of ways.

When you fail, you learn so much about the epic fail. What happened? What transpired? What caused this failure? And then you can take all that negativity and sculpt it and fix what you need to do. It's instant gratification in a bad way, but you're able to change your messaging, change your product, do whatever you need to do to rectify it. And that's a good thing. I'd rather know what doesn't work than not know it.

I have so many ideas coming down the pipeline that my mind is always on new ideas. But I'd be more than willing to help somebody when they come knocking on my door. My ideas change industries. In a sense, they're a disruptive innovation, but any idea is excellent. A new bagel to just something fresh, looking at something and reimagining it and making it simple. It's all about life simplified by design, and I want to simplify things.

We've all fought with plastic wrap forever, so I invented the cutter for plastic wrap. And then, for gift wrap, same thing. How much do you hate gift wrap? But I simplified that. My theory is that you have to focus and stand for one thing. I'm narrowly focused on dispensing and cutting. My mission is simplifying processes and dispensing anything on a roll that need to be cut. I want to streamline that process. So if you have that focus and that mission statement, you know where you're going. So think of all the things out there that come on a roll that we hate to use. There are many.

I love books, and I love to read. Now you can get them in so many different mediums, so it's all good. I think people are hungry. There are so many young entrepreneurs coming up that need that knowledge. They're not coming to me, so they're getting it from somewhere, such as the Internet and reading. But power to these guys! A lot of them are killing it. There are some talented young people out there.

They're driven, and they're resourceful. I think the phone has changed everything. Back in the old days, I had to deal with people face-to-face because there was no Internet and had to dig and go to the library, so maybe that's the significant change.

Joel Butterly
Ingenius Prep
Ingeniusprep.com

I'm the co-founder and CEO of InGenius Prep, which is an education consulting firm based in New Haven, Connecticut. We started the company about six years ago when we were all in law school. Two of us were at Yale, one was at Harvard, which is why we ended up in New Haven, which was maybe not our best decision, but so be it.

I started this company and a real estate company at the same time. The real estate company still exists. It's a smaller deal, I think, than the consulting firm. With InGenius Prep, the idea behind it was to see if we could find a way to reach a higher level of scale with these kinds of services, with admissions consulting services.

Generally, we help students apply to US colleges and graduate schools without compromising consistency or quality. The bet was that if we invested heavily enough in our intellectual property and our curriculum, we would be able to work with five, ten, fifty times as many students as our competitors while maintaining an extremely high level of consistency and quality. So that has borne out well into practice.

Today, the company has about 150 full-time employees. We have eleven offices around the world, including six in China, one in Korea, two in Canada, and two in the United States. We're not a funded enterprise. We bootstrapped the company. We started with $5,000 and have scraped away over the last six years, so it's been a bit of a slog, but it's been well worth it.

As far as I can tell, in the absence of mentorship generally, it's hard for some aspects of corporate culture to trickle down from the senior leadership down to the entry level. This has been especially true because we have so many people scattered around the world (we're not centralized). It was influential in the beginning that the members of the senior leadership were directly mentoring our early employees when we had like ten, fifteen, twenty people. We wanted them to have this same vision of what the company would be and the same basic work ethic and approach to tackling problems that we did.

There was a one-to-two-year gap, probably from 2016 to 2017, where we noticed that the entry-level employees weren't developing in the same way the early employees did. So the plan from there was to pair the entry-level folks up with mid-level or high-level director-level staff so that they could serve as mentors to them. Then the senior leadership has imparted our experiences, vision, and work ethic to the next level down, and they have done it with the newest hires.

Mentorship has been important, equally for the training of specific skills, as it has been necessary for the inculcation of corporate cultural values. We have a long way to go to be better at it, but the more we can disseminate the responsibility for mentorship from senior leadership and expand the population of people who are capable of mentoring others, the less rickety the .organization becomes. Being less dependent on the top, the organization grows more stable.

I learn from my mistakes. I come from an academic family, so my family and my family friends weren't of much use to me. I feel that I would benefit tremendously from a good mentor. I think the difficulty is that the bigger the company becomes, the more senior and more experienced the mentor needs to be. The more difficult it is to find somebody willing to invest that time unless they have some strong personal connection to my family or me.

So I have not learned much from mentors, and I wouldn't advise that. There were a lot of mistakes I could have avoided had I had good mentorship. I didn't prioritize that early in the company, so I didn't develop over time the kinds of relationships that would have blossomed in that way.

Also, I haven't learned enough from peer groups. I haven't made use of my membership in the various young entrepreneur organizations to which that I belonged. So I wouldn't recommend that, either. I've learned most through making mistakes. We've responded pretty diligently to them, so we've not suffered too much.

There have been a few critical times in the company where I've gotten some good advice from people. I wouldn't necessarily describe them as mentors as I've only spoken to them a couple of times about these issues. But because of the importance of their input, it probably bears mentioning.

One of them was Chris Jenny, who was, at the time, the president of the Parthenon Group in Boston. Now, I believe, it's been acquired by Ernst & Young, and I suspect that he has since retired. But he was extremely invaluable in helping me narrow down the focus of the company early on and identify why I was so tired, especially in the first year of the operation. He had also helped me understand that no matter how talented someone is, they can be in a role in which they will fail catastrophically. No matter how smart or talented someone is, failure is always a possibility.

So using people in the right places is as crucial as getting the right people to start.

Then my uncle gave me a piece of advice, right when I was thinking about starting the company. I hadn't incorporated the company yet. He said that throughout his life, he'd always been at the same place among his peers. He'd always felt like he was in the top 10 percent in high school, then in college, then in medical school, and now in his private practice. He said, "If I could go back in time, I think I probably would have started with the question, 'If I can be in the top 10 percent of anything, what do I want to be in the top 10 percent of?'"

That was interesting because, at the time, I was in law school. I was planning on being a lawyer, and I asked the question, "If I can be in the top 10 percent of anything, do I want it to be law?" And I looked around and was like, "Absolutely, no, I don't want that!" But the infinite amount of upward potential in business was attractive to me. So that was valuable and why I chose this path over selecting law.

His was a useful way of framing it, and it put a lot of things into perspective for me and made my decision not to pursue law clear. Other than that, the best book that I've read on leadership and management, for sure, is *Good to Great* by Jim Collins. Which I know is, at this point, almost a trope, but it is the best.

Within the company, I have a handful of people every year with whom I work directly that are outside the executive team. I put a relatively high emphasis on identifying people that have skill sets that I can help develop and then mentoring them. I think I have a lot of friends who started companies of their own, and I've been fortunate to have seen a lot of success early in my entrepreneurial career. So I've helped them a fair amount in fine-tuning their products and thinking about marketing and the development of their platform. And that's been a lot of fun. I've enjoyed that, and I learn a lot in the process of doing it, so it's been informative at the same time.

The best advice I can give to people most of the time revolves around the importance of sales and developing a sales strategy early on. Also, hiring and firing. People struggle with that early on because a lot of entrepreneurs are hiring people who are older than them. It's an uncomfortable dynamic, and they aren't sure how to determine whether somebody's doing a good job or a lousy job.

If I had to choose one area where I feel entrepreneurs need the most help, I'd probably say hiring and firing. But a close second is sales and sales strategy. I think people tend to assume that, "Oh, this is such a great idea, so everyone's going to buy into it." They don't understand that no matter how useful what you're doing is, anytime you're adding something new to somebody's life, there's an inherent transaction cost. So what you're offering needs to be obscenely valuable and obscenely convenient. Think of things like Uber, which is so convenient that it's unavoidable.

Or it needs to be well marketed and sold. I've spoken to many people who have a good product and a great idea, but no strategy for selling it. They feel disheartened when they first go out into the open market and realize that customer acquisition is hard. That seems to be a common flaw.

When hiring and firing, there are a lot of questions. How do you vet people? How do you hold them accountable? How do you fire them? How quickly do you fire them? How do you promote them? How quickly do you promote them? I think that's a big part of it, and it's not well documented online. The resources I've seen online are worthless.

I've been fortunate because the first time I took a foray into entrepreneurship, we saw a lot of success and built a large, profitable company. Obviously, that's not commonplace. To some extent, that has to being luck, being in the right place at the right time, and having the right personal background for it. So it's not like I can claim full credit for all these things. That would be foolish.

The things I have found most valuable include having a healthy skepticism of raising money early on. For some people, it's an absolute necessity, but generally speaking, I think you need to learn how to make money first before you should raise money. Otherwise, you're a statistic to an investment firm. The chances of you succeeding are extremely low, and they're waiting for the one that hits. We may raise money in the future, but the fact that we didn't taught us a lot about business fundamentals, such as maintaining profitability and maintaining sustainable growth. That was very important.

The second thing I would talk about is hiring. You could have a crap idea but a stellar team of people, and you will succeed. And you could have an incredibly good idea and have a crap team of people, and it will not succeed.

So being able to find, select, and mentor talented people early on is a challenging skill. The proposition that you're giving them is, "Hey, I'm going to pay you less for a higher risk job." Being able to do that is essential. Because once you reach a certain point, you can't do it all on your own. So if you don't have a talented group of people around you, it's impossible.

Probably the most valuable lesson I've learned is that if I have the right people in the right places, I can do nothing, and things will succeed. If there's the wrong person in the wrong spot, I can work eighteen hours a day, run myself into the ground, and it's still going to be a mess at the end of the day. So that's been the most cogent lesson I think I've learned.

My general perspective is while I'd like to think I know a whole lot, but if the last six years have taught me anything, they've taught me how little I do know. I probably want to spend some more years making mistakes before I can speak confidently, but that doesn't necessarily mean that I'm right. I still have a while to go before I think I've crossed the modesty boundary and can feel comfortable propagating my ideas in that way.

I think I was incredibly arrogant when I first went into business. I thought that since I was coming out of this fancy school with a high GPA, I was so sure I knew everything I was going to talk about. And I was so smart and all those things.

But honestly, during the last six years, probably the best thing that has happened is that it has been incredibly humbling.

Most of the truly successful people whom I've spoken to are often humble. These people did not raise a lot of money but rather wrestled with the challenge of creating an enterprise that is stable, profitable, and sustainable. Successful, but with longevity.

There's always a tinge of arrogance to them, but they are usually pretty upfront about the myriad ways that they are inadequate and the countless ways that they have screwed up.

I've found that to be an interesting gauge of whether or not somebody's gone through it. Because if I came out of the last six years more arrogant than I went in, I have missed something.

Kevin Wilkins
Trepwise
Trepwise.com

Trepwise is a growth consulting firm based in New Orleans. Our mission is to power organizations to maximize their potential, and what that means is we work with organizations to build capacity to help them focus and excel on their goals. We do so by focusing on three key areas: people, planning, and process.

I say to people it's about the culture. It's about organizational structure. It's about goal setting. It's about performance management. It's about the feedback mechanism. It's making sure you have the right people in the right chairs doing the right jobs because the best plans will not get executed unless you get the culture right. Mission, vision, and values are so important. When we talk about planning, we focus on strategic planning. For nonprofits, we focus on growth planning. For for-profits, we also do crisis management planning.

Then, finally, when we talk about the process, it's about implementation. We always state, "The best ideas poorly implemented get you nothing. But a good idea flawlessly implemented can get you a lot." So we help train organizations to implement against their goals and against the plans that we create.

Mentoring is so important, and I believe that so much that we built an organization that focuses on coaching and mentoring executives and leadership teams. We work across the for-profit, non-profit, and public spaces. Our vision for our firm is a thriving community where good ideas spread. We believe good ideas can come from anyone and anywhere. So, by mentoring and coaching, we help individuals not only strengthen their skillset but also focus on the goals for their organization.

New Orleans is a unique market. I'm not from here, but I married a woman who is from here. Often, people leave New

Orleans, but many love to come home. We spent most of our married life in Boston, where I was in financial services for over twenty years. My wife's a professional fundraiser. We decided to move back to New Orleans in 2010 to be part of the resurgence of the city.

It's a unique city that has a deep cultural heritage and had to be reimagined after Katrina. New Orleans is like no other city in terms of opportunities and the idea of reimagining all aspects of the city. Out of the horror of Katrina came some good, but the good was how do we build a city that can meet the needs of its diverse population?

When you come to a city like New Orleans, you need to understand the dynamics and history. You need to know where the support systems are. Mentoring has helped me understand what the city's all about. I raised my hand and said, "I want to help. I want to create an organization that's going to help build a community here. But before I do that, I'm not going to come in with my East Coast mentality, like the East Coast people know all the answers."

But first, I needed to understand what's required in New Orleans. What does reimagination mean? Who do I need to know in the city? And whenever I reached out for guidance from anyone in the city, no one—and I mean no one—said no to me. They always made time to have coffee, have a meal, or talk about it, because they were excited because people were moving here. They were excited that people cared about their city. They were excited that people wanted to help them make an impact. So mentoring was huge in terms of the launch of our company.

I've had mentors throughout my career, but the most significant mentor in my life was my grandfather. He never got out of grammar school and only went through the sixth or eighth grade. That was back in the early 1900s, and they had no money, so he had to go to work. I remember him saying to me constantly, "At the end of the day, they can take everything away, but what they can't take away is your character. That's what you have until the end."

That was a key message: always do the next right thing. Another thing he would say was, "Always know that people are not going to remember you for the meetings that you run, but for the person that you are."

When I was getting into different types of colleges, I remember him saying how proud he was of me. But he would say, "Remember, it's not where you go to school—it's what you do with where you go to school."

So it's these messages that stick with me. I'm now in my fifties, and I heard these messages in my teens and twenties. They stuck with me, which shows the power of mentorship and the power of voices.

Throughout my career, I often had jobs where it was a stretch. People believed in me, and they would put me into positions that maybe I didn't know exactly what I was doing. However, you learn as you go, and I've had incredible mentors throughout my career. When I was at Procter & Gamble, and when I was at Fidelity Investments, I had people who cared about me individually. They knew how much I cared, and they knew how hard I worked. So they always wanted to provide that guidance.

The biggest mistake you can make along your career path—and I've made this mistake—is to forget to ask for help. You forget to ask for guidance. You get into positions, and you think you should know how to do it, so you go full steam ahead, and you might stumble a bit. So I think it's essential to ask for guidance, no matter where you are, especially if you're running organizations like I have a history of. Also, it can be a little lonely at the top.

Who are you going to talk to? You're the person who's supposed to have their stuff all buttoned up. Where do you share that vulnerability? Where do you reach out to say, "I might need a little help. I'm not sure"? Whenever I did that, it was most always often successful. When I failed to do that, I later realized I should've asked for some guidance there.

Many people feel like that's a sign of weakness if you don't know everything, and you're not showing your lead. I often say that asking for help is the most significant sign of strength. It's about strength, and it's about humility. And you never get caught up in titles. You never get caught up in position. It's not about power. It's about doing the right thing for the organization. It's about inclusion. It's about making sure your team is in control. It's about making sure that you are asking for that support and help. If you can maintain focus and maintain humility and ask for assistance, it's a fantastic recipe.

I've benefited a lot from mentorship throughout my career. When I had the opportunity to come to New Orleans, I had the chance to build Trepwise. My goal was, since it began with me, to help organizations be more successful.

New Orleans didn't have a lot of industry here, but they had a few. Hospitality is huge. Oil and gas were huge. But there wasn't a lot of diversified industry, and therefore, there wasn't a lot of diversified industry experience. So the question I wrestled with is, "How can I use my industry experience to help a new New Orleans that's focusing on entrepreneurship and startups and new ideas across all sectors, private, public, and nonprofits?"

Trepwise was founded on mentorship and on how we can help young leaders. How can we help professionals navigate a changing environment, landscape, and ecosystem to allow them to be successful? And then "I" became "we," and we became much bigger than me.

Now I have a team of skilled practitioners who are focused on our vision: this idea of a thriving community where good ideas spread while focusing on helping individuals and organizations frame their ideas, develop their ideas, plan around their ideas. And not necessarily do it for them, but help them do it, and I think that's the nuance there.

Sometimes consultants are brought in, and they say, "Do it, and get back to us." We're not that consulting firm. We're a consulting firm that's going to partner and mean it. It's going to help guide and train and develop the skills for these organizations to succeed as they continue to grow. It's part of our culture and fabric.

I would probably say that most entrepreneurs need mentoring in structure. How do they scale their ideas? Entrepreneurs tend to be visionary and envision a world that does A, B, C, and D. Getting into the details and being able to scale those ideas can often be challenging.

So how do we make sure that you're organized correctly? How do we make sure that you have the right plans in place? How do we make sure that you have the right people surrounding you? How do we think about funding? (Funding is also another challenge that many entrepreneurs have.) How do they access capital? We believe in an equitable community and society.

While New Orleans on many metrics is thriving, on other metrics, it's not thriving. Not all populations are having access to some of the success that's going on in the city. So how can we help people of color? How can we help women-led businesses achieve the same success as other entrepreneurs? It depends on who you are and your background and what your goals are that dictate what they may need from a mentoring perspective.

My advice is not to be afraid of failure at all. Take risks. However, make sure they're calculated and make sure you learn from them. You will fall. It's not how you fall; it's how you get up, and how you keep going. It's all about implementation. You can have the best ideas, and if you cannot bring them to the market, they are meaningless. So the best ideas poorly implemented get you nothing. But a good idea flawlessly executed can get you a lot. So focus not only on the concept and why it's relevant but what you need to do to bring it to market.

I went to Harvard Business School, and Harvard is all about case methodology where they give you a new case every single day, and you're supposed to analyze the industry. That's how I've lived my career. For me, it's about experiential learning. There are some innovative books with some frameworks in them, and Michael Porter has all his templates and stuff. They can be helpful, but I'm a big believer in life experience and ensuring that you can apply your life experience appropriately.

Erik Kaeyer
KG+D Architects, PC
Kgdarchitects.com

An ex-employee of ours named Dan Jaconetti was with us for years, but he left because he got married and moved out to Chicago. We recently reconnected, so I asked him what his thoughts were, and he had an interesting observation.

It keys into my personal experience because my first experiences in architecture were with big firms. A big-firm experience is different from a small to a midsize firm, which is the practice that we have here.

In a larger firm, you tend to get quickly put in a specific role or position, and that's your experience. Architecture has such a wide variety of skill sets wherein you need to be successful, so when you're in a big firm, they take one of those skill sets and take advantage of it, whether it's design or technical or marketing.

When you work in a firm like ours today, which is a twenty-five-to-thirty-person firm, we do projects that any large firm would be proud to call their own. We compete against large firms, so I understand and know that type of experience. What the employees have in our firm that's special here is they get that large-firm experience, but they're also experiencing the full spectrum of skill sets that you need to become a successful architect.

As mentors, we expose young architects to the full experience. What we mean by that is every week, we get together and talk about the projects, practices, things that worked, lessons learned, and how the business of architecture is run.

Through osmosis, they learn quite a bit. So this gentleman who left and went to work for a big firm said, "Experiences in your firm far exceeded the experiences I'm getting here because now I have a specific role. Even as a more senior person in this company, I don't get to see the full spectrum. I don't understand or hear what the partners are doing or how the principals bring in work. Your firm exposed me to the clients and consultants."

Since we work collaboratively, it was a vertically oriented experience where he saw a project from beginning to end and all aspects of it. Through that, he had such a wonderful and excellent learning experience, but he isn't seeing the young people in his new large firm having that same exposure. They don't have the same understanding of all aspects of it. From a mentoring point of view, we expose people to the full spectrum of skills and issues we have to address on a day-to-day basis. I imagine that having that well-rounded perspective makes you a better participant in the architecture industry.

You're dealing with lots of different personalities and people. You have to understand how to treat people and work well with them. Everybody has a self-interest, so one thing about mentoring is that you have to get away from it not being about you; it's about them. It's about this person that you're working with and how you can help them become better at whatever it is that they're doing.

You have to pay them well and treat them like they're professionals. You want to have as few barriers as possible so that there aren't walls between the people that are bringing the projects and the people that are doing the projects—there must be direct communication. You want to have internal training.

However, you also want them to have the opportunity to have external training so they get the experience of realizing that what they're learning in your company is a wonderful experience. They get to meet people that have other experiences and other practices to determine whether what they're doing in this company is what they want to do for life or whether this is one step along the path. Perhaps they would be better off in a different environment.

There are experts out there who are experienced in whatever your interest is. So you want to get them to get out there, have that experience, learn something, and then bring those new skill sets that they learned back to the company and share it with everybody.

Part of the learning experience is being able to explain what it is that you've learned and teach other people. What was it that jazzed you up about it? Be excited about it and share it with everybody else.

One of the reasons why we've been successful is that we show enthusiasm for the work that we do, and we share that excitement with our employees. We share it with our clients and other consultants. You've got to treat everybody well, including your employees, clients, and consultants. When you're with them, they're the most important person at that time for the job that needs to be done. It has to be sincere. Make sure that they're fully on board with what it is you're doing.

I like to lead by example. It would be best if you worked hard to be successful in this world. You have to know what you're doing it and be passionate about it. One of the reasons that we've been successful here is that the principals in charge of these projects and I have two partners do "lead by example." We work as hard or harder than anybody else in this company, and the employees around here know it. They appreciate the fact that we're not just giving them tasks and disappearing. We've rolled up our sleeves, and we're part of the action, and we see it from beginning to end. We're trying to give them the tools they need to be successful. When they achieve something or create something unique, it's rewarding to acknowledge them.

Part of that, I get from my experience with my parents. My parents would be on my list of mentors. Sometimes people will say it's one parent or the other, but both of mine had a similar approach. I was loved, but I wasn't coddled as a child. Some friends of mine even joked that they don't think I was ever hugged, which I don't think is the case. Rules were set, and expectations were created. But there was a full level of support, and generous praise was offered whenever there was a success. They were there to share in that success and be proud.

As a leader in a professional architecture firm, you need to be the same way. We treat the employees professionally, and they know what's expected of them. When they achieve that level of success, create the project, and develop beautiful renderings or whatever phase of the project gets built, everybody thinks it's wonderful. We make sure that they're sharing in that success, and they realize that they were a big part of the success of the job.

In terms of other mentors that I had, I worked for a few different firms before coming here. I've been back on the East Coast for twenty years, but I had a couple of mentors back in Chicago when I was there. Angelo Kokkino and Andrew Tobisch were both in the same company, McClier, which was bought out by a much larger firm about the time I left.

They recognized and realized what my talent was and provided me the opportunities, support, freedom, and space to be successful. They shared in those successes because they took a personal interest in me. They provided excellent, thoughtful criticism along the way, which wasn't demeaning in any way. They gave the direction needed to keep the project moving in the right way. When I said, "Well, should we go this way or that way?" They were thoughtful in terms of which direction it should go and why, without forcing it. They wouldn't say, "We have to do it this way." It was a conversation, and collectively, we came to the right solution. Because of that, I was grateful and continued to go back to those mentors for advice.

They recognized my skill as an exceptional designer, as those weren't their qualities. One had quality in terms of management and technical architectural expertise while the other was skilled in sales and people and the overall creation of projects. Between the three of us, we were able to create some exceptional projects because we all worked off each other's strengths. They helped strengthen mine and facilitated that ability, even when I was a young architect. They were able to find support so that I learned other aspects of the business but didn't have to struggle through them.

I had some wonderful experiences. When I was in Chicago, we were doing work all around the world, so they exposed me to different clients. I can talk about meeting multibillionaires in the Middle East and having drinks with them at their house and giving private presentations with peacocks in the background as a young professional. Those are experiences I cherish, so I've kept in touch with those people because they were special to me.

One thing I'd say about mentoring is that I've found that it's easier to be a mentor or mentee when there's a sizable age difference between the two. It's almost as if it's a generation apart because you have the person that's wise and doesn't feel challenged by the mentee.

Sometimes when your mentor and mentee are just a few years apart, it's challenging to have that role because there can be a conflict as if it's an older-brother-versus-younger-brother type of thing. Maybe the older brother expects you to be at his level when you aren't necessarily there yet. When you have a generational separation, both sides are interested in the other's success.

Also, when you're starting to mentor somebody—especially someone right out of school—there's a transitional period from school to work. You have to understand and appreciate that people mature at different speeds. As a mentor or coach, you have to recognize that transition period and help them transition from that school-focused, educational, academic world to the professional world. Suddenly, this person realizes that they make money, which is fun, and they have a little bit more freedom. But then they realize that they're going to be working for the rest of their life in a career that they have now decided to dedicate themselves to, whether or not they're fully prepared to do so.

They might've been good at art or drawing in school, so they went into architecture. But now it's real. Some people jump into it. I would say that I knew earlier that I wanted to be an architect. I have a history of architects in the family, which isn't necessarily the reason why I did it, but I was good at art and creativity, and this is a wonderful field to express what I want to express.

But many people graduate from college in a specific field like architecture, and they're not necessarily ready to fully embrace it. Those are the people that need a higher level of mentoring, and they're a tougher group to work their way into how to do it. It takes time, and you have to give them space to grow. It's a tricky thing. Every person is somewhat different in how they grow and learn and how you should mentor them.

Some people need to be coddled, so you give them little pieces of things. Others, you have to beat them up a little bit. Not physically beating them, but you have to say, "Hey, this is your life. Start acting like you care about this because you could be excellent. I see the potential. I've seen the work that you've done in school. I know that you're jazzed up about this aspect of this business. Jump into it. Get excited about it. Because if you do, this will be rewarding for you. And if you don't do this, this could be a real struggle."

It's not just architecture, as most businesses out there aren't easy to be successful in. You have to be passionate about it, and you have to work hard, and hopefully, you have a couple of lucky breaks, and things turn out well. If they don't, you keep working at it until you find the one that gives you a big break.

It's important to leave room for your mentee to make mistakes. They're going to commit a couple or more. We all make mistakes. I made one the other day when writing a proposal. I forgot to edit something, and it went out to a client. We're all going to make mistakes. You work hard to try to do your best. We allow people to make mistakes that aren't serious. You give people a little bit more, you challenge them a little bit more every week, month, or year. You give them opportunities to succeed and opportunities to fail, but you don't want them to fail too big. You want them to fail a little bit at a time, and by failing a little bit, they grow. They won't fail at that same thing again. Next time, they'll fail at something a little bit at a different level, and that's okay. I will also say that because of speed and technology and the way that people operate, the world is a little less forgiving now than it was ten or twenty years ago at making mistakes.

People's expectations are high. Our clients' expectations are high, and we're constantly challenged to be perfect daily. That's a tricky thing to accept. I think that because the world is becoming smaller in certain aspects, and more challenging in terms of the speed that you need to complete a task, that it's challenging to get it done as quickly as it needs to be done—to the satisfaction of everybody out there who expects it to be done.

We all work together to collaborate to get that project or task done accurately. I think as a mentor or manager, it's essential to work with the younger folk to help them and help each other succeed at the task that's at hand.

Our senior staff did a professional sales seminar on marketing with Sandler. But one thing that the course brought into focus was that it's not about you or it's not about me when you're selling.

It's about the person that you're selling to. They're the most important person, whether it's the mentee, client or consultant. Whoever it is that you're with at that time, that's who it's about. Over six months, we learned that to focus on the people or person in front of you is a critical life skill. Whereas before, we may have gone into an interview and talked about ourselves before talking about them. We flipped it on its head and entirely focused on them. If we were going to show a formal project we worked on, we were going to relate it to them and the problems that they were interested in solving. I've read some self-help books, but I would say that the meeting every month and discussing how to work was probably more valuable than anything else I've done over the last few years.

The person whom I spoke about at the beginning of this conversation, Dan Jaconetti, came in as a bright young architect right out of school. He worked with us for a few years and quickly learned that his skill set wasn't necessarily at the design end. His skill set was in developing projects, detailing projects, and he had an excellent way about working with others as he was personable, and people liked him.

Dan was a great person to not only serve as a right-hand person to me. I could work with him and show him how I design, and he could dive into the technical and specification aspects. But he was also a wonderful person to take to meetings. Through osmosis, he would listen to how I worked with clients and engaged with them. We did a couple of projects from beginning to end, including the Jacob Burns Film Center in Pleasantville, which is a marvelous facility. We did their Media Arts Lab Twenty-First Century, a next-generation institute that works with students and teaches them how to communicate in the world today.

Dan took that project through my guidance and leadership, and by the end of the project, they were counting on him. He was the person they wanted to talk to, and not just the owner, but the construction manager. The board of directors looked to him as much as they looked to me. I take credit for that, but I give him a tremendous amount of credit for being a part of that and wanting to be an active participant.

That led to another project, which was Guiding Eyes for the Blind up in Patterson, where we did their K-9 development center. He was terrific at doing the research, and I recognized that right off the bat. We would work back and forth as to how to develop spaces through his research and my design brain to come up with the right solutions, then sit down with the client.

By the project's end, Dan was the guy the client called, went to, as he helped lead that project from its inception through its completion. For a young architect, I guess the mentoring aspect of that is finding what the skill set is of that individual and exploiting it positively so that they learn, and everybody has a positive experience.

Our slogan is to listen, imagine, build.

The first thing we do is listen, and that's a massive part of our business and how we've become successful because we don't have any preconceived ideas. We don't have one set design style. We listen to the clients and look at the environment. Through both, over time, we come up with a solution that fits that specific site and client based on what we're hearing. Then once we have that information, we can start the imagination process.

One of the wonderful things about being an architect is that you can affect the environments wherein people live. Our practice here is about the place that you go to, whether it's a school, library, church, community center, or an office. Those are the environments that we want to shape. We love working with committees in large groups because we want to affect the communities that we're in and that are around us. That's something that we instill in our employees, and we mentor people on because we want people to not only be great architects but also great citizens of the community and environment around us. We want people to be active participants, and one way that we see that we can be active participants is through this wonderful thing that we get to do, which is to design spaces that people can get to love and appreciate.

The area that I think most entrepreneurs need mentoring in is the transition period of getting mentees from academia to their professional careers and helping to ensure that this is where they want to be for the rest of their life. If you look at the architectural schools, in most cases, they're relatively small compared to other programs. I graduated from Cornell, where we started with ninety students and graduated with thirty (two out of three people that started the program left).

On an annual basis, Cornell's undergraduate program is ranked first in the country. even so, Of my thirty classmates that graduated in architecture, probably only a third are still practicing architecture. We started with ninety, and now we're down to ten. So 10–11 percent of the people that thought they wanted to be architects are still architects—and that's in the world-renowned program.

If you go into the design industry, you may ask, Where did these people go? Well, there are lots of different ways that you can still be in a similar profession, whether it's construction management or set design. Many people go into graphics or computer design industries. They design video games, or they go to Hollywood to develop sets, or they go to Broadway to design that type of set.

There is an infinite number of design trays that they may go into. Or maybe they find out that they're more of a technical person, so they go into the construction field and become construction managers or build other things.

There are lots of ways to express the creative design that you thought that you were going into when you started architecture. I think part of the mentoring is trying to help those people right out of school find what they're best at, and whether this is something that they want to do, or if it's something that they ultimately realize is a little off track. If so, maybe they should find something else.

If I were to write a book, I would advise others to work hard. Lead by example. Treat the people around you well. Be excited and enthusiastic about what you do and share that enthusiasm with others. Don't compromise more than you have to, as there's always a compromise. Come up with your ideas, and do the best you can to stay on that path because you have to find your way in the world. If you compromise, ultimately, you won't be happy with who you are, so be true to yourself.

Justin Bakes
Forward Financing
Forwardfinancing.com

I'm the co-founder and CEO of Forward Financing, which provides working capital financing to small businesses throughout the US. Founded in 2012, Forward Financing is headquartered in Boston. Throughout the company, we have almost two hundred employees. Half of which are in Boston, and we have an international office in the Dominican Republic.

One unique way in which our company has been affected or improved upon by mentoring is with the new hires. Most people talk about customer experience, but at Forward Financing, we talk about the employee experience.

We use mentoring for new hires for their first day, week, three months, and six months to make sure they're successful. We've found that, historically, when starting a new job, a new career, a new company, in a new city, it's an intimidating, stressful change. Having a mentor and someone they can work with to make sure their transition is successful is essential.

The benefits of that success are improved employee retention, and we have less than 5 percent regrettable turnover. The other benefit is that new hires can get up to speed faster and be able to contribute at a much earlier stage than they would otherwise. The third benefit—which is just as important, if not more—is that through mentoring, we're able to retain, maintain, and grow our company culture. Adding new hires, growing quickly, and having a mentor at the company does us a lot of good in being able to maintain and positively improve our culture.

When someone comes into our company, each new hire is immediately paired with a mentor. We use relationships and mentors throughout the company. Some of the most significant impacts have been that we've seen improved retention, moving faster up the learning curve, and being able not only to consume and learn information but also to contribute positively to the business. Then the third is the culture.

My biggest mentor was my father. My father was a terrific leader and a great father. Before and during my professional life, he gave me a lot of support and insight. One of the sticking points or biggest takeaways I have taken from him is—and I use this every day—is to put everything possible into relationships without looking for something specific in return.

Whether it's personally or professionally, I look and drive to put what I can and see how I can impact positively in a relationship without looking for payback. Frankly, the nice thing is that no matter what happens, it ensures long-term success, prosperity, and positive things do happen. So that was one of the critical lessons learned from my father.

My father was in a different business; he was the president and CEO of large public companies, and he was also an entrepreneur and started successful companies. He was a professional manager and had a completely different career path than I did. But this lesson, and him being able to mentor me throughout my career up until a few years ago, is a significant part of why we've been successful here at Forward Financing.

I've done mentoring outside of business and nonprofits, specifically for children in the foster care system looking to go to college. Within the business, my form of mentoring is effectively trying to create ambassadors throughout the company. It starts with our leadership team. We have ambassadors spend time with leaders of the different groups and departments so that they're effectively an ambassador for myself and the goals, priorities, and path of the business.

What that does is allow the ambassadors to create below them a strong and aligned team, so that communication flows down, and we're all aligned on priorities. Again, that maintains and reinforces our culture. As a mentor, I first look after my direct reports so that they can effectively be ambassadors, and so they can appropriately disseminate information, priorities, culture, etc.

How we do that is not just via one-on-one meetings but also via weekly tactical meetings with our leadership team so that the messages are clear. We also do daily calls with our team, which we call huddles. We want to have constant increased communication, not only individually but across the organization, so that we have consistent messaging priorities across the company.

I feel the area that most entrepreneurs need mentoring in would be on how to build an organization and properly plot out an organizational chart, which makes sure they're hiring the right people and proactively thinking about that. The second area I feel would be essential to bolster would be specifically around hiring, such as how to hire the best people and retain them.

If I were to write a book, my key theme would be to maintain a relentless focus on your hiring process. You should have a robust hiring process as an entrepreneur, CEO, and the company as a whole, and invest as much as possible from a time perspective and process to your hiring process.

Don't cut corners as an entrepreneur or CEO. Take a personal interest in who you bring on and create and recruit candidates. Spend the time upfront, sourcing, interviewing, and especially onboarding candidates. What we've seen is that practice generates terrific rewards for the company as well for other employees and me.

Adam Phillips
American Business Systems
Absystems.com

We're in the healthcare space, on the billing and revenue cycle management side. We've built a training and support company (similar to a franchise) that helps people start their own independent healthcare business providing outsourced services to private practices. We provide all the upfront training and marketing assistance to our licensees as well as the back-end training and support. We've been doing that since 1994, so we're coming up on twenty-five years in business.

We have a suite of products and services called revenue cycle management services. The primary offering that we have, which you can read on our website, is nine different services with which you can help private practices. They are various things related to the bottom line, such as assisting them to reduce their insurance claim denial rates and helping them get paid faster and more efficiently. Plus, it makes it a lot easier for patients to pay what they owe.

The doctors who end up using our licensee services see significant increases in overall annual revenue: 20–30 percent in some cases. We have a document management system that they can use. We have audit protection services. If doctors are concerned about making sure that they're doing their coding and everything correctly, we have services that can help them with that too. Doctors will typically see their claim denial rates reduced to less than 2 percent when using our system. The national average for insurance claim rejections hovers around 30 percent, so getting them down to less than 2 percent is quite a big deal.

My parents founded American Business Systems in 1994, but my parents started a medical billing business in the '80s. Our family has been in the industry for so long that I have memories of my mother using a typewriter to make medical claims. I came from a mortgage background, and I came on board with ABS about thirteen years ago after deciding to help my parents grow the business. Every year, we see growth, and there seems to be no end in sight. Doctors are having such a hard time with all the different rules and regulations, medical codes, and new payment models that they have to follow to get paid from insurance companies. They realize that it makes a lot of sense to have somebody outside the office doing some of this stuff that they're trying to manage in their offices.

I want to share the story of consistency and persistence I learned by watching my father. During his childhood, his parents and peers told him that he would never amount to much. He had overcome those with consistent mental reprogramming and positive thinking and not to being afraid to fail in new ventures. I witnessed him start and fail at many different opportunities and businesses until he finally found one that stuck in healthcare, and here we are today.

My father is my significant mentor, and I also have my two best friends who are in the business with me today. I hired them because I learned early on that to succeed, I needed to have people around who I felt were smarter than me in different areas. One of my good friends is our chief operating officer, and he's a numbers guy, so he helps out quite a bit in that area. He runs the day-to-day operations of the business, and I'm thankful for his assistance.

One of my best friends is a master salesman and business coach, and so he's been instrumental in bringing new business to our company. I've been able to witness his journey through our company and learn a lot about how he does things. He's good at dealing with people who are looking into the business.

My friends are both super smart guys, and we're fortunate to have them as part of the team to help us grow. Whenever we're in the office, I feel like I've got people around to show me the way to go and the way to do things. My father and friends help keep me from making stupid decisions, which I appreciate.

My father and two best friends are continuously mentoring me even today, even if it's not directly presented as such. I observe how they interact with our clients, licensees, and technology partners.

I'm able to draw from their expertise and responses to any issue that comes up, which has been helpful for me.

My big "mentorial" moment with my father would come back to what I witnessed and observed in his overcoming adversity to be the successful man that he is today. I would say that I learned best by watching him go to work every day.

Before he started this business, he was doing some computer training for the government. He had to travel all over the place, and he was gone a lot, and he hated it. I knew that he did, but he did what he had to do to get where he is today, and it was being that responsible person and doing anything that it took to make sure that his family was well cared for, and that influenced me.

I did some community college at a high school, but I went right into the workforce at fifteen, and I've had a job ever since, working in various industries. That was my direction, that was my path.

I emulated my father because he went to college but never graduated, and that was not a hindrance to his success. He's a successful guy now, and I'm looking forward to walking in his footsteps. He embodies the kind of persistence that leads to success.

Many books have also served as mentor texts for me. Anything by Zig Ziglar. Robert Cialdini has got some great stuff on the science of influence. Recently, I've read some *The Compound Effect* by Darren Hardy on how to be more productive and how to make small incremental changes in your life to become the person that you want to be.

The Compound Effect teaches you that you don't have to make massive changes in your life for anything that you want to do or stop doing, such as bad habits. All you have to do is practice small incremental changes daily to see change, and that was true in my life.

I also read the classics such as *The 7 Habits of Highly Effective People* by Stephen Covey. *Lifetime Plan for Success* was a Dale Carnegie book, and then, of course, *How to Win Friends and Influence People*. I read that book when I was a kid.

I have not dipped into mentoring yet. I've been so focused on building this business, but I want to go down that road. I feel like

I still have a lot to learn myself, so a lot of it is knowing that there are people out there who could benefit from the things that I've learned. I think the focus would be going back to demonstrating what I mentioned above, which is being consistent and persistent in anything that you're involved in and making sure that you can be a reliable person, in your personal life and work life.

When I look around today and look at new entrepreneurs starting, I'd say that consistency and persistence are the two most needed lessons for those starting out.

I learned early on to be a reliable, consistent employee. When I was fifteen, I worked in a sandwich shop. The owner told me that hands-down I was the most reliable teenager he had ever seen, and he was so glad he had found me. I heard him bragging to people that there are not many fifteen-year-olds who always show up on time.

By the next year, I had the keys to the business, and he trusted me to open and close the shop. Every job I've had—whether it's sweeping floors or bringing in new licensees to our unique opportunity that we have now—people know that they can rely on me to always be there.

I've made some mistakes. For example, it was a mistake not to be fully prepared when I was transitioning to a new position and looking for new employment. I didn't prepare well for the interview process and made some mistakes, which ended up with me not being hired. I didn't say the right things and didn't know what they were looking for in a new hire, so that was something I had to learn the hard way.

I didn't prepare myself for the type of questions they would ask, like why I had wanted to leave my current position. I didn't give them the right answers, so I learned that when you're looking to find new employment, you should role-play with a friend or a family member on what you think you'll be asked and what should be the responses to those questions.

We have also written books that help doctors thrive in private practice. One is called *The New Thriving Medical Practice*, written by Patrick Phillips and Dr. Vicki Rackner. It's a marketing tool that our licensees can use to help educate doctors on the need for proper revenue cycle management and why it's a good idea to have somebody outside the office doing this work for them. There's another one called *How to Reprogram Yourself for Success*. They're the two big books that we push that licensees get when they become a licensee of our company.

COMMUNITY

As this next group of entrepreneurs will inform, mentors can be found in all areas of life. The chapters from the following business leaders describe how they were fortunate to find teachers in a variety of spaces with their communities. Accessing mentors in your area can help you identify those within your industry who are willing to invest in you and your success.

Community mentors can offer their experience to guide you throughout the unique challenges that many leaders encounter, such as how and when to scale, and the crucial seats you'll need to fill ASAP in your company. Also, community mentors can offer access to their networks, include you in networking events, and introduce you to others who can help you.

Maryann Donovan
Impact Personnel, Inc.
Impactpersonnel.com

I opened my business—a staffing and recruiting company—thirty years ago. I was in my late twenties, which gives you an idea of how old I am. I spent many hours speaking with a mentor of mine, who was a recruiter.

I was in Fairfield County at the time, and she was in Manhattan, New York, and she helped me think through the process and mentored me throughout the opening of my business. Though retired now, she's still someone I call upon from time to time, and we've stayed in touch. If I didn't have that support, I wouldn't have my company now.

In the beginning, you need to have strong mentors. I think you need them all the way through, but most especially at the beginning. Back then, a female couldn't get a loan by herself, so I had to rely on a line of credit on my house. That has changed, thankfully. But if you think about it, your accountant, your lawyer, and maybe your landlord can take care of all the finer details of opening a business. But you still need the big-picture person to help you through, and that's where my mentor came into play.

It was a big leap, especially considering how young I was, and it was a risk. I was married. I had a child. I had a mortgage. So it wasn't like I was free to do whatever I wanted financially. I do think by having my mentor nudging me forward and reminding me of what I had done in the recruiting business and that I had the potential to build made a difference for me to leap.

I knew how to recruit, and I'm good at it, and I knew I was good at it, but I didn't know how to create a logo or to set up an accounting system or how to pay my temps or my employees. I had to do all that and get all that into play. It was hard for me at first.

You're always learning. I think you should, as an entrepreneur, continually be growing but at the same time learning. Every day, there's something to learn. That's why I like it, because I deal with different people and different companies every single day of my career. It keeps it fresh and exciting. No day is the same in my world.

I've said this over and over again to people starting businesses: my biggest mistake was, in the beginning, I thought I could do it all and be it all. I also wanted to save money. I would write the temp payroll, on my dining room table on Friday nights, and figure out deductions. Of course, I'm neither a mathematician nor an accountant, so I've made mistakes. Those penalties probably cost more than a payroll service would have cost. You have to get professional help and rely on professionals as soon as possible. Doing my payroll was not a good thing to do, and I learned that lesson the hard way.

I think I've read all the books. I've read *The E-Myth* by Michael Gerber and Simon Sinek and everything in between. I'm a big reader anyway, and I read anything from biographies to novels to business books, so it would be hard for me to say, "Oh, here's the one book that made the difference for me."

Back in the day, I used to subscribe to *Inc. Magazine* and *Success Magazine*, which was big for me then. My idea is that if you get one glimmer, one noggin of info, or one takeaway from a book, that was time well spent.

In my world, because I have employees here, I think I've mentored every single employee who's ever worked here. Whether that employee was here for three months or six months or ten years, I've mentored all them, because I think that's what you do as a boss. I've had situations where people have been here for three months and said to me, "I'm not sure that the world of recruiting is right for me."

It's not for everybody. It's tough. I've helped those individuals figure out where they could be better placed, and I've placed a lot of them through my company. I still have tons of contact with people who have worked here in the past for that reason. But I think you're always a mentor if you're a business owner. I don't think it ever stops for your employees, as that's how they grow.

I've had employees go into other recruiting situations, mostly corporate, and then they become my clients.

That has worked out nicely, so it's okay. This side of the business is not for everyone. Some people would rather be in a more stable environment where you get a salary and work the corporate. That's how I started in this world, but I didn't like the corporate. I like this side better, but it's not right for everybody.

We work a lot on the East Coast, so it's not as local as people might think, especially now with technology. Because of FaceTime and Skype and all that, we don't have to meet in person. I don't meet a lot of our clients in person. We filled a job in Washington, DC, and I've never set eyes on the client, but that was fine because we did it all by phone and email. That part of the world has changed a lot.

I've watched the business evolve from thirty years ago in so many ways. The world has changed, but it's mostly for the good because, as I said, I can fill a job in DC. Thirty years ago, that would have been very difficult because it would have had to have been done by phone. The fax was somewhat useful back then, but there wasn't any email.

If you think about a life without email, we had to send a resume by snail mail or fax, so that has changed for the better. LinkedIn has made a significant impact on our businesses. All the job sites have changed things. But it's still based on human relationships. You still need mentoring. You still need human relationships.

Now the next big topic of conversation in our world is AI, and is that going to change things? It will, to some extent. But you still need a human at the end of it. A computer can only have screen skills and resumes so far. You need a person at the other end to screen for the cultural and behavioral aspects of placement.

Twenty years ago, you would drop your resume off or mail it and look in the Sunday *New York Times*. The first thing I did every Sunday morning was to get the job pages in the local papers and the

New York Times. That's what I did to see what my competitors were doing. We used to call in our ads. So it's all changed, but it's still all about relationships at the end of the day. That's how I've grown my business for over thirty years. It's all about relationships, which is mentoring and being mentored.

The area I think most entrepreneurs need mentoring in—and I would hope most entrepreneurs would agree with me—is that mentoring is implicit in how you work. It builds relationships. It creates honest conversations. My message would be that entrepreneurs need mentoring in how to keep it going. When you open a business, you need to know what to do.

As the old story goes, "I like to eat, so I'm going to open a restaurant." No. You have to know what you're doing. I knew how to recruit. I knew what I was doing from that aspect. I had worked in corporate recruiting and agency work, so I knew my craft very well. I knew the demand was there. I knew the economy. I knew my numbers. But I needed an accountant to help me with that kind of thing.

As I grew the business, peer-to-peer support was helpful, and I think most entrepreneurs would agree. I joined the Women's President Organization (WPO), and I've been involved with them for about fifteen years.

You're invited to join by certain revenue constraints, and it's a peer-to-peer advisory. We meet once a month, we do an annual retreat, and there's a big global conference every year that's been extremely helpful. That's more peer-to-peer advisory and mentoring, and that's been fabulous because it's all females. In my group, you can't be in the same discipline, but outside, you can be. But the whole idea is that everyone has the same problems (maybe not at the same time), so you're helping each other weed through all these situations and giving advice and receiving advice. You're mentoring and being mentored at the same time.

I would advise any business owner or entrepreneur to be mentored that way because I think it's a win-win situation. Again, you need someone who will give you real feedback and not say,

"Sure. You're going to be great." I had people thirty years ago tell me not to open my own business, and I respected that.

Then I had a friend who sat down with me and went over points and how I was going to do certain things. He wasn't in recruiting—he was a friend looking out for me. I appreciated that because it's not easy and you do need somebody who's going to help you see the hidden costs. You need people who are going to support you but give you honest feedback.

If I were to write a book, my key message to entrepreneurs would be to stay focused. But also, from a mentoring standpoint, from a people standpoint, it's all about relationships. I think you can never stop being mindful of that. I would focus on building and maintaining those relationships.

I think for us, the relationships have been what's helped us grow the business. We have to know what we're doing. People move. You might have worked somewhere twenty years ago, and then you leave, and maybe five years will go by, then you end up somewhere else, and we might work together, or I might place you. I still work with some of the same clients that I started with when I opened the business.

Time is what helps build those relationships. I think people sometimes forget that relationships take time. The same is with your employees if you're mentoring them. You have to give them your time. You can't say, "Go out and figure out what you're going to do next." You have to help them, and that time is essential.

Every relationship can be valuable. The way I did it over these years for my business is that I treat everyone well. I treat clients the way I'd want to be treated. A lot of my competitors don't. I treat my candidates well: I call them back, and I take their phone calls. Even if I can't place them, I try to help them with their resume. That's come back to me because people know that we are going to treat them well, and they remember that. That was a big part of it for us.

In some ways, we mentor our candidates because we're taking them through the process. It's scary. If you're working somewhere, and you're going to give up a job that you've had for five years, and you're going to join my client, that's scary. So we help our candidates with the onboarding process. We help them through the whole recruiting process and hopefully get them the right opportunity so they're going to be successful. My client will be happy, and my candidate will be happy. It's all a process, and it's all based on time.

Once in a while, it doesn't work out on the client's side or the candidate's side. But that's how it goes. Sometimes people aren't appreciative, but that's okay. Usually, they are, and most people appreciate it.

To return to mentoring, I know I wouldn't be here if I didn't have the woman who I mentioned earlier and then my former boss, who taught me the business. Even though she didn't directly mentor me, once I opened the company, she did when I worked with her. That's how I learned the business. Then, indeed, I've enjoyed mentoring the people who have come my way through the company. I think it's contributed to my success and impact to pay it forward.

Erick McCallum
CG Environmental Cleaning Guys
Cleaningguys.com

I've had a lot of influences in my life, but they were influences on how I didn't want to be.

I had examples of people who did things in ways I knew weren't right—to the point of misleading me on information so they could enjoy my failure. People should understand that the people whom they take advice and information from need be trustworthy. They need to know, in their heart, that they're going to lead them to the right direction.

I've had some mentors in my life.

Bob Adams was a gentleman who was a father figure to me. I lost my parents early in life, and this gentleman held a position with Lockheed Martin before they built the multibillion-dollar stealth. He's the guy who made a scale model to go in the wind tunnels to be sure it even worked. A lot of our equipment is patented and proprietary, and many times I was told that it couldn't be done.

Bob is the one who instilled in my brain that anything can be done if you put your mind to it. I had a good mentor in that regard from him, but not too many throughout my life, honestly. It was generally me taking information from people and deciding if it was good information or bad, then going from there.

I think nowadays a lot of people are looking for shortcuts, and I think if they focused less on the information being given to shortcut their way to success, it would benefit them the most. I'm the father of three, and they've all graduated from college, or still in college, and working at the same time. Honestly, I think if there's an easier road to take, I would be more suspicious of it. So be sure that who you're speaking to is honest in their everyday dealings, and if they're willing to take the time to mentor you and to give you the right advice on life.

One lesson I had to learn late in life—and it's very serious—is never to allow a millionaire to pay for your lunch. The reason for that is because in that period you're going to have lunch with this person, the information you will get out of him or her will be worth a hundred lunches. The way I live my life is that the people I want to surround myself with are the people who I can trust.

The negative experience of having people around who were not trustworthy has affected my business directly. You learn lessons on how to be cautious about who you listen to because caution is the shortcut. Many people want their success today, and that doesn't happen.

For some people, it may happen whether that's an inheritance, or they fall into it, but it's no different than a scholarship at a college or an NFL contract. The likelihood is slim. People need to understand that it's going to take hard work. If you've got to quit in your being an entrepreneur, then it's not the way to go because you can't quit, ever. You have to work very hard, and you have to have the ability to do everything.

I've got a story about a good friend of mine. He ran everything for CompUSA, but he started in the box room. He ended up running everything in the Americas and the Caribbean. We went to high school together, and we share stories of moving up. The one story that everyone has to understand is that you don't start as CEO. As CEO, you have to know what they do in the box room, at the registers, and in sales, or you can't run a company. You need to be familiar with every level of your organization, inside and out.

I learned most of what I know from the school of hard knocks. I made mistakes and learned from them the first time. There hasn't been anything that I've read, but I've done an excellent job of learning from my mistakes and other people's mistakes. I've made a ton of them, but that's what it takes. There haven't been any manuals or books. I think there are some helpful books out there, but it will come to a point where that book might not fit for every industry.

Some leadership books from some well-known successful people probably have a lot of good points in them. The main piece is to never quit, and you're going to get discouraged from time to time, but don't let that stop you. You're going to have people who are going to spit in your face, or they're going to talk bad about you behind their back, or there will be jealousy issues. You've got to keep moving forward and keep your nose down and working. That's the biggest thing that I've seen in most of the books: never give up.

Also, if you tried something, and it doesn't work, the definition of insanity, of course, is doing the same thing over and over and expecting a different result. You've got to change it up. You've got to be quick on your feet and always admit you're wrong or at fault. We work for *Fortune 100* companies, and we work with some of the top-tier people in these companies, and they all know I have no problem with letting them know if I screw up, I'm going to fix it. When people start pointing fingers trying to divert their faults onto someone else, that puts a bad taste in people's mouths.

You've got to admit to your faults and learn from them. I don't know how this would fit with a lot of people, but I have this impactful quote that I mention to people: "You can't tell a grown man what to do." What that means is you have this idea, you know it's going to work for them, or a product, but they must make it their own. You have to make it where it's their idea because you don't tell them what to do. You can't be that bull in the china cabinet, which is what I've been called many times. I have to reel it in and allow them to see it on their own. That's a big lesson to learn, and that takes patience.

You have to put your convictions in your drive forward and what you're doing and put that energy toward it. Just because it's six o'clock in the evening, it doesn't mean you're done for the day. Just because it's six in the morning doesn't mean work hasn't started yet. Entrepreneurs and people that own companies who are successful realize that it's much easier to punch a clock somewhere.

I'll tell you a story. There was a gentleman working on a ranch. The rancher was sitting next to me, watching the guy dragging and not doing a whole lot. Well, there was an opportunity for this guy to do more things for this rancher, but the rancher said, "He's got a lot of quit in him."

Well, if you got a lot of quit in you, you're not going to go anywhere. A lot of people think they're going to get their success today, so they end up having a lot of quit in them, and that's why they jump from job to job to job. My recommendation would be to put all your effort forward, especially in today's market, because you will stand out in a good way against the others. If you're going to do it, do it 100 percent—not 60 or 70 percent.

I've been a scoutmaster and other things of that nature, which have been leadership roles. I own a company called Beard's Wrecker Service, and it's the largest wrecker service in all North Texas now. When we bought that small company, it was in bankruptcy, and it was in terrible shape.

My partner there is James Bennett, and he's a good friend of mine, and I think of him as my brother, quite frankly. He came to me one day after being done wrong by another company and brought the opportunity to me. He didn't know how to run a company, he didn't have the means to buy it, and he had nothing. Now in this company, we have trucks that cost $1 million for just one truck. To get into that industry is expensive, and it takes a lot of commitment, as it's a 24/7 business, because you never close.

To make a long story short, we bought the company, he leaned on me a lot for the information, and that's my point: it's essential to listen to somebody who's going to lead you correctly and not down a dark path. We were able to grow that company in less than six years to the biggest wrecker service in North Texas, and that's against guys who have been in business for thirty or forty years or longer, so that's a big deal.

As a mentor for James, I was always there for him, and I always gave him the correct information. He now runs the company. He's never owned a company, and now he has this huge monstrosity thing, and he's doing a great job. I'm sure other people would tell you a hundred stories of me helping here, helping there. There are so many ways to mentor somebody, whether it's kids in scouting, a Sunday school class, or in business.

Even in business, you're dealing with people's personal lives because they have personal problems. They come in and ask for your advice about certain things. I have an open-door policy at my company, and any employee can walk into my office, shut the door, and talk to me about anything, and I've heard a lot of things.

We have a strong company culture—very strong. With as many employees as we have, it's still a family and a tight-knit company. We all know each other, and we know each other's families and kids. The bigger it gets, the harder that is, but I try to keep that part of the company culture at any of the companies with which I've been involved.

I purchased that wrecker company because I knew that James had the drive that he has. We all have stories to tell about our growing-up times and our home life as kids.

James came from an extra-rough area. He has a lot of drive, and honestly, he had the vision, and I could see the vision through him. At first, I couldn't see the vision that well, but I invested the time because I knew nothing of that industry. He was a second-generation tower, so it was probably a leap of faith, but I had faith in James and the possibilities that could come.

It was like another case of choosing to believe in the correct person and having no doubts about him. Every company is built on its people, and if you've got a bad culture and bad attitudes, then you'll probably go nowhere.

The area that I feel most entrepreneurs need mentoring in is the drive. I hate to say it, but we have a lot of employees, and I see a lot of different people, and my answer to this could upset a few, but it's the lack of drive that's the problem. Another one of the biggest problems I see today is that everybody wants it now. We all would like to have it now. My back and joints would love for me to have had it now and not have built a company. I was the guy that did everything in the beginning, so it doesn't work that way.

People need to decide on the direction they want to go in their life, and then they need to plant those feet down and go and do the best job possible. We raise guys in the ranks pretty darn fast when they show that drive and can-do effort and thinking outside of the box. That's highly important, but a lot of people would just as soon sneak in the corner, get on Facebook, and not do their job while they're being paid. That's why you see businesses with thirty to forty cameras everywhere because they have to babysit their employees. So be the person that stands out and help the company push forward because if you've got an owner or a boss that is thankful for good people, he"ll reward you.

Are motivation and drive something that you can teach? I think parents today—and I am one of them—are at fault for the way the youth thinks today. I came from not a lot, and if I wanted something, I had to work and figure out how I was going to get it. Well, I've used that in my business life today, and I'm sure that's maybe why I'm where I'm at today.

When it came to my kids and when they wanted something, I lived my life through them and I wanted them to have things. Now, I'm harder on my kids than most parents are. My kids have more grit than most, but I have been easier on them than I should've been.

A lot of the youth today have been given everything and anything. Expecting them to progress in life on their own makes it much more difficult on them because they weren't brought up having to figure out how they were going to get those fifty-dollar tennis shoes—they were given them. They didn't have to figure out how to get that Gucci handbag—they were given it. That's a massive problem in today's society.

Kids don't get on their bike and ride miles away from home because the news has parents so scared that their kids are going to be kidnapped, murdered, or raped. They're stuck in the house playing Nintendo, PlayStation, or whatever it is today. I fault myself too, so I want to make sure I'm clear that it's not the "other" parents. I have also been at fault for this as well, but that is, in my opinion, one of the biggest problems today, whether it be a broken home and/or giving kids what they want without them working for it.

It's like the picture you may see hanging somewhere with a farmer with a piece of wheat in his mouth chewing on it and saying, "That boy's got a lot of quit in him." You can't have a lot of quit in you. If you're going to own a company, you're going to do everything you can from eight to five while people are at work, and in the morning and at night, you're going to be doing everything.

During the day, reach out to your customers or do the paperwork that you could do at night.

Time management is a huge piece of being an entrepreneur, and you have to master it for your field of business. There's only so much time in a day. You can't add to it, but you can sure take away from it.

John Aronson
AATA International, Inc.
Aata.com

There are so many areas of mentoring when you're in a rapidly developing business and working in many different areas. Our company is an environmental, social management, permitting, and technical services company, and we work in fifty countries.

Some of the mentoring that we depend upon is related to partnering, identifying, and working with people from a broad spectrum of different geographical areas. Also, our environmental consultancy covers physical, chemical, biological, social, and regulatory issues. So this involves a wide range of disciplines, experiences, and applications.

We take it seriously when seeking advice in mentoring and guidance from many different types of people from many different technical areas and procedural areas. The best mentoring we get is from people that have "been through the wringer" in different regions before.

Probably the most important thing is identifying and securing the best partners possible when you're moving into a new area and need an understanding of the idiosyncrasies of the rules, laws, regulations, and social mores.

We operated a branch office in Colombia for quite some time. We have had branch offices in Kazakhstan, and many times, we have set up project offices in different areas. So the use of local mentoring is more of an advisory capacity of getting up to speed quickly and understanding the specific aspects of doing business in different countries. We work a lot with the various World Trade Centers. We're members of the World Trade Center in Denver. The Colorado International Trade office has been a big supporter.

Mentoring as a term covers such a broad range of topics. I think we have to depend upon excellent advice from both the business and technical sides. It's essential to understand the tax implications. Taxation from an international perspective requires a broad, deep understanding. So that's one area where we are particularly serious about seeking local mentors.

We seek local partners who are plugged into the customs and language and know the specific dos and don'ts of conducting business in certain areas. We worked diligently and for a long time in Indonesia, the Philippines, and Africa. We were one of the principal experts on permitting joint projects in Russia and the former Soviet Union, Kazakhstan, Moldova, Azerbaijan, and Ukraine. We've done many large, complicated projects, and we have had some excellent top-drawer mentors.

Unfortunately, due to the latest political issues mainly related to Crimea and some of the sanctions against Russia, that entire segment of our work in Russia and the former Soviet Union has dried up because of that sociopolitical relationship. You have to be tuned in to the broadest range of social, political regulatory aspects to be able to work in a global environment.

I read a great deal, not just business books, but also technical books. There have been many different types of excellent business books as there are so many being produced now. But many books I read are specifically geared toward people, in trying to understand the sociocultural framework and how fast that's changing around the world.

Some cultures are leapfrogging and skipping entire developmental segments. One of the regional publications—which is quite old now—was in the *Harvard Business Review* and was called "Evolution and Revolution as Organizations Grow." We've used that as an anchor point for much of our strategic thinking for over thirty years now. This was produced in the '70s, about forty years ago.

Now the rate of change is so fast that it's essential to keep up on the more-recent developments.

I was one of the first people to have a cell phone, one of those giant Motorola brick phones. I was in the San Francisco earthquake during the World Series in the late '80s, with my cell phone. Well, I walked around downtown San Francisco as I was interviewing with our catastrophic risk assessment manager at the time. I got out of the building during the earthquake, and there was still a lot of confusion. I remember lending my cell phone to the security guard at the Hyatt hotel so he could summon the earthquake inspectors and coordinate the evacuation.

This was quite a revolution to have your own cellular capability, but now you look at some of the cultures and the massive amount of communications and computing ability. It's challenging to be able to select and to focus on the things that are important for your business because you get inundated with so many things.

Part of our problem and challenge is working with so many different cultures to understand the core values, the basic principles, how the society stacks up concerning these changes, and I can tell you it's changing so rapidly that you have to be sensitive to that.

We're not a big company, but we do network globally. We've divided the world into three eight-hour zones. North, Central, and South America are eight hours. Europe, Middle East, Africa are eight hours, and then zone 3 is all the Russian Far East, India, Southeast Asia, Australia, Micronesia, China, and Mongolia. By far, zone 3 has the most population, with at least 3.3 billion people. So that's the one that will keep you up at night because when you're going to bed, they're getting up. It's across the dateline. And so keeping those three zones integrated and functioning is a lot of fun, but a big challenge too.

I founded the company in 1989, and we celebrated our thirtieth anniversary in 2019. We've done about four hundred major projects. We don't do thousands of projects. We do some projects that may last for ten or twelve years. We worked on one, which at the time was the world's largest oil and gas project.

We started there in the pre-baseline period and took it through to production, and that was about twelve years. With those types of long, extended projects, you're learning things every day.

We've only had two projects that have turned out to be negative on the overall performance of the company. Not because of any fault of our own, but because of various idiosyncrasies of the client and their economics. I think the most significant challenges have been related to clients who have tried shortcuts or haven't understood the proper way to do things in a cultural context. Specifically, this is related to the overall financial management, as it's especially important to understand taxation.

Some of the countries have completely confused tax policies and applied them arbitrarily. This has happened to us a couple of times where people come up with arbitrary tax assessments, and you ask, "Where did that come from?" So the biggest mistakes we've made are not fully understanding how to deal with the application of rules, regulations, and laws. We still don't know how to deal with the arbitrary government and quasi-governmental decisions that can be applied out of the blue.

They want you as a partner, and if they value your activities and contribution, then usually, there's a way to work it out. But if somebody is competing with you to try to get you out of a particular financial arrangement then generally in most of the countries, there's some pathway to deal with it, but with a lot of them, there is no pathway. It takes a lot of understanding in that regard in the effective taxation application of taxes fairly and equitably.

Right now, we're working mostly on international arbitration of projects, and these are starting to be quite a significant force, especially if countries evolve into modern legal, demonstrably legal frameworks.

We do quite a bit of work in international arbitration, and that has been a satisfying and vital area of our work because it challenges the legal context in which a lot of these projects operate internationally. That's a bright light in dealing with these arbitrary rules and regulations.

I started early, working here locally in Fort Collins in the Poudre School District. I supported the Poudre School District with lectures at the elementary and junior-high and high school levels. I've taught courses at the university level, and every year, I give a couple of talks at various society meetings.

But there is now so much good inner connectivity using social media that people seek advice for counseling around what to take in school, understanding environment science, how they fit in, and the future of environmental consulting. Often I give a show-and-tell to students, prospective employees, and the people seeking out information on how to decide on a career and what to study for in a job.

I do maybe four or five significant interactions a year on helping people decide what areas to study, what types of university courses to take, and what kinds of experience to seek. We have had a reasonably active program for internships and referrals to internships. We're networked into a broad spectrum of companies and activities that have those types of opportunities. We get quite a few requests for that type of information every year, and we're happy to share our experience.

There's so much to learn, and given the fact that we work in so many different areas, it's so valuable to be able to sit down with local partners and get to know how things work. We've had some partners that have been with us for thirty years. We have relationships with technical specialists around the world. It's gratifying to see how these long-term relationships can be maintained through the good, the bad times, and the challenging times.

But once you go through the mill a few times with these people, you gain high respect for them and their cultural and social and educational backgrounds.

Many people ask, "What is it that you do?" I even remember my mother—God rest her soul—asking that question. When you talk to people that want to get into the environment, it's not just saving the whales; it's all types of activities for conservation organizations and global climate change. There are so many opportunities, and I think most people are interested in knowing the one area where they could excel.

People have gotten into threatened and endangered species, plastics in the ocean, or Arctic ocean changes due to the melting ice. You go down the list, and there are so many. I think the biggest challenge is finding that area where they have a particularly keen interest and motivation. It's a lot of fun because our company deals with physical, chemical, biological, social, and regular chores. It's challenging, but it's also a lot of fun to help people try to find that niche that suits them.

I recall when I took a high school aptitude test. I knew I liked the outdoors, but there were only two categories: farmer or a forest ranger. Now there are probably thousands of different areas you can go into the environment and have a meaningful contribution to society. The most fun for us is that we work all around the world, and we get to go to some of the most beautiful, challenging, pristine, and polluted places on earth.

We worked on the Chernobyl incident. We went to Gomel, the evacuated city. We worked in support of Belarus, which had the highest deposition of fallout of any country. We've worked in some of the most pristine areas that you could ever imagine in the Russian Far East, in the high Andes, in Argentina. So we've gotten to see quite a lot of the world, and I think the thing that strikes you most is the diversity. As an example, Argentina has toucans in the tropical north of the country and penguins in the frigid south.

So in mentoring people that want to get into an environment, the diversity of the world, it's hard to explain to people how unbelievable and how challenging it can be to understand these different areas. The fun of mentoring people and trying to find out what gets their juices flowing and what they want to contribute and what areas they want to help is gratifying. We have a platform that provides a lot of that information that people can use on a practical basis.

I spent much of one winter in the Magadan Oblast, Russian Far East, in the far north, near Omsukchan and over to the Kubaka area, and it got down to fifty-four below zero centigrade. Minus forty degrees Fahrenheit F and minus 40 degrees Celsius are the same temperatures. So they crisscross it at forty, but minus fifty-four was the coldest day, and breathing that in, you've got to be careful because it's so cold.

The next year, and this points to the diversity of our activities, I worked in Myanmar, Indonesia, and Argentina. The coldest temperature was coming back from Myanmar through Narita Airport, Tokyo, and it was plus forty-three degrees Fahrenheit. That last winter before, I was almost a hundred degrees colder, and that was the coldest. So one of the things you find is how adaptable are you to the climates of the world.

We've been in some of the most pristine areas on earth, but I can tell you for sure it is a global situation. From the horrible fires in California, the smoke could be seen from a satellite in New York. You can say, "Well, isn't the air in Colorado beautiful and pristine?" Yes, but we get the inputs from a global atmospheric situation.

Even in the far north above the Arctic Circle, scientists are finding some airborne pollutants are getting into the Arctic Ocean. There are going to be so many environmental challenges as the population continues to expand. You develop an appreciation for how the world works when you see so many areas that have been decimated—such as burning forests in Southeast Asia and clearing the rainforests in Brazil and South America.

There are many forms of impacts, and we have to be dedicated as a human race to keep some stability. But it's a challenging situation to have seen so many different areas around the planet. Some people are living on the edge. We worked in Niger in sub-Sahelian Africa, immediately adjacent to the Sahara Desert, and the people there live on so little.

They grow millet, and they drink high saline waters. It's hot, and every few years, the locusts come through and wipe them out. To see where the human condition is and how it's located and how it's surviving is impressive.

We write extensive reports, and now and then, someone says, "John, you need to write that down. You need to say something about that situation." I think back to some of the first international projects we worked on, on the island of New Guinea, and we went to places that local people have not advanced beyond hunter-gatherer.

We looked for lowland tribes and highland tribes in Indonesia, on the Indonesian side of the island of New Guinea. There's an equatorial glacier on top of the island of New Guinea. So there's not that many of those around in the world, but it's almost fifteen thousand feet up there. The glacier has advanced and receded many times over the last thousands of years.

That experience alone is something that I think I should write down and share with people because I'm grateful for the opportunity to be able to go to some of these places. We've been hired to go to some of the areas that others pay a lot to see. Some of these places are so remote and difficult to get to that it's probably worth writing down.

Also, the photo documentation we have probably should be maintained somehow. We've taken thousands of pictures of some of these places.

When you look back, you realize how much you didn't know. There's so much to learn and understand. So my first advice is to be an active reader. Nowadays, anything that you want to get into, you can learn from the Internet. You can do searches on almost any topic. So the one thing that I would say is, be true to yourself and find the things that interest you. Whether it's ornithology, ichthyology, soils, physics, or some specific kind of engineering, the sciences are so broad, and there is so much to learn and understand.

I went to undergraduate school with one of my best friends. We went on searches for graduate school together, and he got into an area that was of interest to him, and I recall trying to understand how he came to this conclusion. He got into a specific area of Messenger RNA research, became a university professor, did research for over thirty years, and got to go to some of the most unbelievable places to do his research.

He taught me a lot because he focused so intensely. So I think understanding yourself is the most challenging thing, and finding out how you can contribute and feel good about what you're doing is probably the biggest challenge. There are so many avenues, and they're high speed, diverse, and you can do so much by getting online and researching things that you're interested in.

You've got to network into those organizations and societies and clubs that ring true with what you're interested in. I think that reaching out and expanding your interests and expanding your networks into areas that you might be a little uncomfortable in is also rewarding once you find those avenues that you can pursue and understand.

I grew up on a farm in Nebraska, went to college, and the first thing I did was try to get to the ocean because I have a keen interest in water and the oceans. So as an undergraduate, I went to the Mote Marine Lab in Sarasota, Florida, traveled to the West Coast, went up to Oregon, and got to the Pacific Ocean.

My background is that I'm a water specialist, so anything water is of high interest to me. I think you have to pursue those things that resonate with your interest.

There's so much information out there nowadays that focusing on the areas that you want to contribute in is the biggest challenge, as well as sorting through the number of different opportunities that are out there.

Mary Feury
Altec Systems, Inc.
Altecsystems.com

A unique way our company has been affected by mentorship is by learning the pitfalls of our particular industry. Every industry has a niche. In the commercial security world, our company was positively impacted by having access to our buying group, which is a whole plethora of other security integrators. Having this wealth of knowledge available as a mentoring source for us has been instrumental over the years. They've been able to point out pitfalls, things we should be aware of, little need-to-knows and nice-to-knows about our industry. Mentoring, by this buying group, PSA Security Network, has been instrumental for us and invaluable to the company.

There's a small little book I often refer to, because it's short, sweet, and concise—one of the John Maxwell books called *How Successful People Lead*, which I like because it keeps you on point. As you're mentoring people through the various levels of your organization, it helps you assess where you are and where you are going in the organization. This book gives insight on how to move to the next level, what to look for, and what leadership is necessary at every level. There are leadership responsibilities within all levels of an organization, all the way to the top, and that's an excellent book for defining and helping people understand that you take on leadership responsibilities, personally, at every level of an organization.

I had a boss at a prior organization, and he was an excellent mentor when talking about negotiations. He emphasized the importance of making sure—whether you're dealing with companies, customers, vendors, or people who are supplying services to you—that all those relationships need to be win-win.

My mentor didn't feel it was good for the company to feel like we won and got what we wanted—and too bad if the other side did not. He emphasized that it was always essential to ensure we were all winners. If everyone wasn't comfortable, then we weren't done working yet. His mentorship was an instrumental learning scenario for me. Now that I run the company, his teaching created for me the groundwork rule that when you're dealing with others, regardless of the relationship, that win-win needs to be part of the philosophy.

Additionally, my boss emphasized the importance of learning from your mistakes and moving forward with that knowledge. One of his favorite phrases was, "When you are in your car, there is a reason why the rear-view mirror is so much smaller than your front windshield. Keep an eye on where you've been but remember to stay focused on where you are going!"

I can probably think of a hundred mistakes I've made, but the most significant thing—especially when running your own business—is keeping an eye on the cash flow. It's different when you're a cog of a wheel in a large organization and don't have to watch how the whole business is doing. Early on, one of the mistakes I made was thinking, "We're great. We're profitable," but I wasn't watching from a cash-flow perspective, and that can get ugly quick if you're not watching it closely.

I had to learn to watch the pendulum between the two: watching cash-flow needs and profitability for the organization. You can't look at a P&L and say that you're profitable, because you can go bankrupt three weeks later if you're not watching your cash flow. That was significant learning about how to be aware of both sides of the pendulum. You must be aware of how well your business is doing, where your money is going, and how it's coming in. Pay attention to your flow, your return, your volume turn, and all those other aspects of the cash flow.

It was a rookie mistake not to pay attention to the cash flow, then play catch up, and then learn in a hurry to keep an eye on that ball. That learning was big. I was coming out of thinking that cash flow was somebody else's problem, and I'm not responsible for it. When I moved into an organization where all of it was my responsibility, that aspect of running the business became pertinent in a hurry.

Our employees vary from four to ten, depending on seasonality and the ebb and flow of the business. I augment the company a lot with subcontractors, and those relationships help the ebb and the flow of the organization as well. We can stay lean when we need to and add when necessary.

We carefully scrutinize the subcontractors we bring on. They have to "act as" an actual Altec Systems employee, and they have to have the same philosophy and certifications we do. So it has to be a fit before we even qualify them to sub for us. Once they're a fit, they're in. Once a sub works with us, we'll tend to use them repeatedly, as they become an extension of us.

As part of a buying group, I was asked to do some consulting for them because in my previous career, I was a Six Sigma certified Black Belt and had done a lot of mentoring. I did some leadership consulting and mentored some of their folks going through the Balanced Score Card strategy planning process, which, in essence, is defining the values of the organization, their mission, vision, and goals.

I mentored for them on a group level and then one-on-one one as people called and asked for some insight into how to push that strategy planning forward.

From time to time, that organization will reach out, but it's not a formal mentoring program anymore. If they want to go back and tweak something, and they don't remember how we did it or what we were talking about at the time, they'll reach out to me. My business still has strong relationships with this buying group, as well as with some vendors that do business with us. They ask for insights to better handle some processes in their organization, so it's more of an advisory than a formal mentorship.

It never hurts to help someone, whether they're a vendor, a customer, or someone who's reaching out. It's appropriate to always "find the time," because it's a small world, and you never know when you'll be the one asking for help or when they'll reach out with other opportunities for you. It's always good to have that positive network, regardless of who it is you're dealing with.

As far as mentoring, the biggest thing I find is that people tend to get "tunnel vision." When they're looking for mentoring, they're looking at their box and the things they're responsible for. Mentoring helps them look up and out, so I think new entrepreneurs particularly need to ask how I focus on the larger picture.

The win-win strategy and defining your focus is essential, so you need to know what your vision is and what the overall goals of the organization are and your part in it. Whether you are a small entrepreneur or a large entrepreneur, you must look at the biggest picture. What's outside of me, and what's outside of what I do? What's outside of the security industry? What's the more significant impact I can potentially have?

Because it's easy to deep dive into the details of whatever you're doing, especially if you're entrepreneurial, running your business, managing cash, and your employees. You can easily get sucked into that granular detail. One of the big things I find is that you must be able to take that step back from time to time and either allocate so much time a week to reading leadership material or reading things outside or within your industry to keep that bigger picture going. You don't want to get sucked under the weight of the day-to-day details, because it's difficult to grow if you do.

In the beginning, I wasn't as conscious of how important it is to stay in touch with current customers. Some customers buy from you all the time, so you sell and move on to the new customer. One of the biggest learnings early on for me was to circle back and make sure I thanked them for their business and let them know I appreciated what they're doing. I learned not to expect that they would continue with me, just because they had in the past.

Everybody needs to know their value and worth. In the beginning, it's easy to focus on the new guys and do what you need to do to get other customers. It's easy to forget about the ones who buy from you all the time. I learned to make sure I said thank you, reached out, and made sure I stayed in touch with all my customers. Because those relationships are vital, and you must be sure to nurture them.

It's easy to place your focus on the new guys and trying to acquire new business. You might think your regular customers are good, and we don't need to pay too much attention to them. That's a minefield you must be careful with. One of my learnings was to make sure everybody knows how much you appreciate them and that you check in with them. Make sure everything's still good. Is there anything they need? Plus, the flip side of that is when you do reach out and make a sincere effort to reach out to those guys, often you end up getting other leads and other business from them. It can be positive to keep your current customers happy, but often they'll reward you with other businesses when that isn't your primary motivation for reaching out.

I think the key message to anyone starting, especially when you're smaller, is to define your focus. Define what are you good at, your strengths, your mission of the company, and then stay within your wheelhouse. Don't try to be everything to everybody in the beginning. Figure out what those particular characteristics and strengths within your company and team and deep dive into that wheelhouse and stay there.

Don't start thinking along the lines of since you're a security company, then you're also going to do IT and other stuff outside the box. You shouldn't be doing that initially. Focus on your core strength. If you're good at customer service, implementations, and project planning, then understand your strengths. Focus, and find out what you're good at, and stick with that wheelhouse and use outside sources for IT, accounting work, and any types of things that you'll provide but where you're not strong. Don't automatically think, "Oh, we can do that too" and try to pull all that in house to your small team. Otherwise, you're going to overwhelm them, and you're not going to be as good at the thing that you say you're good at.

If the company is growing, and you're bringing on employees that are strong in other aspects you want to bring out into the marketplace, that's great, but don't try to be all things to all people, especially when you're starting. It's a mistake that many people make with the automatic, "Yes, we can do that." You must be careful. Don't answer, "Yes, we can do that," unless you have an outside resource that can do that, or you might consult with someone else or have a relationship with someone, but if you try to bring all that in house, you're going to dilute your strengths, and that's not an ideal way to get started. Stay focused on your strengths.

We have many offerings on our website of solutions we outsource. These are offerings that are not necessarily our core business, but we have strong relationships with other organizations that do these solutions well. I don't want be focused on those solutions that are not our core competency, so we have other people that do those services and solutions for us. Whether it's back-office work like accounting, taxes, or other business-related aspects of what we do, we outsource it where it makes sense.

There are so many organizations doing other things well that my first reaction is to ask, "Well, is there a company that we can partner with that does that solution well? Or is that something we have to look at doing ourselves?"

Don Zerivitz
Pro Clean Building Maintenance, Inc.
Teamproclean.com

I started Pro Clean in late 1989, and the company has grown to the point that we now serve all of Central Florida—from the east coast to the west coast. Along with three hundred dedicated employees, we provide commercial cleaning and facility maintenance services.

For the past ten years, I have belonged to a small group of seven fellow CEOs, and each owned businesses in different industries. We know each other's businesses and families intimately. I think of our group as my board, as they've been able to guide, advise, push, and prod me on a myriad of issues over the years. For example, some of the biggest challenges relate to growth—not growing fast enough or sometimes growing too fast.

I view our group as mentors because each of us has volunteered to stick together. The main thing that keeps us together is our commitment to each other and our desire to help one another. One area that they really helped me with is sales management. Two of the CEOs in our group have mature sales organizations with VPs of sales, each managing fifteen to twenty salespeople. Their organizations are extremely well developed.

They were extremely helpful to me in showing how even if I couldn't afford a dedicated sales manager, I could at least put someone in place to begin developing the systems and processes of a real sales department. Then, when we grew to a certain level of revenue, we would be able to move forward much more quickly because the systems and processes were already in place and operational.

I was struggling at that point because there was no way I could afford that size overhead position for the number of salespeople I had. But I also knew I was the worst possible person to be the sales manager, though I was already operating as the part-time sales manager. We have a VP of operations and a controller; both of whom were running their pieces of the business, yet the revenue piece was ignored. The insights my fellow CEOs shared helped me recognize our shortcomings so my team and I could get those integral systems and processes in place.

One very successful member of our group, Mark Israel, CEO of Universal Engineering, a geotechnical and environmental engineering firm located throughout the southeastern US, suggested I speak with his VP of sales, Joe Casha.

Joe spent a significant amount of time with me as he loves to help others be successful. Joe outlined what I needed to do in order to move from a group of salespeople being managed by myself and my VP of operations to a VP of sales position. He said, "Nobody in your company 'owns' revenue, and one person ultimately must do so. You can't afford not to."

And I thought the reality was I couldn't, so how was I going to make it happen?

One book I go back to all the time is called *Power Questions* by Andrew Sobel. Over the years, I've learned to stop talking and start asking and listening, and that's been very helpful to me in my personal development.

Ultimately, I found an excellent consultant, Kelly Crandall, through the organization Sales Xceleration. She has been able to build our sales systems and processes and then step in as our outsourced VP of sales. She has been a fantastic addition and the solution to the advice I received.

I love to mentor friends when they are experiencing challenges in their businesses. Whenever we talk or get together, the conversations seem to always circle back to whatever their challenges are. Through my CEO group, I've learned to question and listen. As most of us know, all problems in every business are either revenue, customer, or employee related. I truly enjoy helping people find solutions to their business challenges. It is so much easier when it's not your pain, but you can empathize with their problems. I've always said if I wasn't in the professional cleaning and facility maintenance business, all I would want to do is help people with their business issues. I don't like the term *consultant* because I don't want to tell someone what their issues are—I want to work with them through resolution. One of the neatest things to watch is when the light bulb goes on for them, and I see that I've made an impact.

Another thing to do is find a group of people who will tell you what you need to hear and not what you want to hear. If you're thin-skinned, don't become a CEO and don't solicit other people's advice and opinions. That leads back to where we started, which was my group of CEOs. Their input can be brutal, and there is no stroking of the ego in that room!

One of the guys in my group was Wayne Gey. He runs Wayne Automatic Fire Sprinklers, a very successful fire protection solutions company with locations throughout Florida and North Carolina. I always looked up Wayne, and during one meeting, he said to me, "Boy, you don't got a clue." Those words crushed me. Here is this guy that I love and respect who's always there for me and provided incredible advice. And then suddenly he said that.

He followed with, "I'm so worried that when your ship comes in, you're going to be at the airport."

Now I was really listening because I knew great advice would follow. I pulled up my big boy pants and asked, "Tell me where I'm offtrack here. What is it? What am I missing?" Most of the time, when you have blinders on in your business and then suddenly something happens, you don't want to take the blinders off. Wayne was effective at that particular point. It was like when you tell your child, "I'm disappointed in you."

Many CEOs who have been running their business for some time are pretty confident in their abilities. But you need to check yourself regularly and realize maybe there is something you can learn here—something you don't know. That was an excellent example of his mentorship. There's no doubt he played a role with me in that particular case. The fact that I remember his words so clearly was my wake-up call to address that specific challenge. He was right because he was usually always right! I couldn't see my problem, but he easily could. That's what pissed me off.

A lot of times, a mentor's help comes from standing on the outside—from their prior experiences or coming at the issue without the emotions involved. At the time, I hadn't had the experiences—hadn't had enough train wrecks. It would be like hearing a train whistle, and next thing you know, you're already in the hospital. But the next time you hear the train whistle, you move. Hopefully, by the third time you hear a train whistle off in the distance, you realize, "Oh, crap, a train is coming!"

There's no doubt that our successes and failures are usually due to people. My biggest mistakes have typically been rooted in not replacing people when we've made a poor hire or when we've outgrown each other. Being in a thirty-year-old business, we have had people who had been with us for a long time. I'm very loyal to them, which sometimes is not a good thing. You must get the right people in the right seats. In our CEO group, we primarily talk about people issues, as opposed to revenue, customer, or financing challenges. We discuss key personnel and what our challenges are—and in many cases, we need to make a change and move.

At Pro Clean, we have hundreds of employees, and I still consider us to be a small company. I have a management team of eight managers, including three direct reports. You get to know them well, so it can be challenging to think of changing. That's probably the toughest part of the business for me. And that perhaps creates the most issues when we can't redirect someone's behavior to the appropriate outcomes we need and don't move soon enough.

You need to weigh the best interest of the individual versus the best interests of everyone else. As we've grown, I spend a lot more time thinking about the best interest of the overall company.

The area that I believe most entrepreneurs need mentoring in is talent selection. The focus needs to be on personal traits and whether those are drivers of the business and the culture first.

The second area is experience. Many entrepreneurs, especially younger ones, are caught up in buying the experience of others when many times it's a terrible cultural fit. If you do only *one* thing well, it should be hiring the right people!

Simply put, without having great mentors, I would never have enjoyed the level of success we have had over the past thirty years.

Chris McCurry
Barkhouse
Barkhouse.com

We work with youth and youth groups, and listening to them helps us forecast what's trending. That impacts not only what we say but also how we say things so that they'll stick. It helps to inform us what's important to them and where they're coming from. We've always had one succinct message and one alignment, so what we do doesn't change. It's how we express our story to people so that it makes more sense to them, and it has personal meaning.

We have such a strong mission here, which is to change the nature of building. It's quite a large idea in a large strategy, so part of that has to do with educating people, understanding where they're coming from and what it's going to take to change the dynamics that are going on within the built environment. It also includes how we're thinking about how products are manufactured and how products can serve people and the planet instead of creating costs for people and the planet. That takes quite a lot of education and mentorship.

We're a nature-based company, co-founded by my husband and me, and we are both strongly informed by nature and complex natural systems. Living within nature, having an intimate relationship with nature, seeing ourselves as not controlling or managing, but co-creating with nature. We do regenerative work, so that's the big capsule that the work is held within. People may call that biophilic design and may relate to that as an element of the circular economy.

Nature was our biggest teacher. Nature is so much more collaborative than we give it credit for, as it's a tremendous system that works to retain balance. We were talking about the weather patterns we're dealing with and the disturbances going on. Nature is talking to us right now, telling us, "Hey, there's some disruption that's happening here, and I need you to pay attention." Hopefully, we'll all listen.

When we back out and look at the bigger picture, we'll see why these holistic views are incredibly important. When you're looking at the entire world and working to keep it clean and livable for humanity, you see the importance of this view.

Somehow, we're so diverted with our technology, with the messaging of the day, and by whatever is being screamed at us about all the different sources out there. We are so dependent on planet functioning that it's hard to think about the idea that we're missing all that.

There's a newly built environment created every month the size of New York, which is staggering. When that's a voluntary investment, when the products being manufactured and purchased are put into that built environment, when those products have one of the largest impacts on what we're doing to the planet and people, when we're voluntarily putting our money toward them, then we can select better products. The impact we can create is tremendous. We can turn things around by focusing on our built environment and what we're doing there and the products that we're purchasing to put there.

The political structure tends to minimize things into simple parts. We hear all the time, "Let's get this through the vote—make it as simple as you can to get it through the vote."

That's not the strategy and the thinking that's going to help us to move this country and this world forward. We have to look at the bigger systems and how they're interrelated. It's not so large that we can't deal with it. We are incredibly creative and imaginative, and the potential is within our grasp. All we have to do is start enacting some of these systems changes.

Nature was my teacher of how to change the strategy of our business. We achieved the world's first and only cradle-to-cradle platinum-level product certification, and we were a B Corp Best for the World–awarded and certified company. That speaks to environmental issues and social equity issues and has also verified our input. When we say that our products are carbon neutral, we've had third-party verification, so it's not just me saying that.

When we say we use zero water in our manufacturing and that we see healthy watersheds, we've had verification of those processes and those systems. It's restructuring, it's using these tools, to help us move forward. When all these ideas first came to light, it was even thought that manufacturers could not possibly integrate them, and we've proven that yes, we can. We've proven that through third-party verification.

The book *Regenerative Design and Development* by Regenesis Group is exceptional. *Regenerative Business* by Carol Sanford is a nice go-to, and she has several books on the marketplace, so those are helpful when we're thinking about regenerative systems and the possibilities for business and the positive benefits businesses can actually bring to the world.

Regenerative design and development is not only applicable to the building industry. We can apply these ideas as we've done throughout our business. We can apply this regenerative concept—we call it Whole Building—into the building sector first, but when we learn the foundation of how nature works, then it can be applied throughout every human system, including business, healthcare, education, and government. This is a process that can be duplicated in many systems.

Along the way, there have been many mistakes, as we've been in business for nearly thirty years. When we want to duplicate processes, one of the things we do here is to encourage other people to strongly think about when you're developing something for yourself, find that which is completely unique within you, that special thing that you love and hate from that space. Don't try to copy other people's processes and systems. Make sure you've verified it. Do the work on the front end and make sure you verify things.

One of the things we've not been able to overcome is the space and the boundaries for intellectual property. How do we both share with people and help uplift other people's strategies at the same time? We are a small business, so we don't have all the resources that a larger industry sector would have as far as legal services, those types of support and resources, or the ability to litigate when litigation would be called for.

For us, that translated into people trying to copy what we're doing, but not doing it in a healthy way. Perhaps they're doing it in an extractive methodology versus a regenerative methodology way. I don't think we've done a good job educating about the difference and the results of when somebody approaches something from an extractive perspective as opposed to when you're approaching it from a regenerative perspective. How can I help build and grow something versus how can I take and benefit and squeeze somebody else?

We do mentoring regularly, as it's a continual process. We've had a number of internships, which have shown up in our space as making a difference. We go out and speak at universities and colleges almost monthly. We speak to industry forums, like Living Products, so we have different opportunities at different levels.

As an example, we had a group of design students who came into town. One of the universities allowed us to work with two classes of students for two full semesters. We were working on a pocket park project in our small town. We're in Appalachia, so the economic challenges are real in this area. When we can utilize a human resource that's creative and mobilize that, then there are real benefits you can see. They created designs for a pocket park that we were wanting to build.

Those weren't designs straight from their own head. The goal was to reach out to the community and create feedback loops based upon the needs. What's important to you? What comes from your center? What does this place inform you that we need that's special here? Then the students created design ideas and interpreted them. We actually built what they designed, which was so exciting for the town and the students, so it was a wonderful experience. It had a lot of meaning for us here. Whereas we can be against new, we had 100 percent town buy-in. We received funding from the town leadership, we received business funding to build the park, and we had a multifocal, large collaborative effort that everybody has pointed to as a large success.

This past week, I met with students at ASU at a Careers for Impact conversation on the campus where a select number of businesses were invited. The big takeaway that students reflected is that these people love what they're doing. It wasn't only us. There were a number of small businesses and larger businesses present. The message the students heard was, "You can love your work. You can love what you do. You should choose what you love to do, and sometimes it chooses you, and that's when it's magic."

We have long precedence set with mechanical processes, starting with the Industrial Revolution, and how mechanical processes informed every human system. The problem with that is that we're living beings, so we can't learn from and apply the same processes that you apply to the making of things to human systems.

It's why we're disintegrating presently. Our systems are breaking down because they were created based upon mechanical thinking. What we need to learn about is living-systems thinking and how that thinking can reinvigorate everything we're doing—every segment of human life—and it's desperately needed. When schools and educational institutions, for example, implement regenerative strategies, their students come to life, and you can see it in their eyes.

You can see their level of engagement change. You can see the life coming through them, and you can see a hunger in these students that you don't experience when we're using those same old mechanical, linear methodologies. The old methodologies are completely reductional, reducing humanity into a machine.

What we're looking at should invigorate us. What enlivens that essence? What brings students to the table? What engages, or inspires, them? What is their passion? What are they wanting to create? What they know, so far, is the old systems that have been created. Don't support those methodologies and those strategies.

So entrepreneurs are important today in changing those structures. We can't be quiet. We have to be out there, talking about these changes at every opportunity we have. We must invest ourselves in changing those old systems, for our children, which is the future. The future is today, so we should make our move right now. Even if we affect only a little change, maybe that will inspire more people to do it, and enough little changes can add up to a big change.

When we're thinking from a regenerative space and taking the time to do some homework on the front end, we get down to what am I trying to create as potential. That's what we're shooting for instead of trying to solve tiny little problems along the way. Problems were created with the same thinking with which we're approaching the problem, and we're not getting anywhere. Such an approach has to change.

We have to think of larger strategies, and those strategies are what we want to apply here. What's the potential? Then we go for that. Changing the nature of building is our potential. That's where we're going.

I wrote a book, which is more of a coffee-table book, called *Bark House Style: Sustainable Designs from Nature* that offers some inspiration. Find that thing within you, that uniquely special element that's within your being and then create from that truth because when things get hard—as they will in running a business—you're going to rub up against a lot of systems that are not functioning. But if you have the passion, and you know you're coming from your own space of truth, you won't be stopped.

You won't be stopped by the difficulties in banking or the government systems or any difficulty that comes your way. You'll find a way through it because you are on the line, your beliefs, your values, and we have to be willing to first formulate those values. So spend some time looking at yourself, spend some time developing your own consciousness, spend some time thinking about how you think about things and how you think about the world.

Ask those hard questions. One of the great things we do here as a method of mentoring is when we're trying to communicate with others, and we're wanting to put our words into action, then if we enter a competition or a strategy, it helps us to focus intensely that which we are trying to say and clarify it.

We look at systems that we appreciate, like the Buckminster Fuller strategy at the Buckminster Fuller Institute, and if we enter into one of the challenges, that helps us to refine our thoughts and clarify our intent to know ourselves better. It helps us to do that through the lens of how others might be seeing us.

When you do find that authenticity, it won't be compromised. It will be the thing that you will hold on till the end of your time because you know it's your personal truth.

Bark is a waste material of the logging industry, so we source that bark within a one-hundred-mile radius of our facility. We call it Reclaimed Appalachian Wood Waste (RAWW). We're located in a part of Appalachia, and all our sourcing and manufacturing happens here. So you know that if we did something that wasn't legitimate, our neighbors are going to be coming and knocking on our door and saying, "Hey, what's up with this?"

It holds us to a standard of being a good neighbor. When your business can say, "We're a good neighbor," it makes you feel pretty good.

I think that books have power, and they have power in the right segment. I can't make my message so compressed that it can fit on Twitter, so that's not my space, but I can go and talk to a group for an hour. Because I'm asking them to tell me what's important to them so my message can be clearer.

It's a lot to talk about carbon and air and water systems. It can get very complex for people, so we like to hear what's relevant to them and then respond to that strategy. It's a lot more work, though, because you're reaching small groups. So the economy of sharing is a challenge, truly a challenge.

I live in one of the most conservative areas, and people are still on my side as far as how we're doing business. They see the benefit of it, and they improve their processes to meet our standards. We've had a real impact on some old industries in this area, but there is such a beautiful story to tell from here because most people don't even realize that the first forest management plan came from North Carolina, that the first person who became our United States forestry service, Pinchot, his forest plan was right here in North Carolina. Everything started here.

It also helps us to learn a little bit about how wood is regenerative, especially when the process is done right. When we're honoring the trees, when we're honoring nature's strategy, it is regenerative. There are so many aspects of this, and there's such heroic work to be told, and even I can see why some of the people in this area have resisted.

They're resisting for a heroic reason, and that's because they believe in nature. They look at these mechanical structures that people have put into place in the larger cities and think, "You are crazy."

It's being proven that they were right. Maybe their strategy wasn't the best, but where they were coming from, it made sense and makes sense, and it's going to be what helps them take us into the future. We've been able to bridge a lot of issues being a different company in a conservative area, and it's forced us to know ourselves pretty well. We have to be authentic here because people can see through you. If you're not, you're not going to last.

We've lasted through it so far.

Katie Fleming
Tenon Tours
Tenontours.com

I can't say I've had one specific mentor. I feel I've had an array of people who influence my thinking and creating my drive to be successful. I utilize other avenues, such as attending conferences, listening to podcasts, watching videos, or reading books to find different people's advice to lead me in various directions and see things from a different point of view.

I get a lot out of conferences and the speakers, then I'm really motivated to buy their books. At the last conference I attended, Brené Brown was there, and it was the first time I had heard of her. I got a lot out of it, bought her book, followed her on social media, and then I realized she's on Netflix, so there's a lot of access to constantly be motivated by her.

I try to go to at least one or two conferences a year, and they can all be so different, which help give me a constant source of growth and ideas. At that same conference where I saw Brené Brown, we had the creator of Life is Good, Bert Jacobs, tell his story. He wasn't necessarily giving advice in an instructional form like Brené was, but through sharing his experiences of the early days of his company, the advice automatically comes.

I could take a lot of things and relate them to creating new ideas for our company, or different things I have gone through that I may not have realized was a learning experience. At conferences, you can realize you're not the only one who has gone through it or experienced it or has had that same issue. What I learn is to see something from a different perspective.

We've made so many mistakes during our time in business. Some of them were around trying to please everyone and give everyone what they want. I have learned I can't do that, especially as we grow. When we were small, it was easier to keep everybody happy. But as we're growing, I realize how hard that is.

When some things were going wrong with individual employees, our business navigator said, "Katie, they have to learn your way. You don't have to learn their way."

That's hard for me to accept because I didn't want to be that person who says, "You have to do it my way, or it's the highway." I think it's more about meeting in the middle where I want them to be happy, and then, if they're working because they're trying to make the company happy, it's naturally going to work out well.

Our business navigator has also done personality profiles with us, which was eye-opening. Using those personality profiles helped me understand myself better and all my employees whom I'm working with, and maybe why employees don't work out. I try not to judge it too strongly, but it gives me a little more insight.

I probably did my DiSC profile about six years ago, and it gives you an idea of how analytical you are, how emotional you can be, or if you're a team player and other different characteristics. It will tell you what your strengths are, what guides you, how you react under pressure, or what you're like when things are going well.

When I first read it, I thought, "Oh, okay, maybe I could see that." And then after a few more years in business, more employees, more ups and downs, I went back to read it and thought, "This is me to a tee."

From the questions they ask, you would never understand how they get this result out of it. I realize how analytical I am and how much I rely on numbers and facts to make my decisions. The owner of the company and I are both numbers oriented, but he's much higher in the emotional aspects. So we can see how and why we balance each other out.

We can look back on something and say, "Oh, that's why I handled it that way," or "That's why I reacted that way." Then you can use it for the future. We use the tests for hiring now because when looking at who we've lost, we see where we may have been blindsided in some cases. So we examine our losses and try to either avoid it or know for the next hire and learn how to approach a specific challenge differently.

I like to focus on my personal development, which, I feel, is working on yourself without relying on someone else to guide you and map it all out for you. I've learned from, and with, others along the way, but I've also taken the opportunity to figure it out on my own.

I'd rather learn from evaluating options, making a decision, and finding out if it was the right one, then learning from it when I'm in that situation the next time. I feel you're missing out on important critical thinking skills when you want to be trained or programmed like a robot to complete a task rather than learning it through the challenge.

I realized that I've gotten where I am in my career by figuring out a lot by myself, and sometimes I wish more employees would take the initiative to do so as well. But then, that's where the personality stuff comes into play, and I understand that everyone's different, and they learn and train in different ways. Now I know that the best way to teach people is the way that they need to be taught, which can be a challenge.

I wouldn't say I've specifically served as a mentor. I'd love if someone looked at me that way and wanted to learn from me, but I don't expect it just because I'm a manager or in a higher position than they are. I try hard to set a good example and show the employees I've done every job here and try to put myself in their shoes if there is an issue. There were two of us when the company started, so I've done everything that the employees have to do at some point.

I show them that my emotions are in it, so while I can make strategic business and data-oriented decisions, I'm not heartless. I try to teach them to take ownership and blame when things go wrong and show them that you can't do everything right, and that's okay. I try to be understanding and kind to them so that it's a safe environment to learn and make mistakes together.

The area I think most entrepreneurs need mentoring in is around balance and understanding various sides or opinions when making decisions. Everybody is different, so if you focus shallowly on one thing, you're going to miss the other side of it. Sometimes I have to step back and not think solely about business, growth, and numbers. I have to remember to take a lot into consideration, including the employees, work-life balance, and if there are outcomes I have not considered.

If I were to write a book, my key message to entrepreneurs for them to be able to replicate my success would be never to settle.

If you get to a point where you're a well-oiled machine, and it works, then you're either being complacent, or something else is up that you don't know that will eventually hold you back. The world and our industries are always changing and evolving so much with technology. There's likely a more efficient way to do something. You should always be wondering how you can get and be better.

I don't think my ideas will ever stop, and I won't ever try to stop changing us. It might not be the best idea, but I will try it, measure it, see if it works. I'm lucky, as I think it's a natural thing to me that a simple commercial could come on, and an idea will spark up. Even if it's not close to our industry, it will spark something that I could replicate in some way for our company. Sometimes it works, sometimes it doesn't.

We're always looking for a way to make something more efficient. I'm still searching for new systems and to see how other people do it, and that helps me. We've had people start here and say, "I'm used to changing, and I like change, and I'm fine with change," but I'm not sure they really know what to expect when we tell them this:

"Change is constant. It's the norm here. When you get used to something, something will change because we've found a better way to do it, a different system or whatever it is. That doesn't mean we didn't make the right decision the first time—it's that we're constantly trying to improve."

Joe Dinoffer
OnCourt OffCourt
Oncourtoffcourt.com

When I started the company in 1994, before launching in any significant way, I consulted with key industry leaders to get their opinions on the concept of the company as I knew their strengths. The funny thing was that all of them advised me not to start my company.

Perhaps they were right at the time with the information I gave them. I started with the purist concept to only develop accelerate learning products to help children build self-esteem through sports—via my background in tennis and physical education.

Within a year or two, it was clear I had to diversify the business by adding equipment beyond the purist approach, to include products for adults also, such as training aids to help people with visual and kinesthetic learning, and help players get a feel for the skill they are trying to learn and improve. Most coaching, as we know, takes place with verbal communication, which is the worst way to teach any physical activity.

While I was passionate about the concept, I reached out to be mentored at the beginning since starting an inventory-based company was new for me. While I learned a great deal from these essential consultations—and I didn't follow many of the instructions of my mentors—I did heed their advice to at least go beyond my initial narrow approach to have a broader line of equipment that a broader customer base could embrace.

One of the foremost mentors I had contact with was Dr. Jim Loehr. He's a sports psychologist and motivational speaker who has appeared on the *Oprah Winfrey Show* and has been involved in the tennis industry for decades. Another mentor was the president of Wilson Sporting Goods at the time, Mr. Jim Baugh. Both were the strongest to advise against my initial purist approach.

From a mentoring standpoint, there's another person whose advice I heeded from a distance, since we have never met—Stephen Covey. I've always been a Covey fan and have embraced his philosophy about setting priorities for years. If somebody has an entrepreneurial spirit and a relatively narrow focus in a niche market, which many entrepreneurs have, business books cannot address their specific audiences and instruct only in general terms.

For me, after the initial concept was establishing and the company was launched, the most positive impact on my company in its early years was to adopt processes that could help me be more efficient and effective.

It was about receiving ongoing mentoring through someone's general voice rather than specific networking with a single individual. Many or most entrepreneurs are the Marco Polos of their fields of interest and passion, daring to embark on journeys where no one has gone before. First and foremost, entrepreneurs need to identify and embrace with great inspiration their individual needs, purpose, and passion.

The two leading tennis organizations in the world are the United States Professional Association and the Professional Tennis Registry, both of which I have master professional status. I believe there are under ten of us in the entire world. They have mentor programs set up, and I participate in both and have been an advocate of mentoring for thirty years. I also mentor in my faith-based community and am a big believer in the process. I've received so much help from so many people in my path that I think it's natural to want to give back.

I'm also a believer in the abundance of exchange concept, which means that if somebody gives me a dozen apples, I want to give back more than the twelve that I initially received. Giving back more than we receive has become so ingrained in my personality that I don't know how to do things any different way. This seems to be the mentality of many successful entrepreneurs since hardly any entrepreneur has succeeded without the advice and consultation from others.

Perhaps the area that most entrepreneurs need mentoring in is team building and creating a unique culture within their own enterprise. The concept behind this is simple.

Human beings need a purpose to become—and remain—loyal. Both concepts, team building and creating a culture for your company or organization have been keys to our success. At OnCourt OffCourt, we have had only two people resign in twenty-five years. One decided to pursue a teaching career in education, the other a wonderful young woman who became a mother of wonderful twin boys. The average length of time our team members have been with us is about twelve years. The only reason we hire new people is when we expand. Other than that, we have had hardly any turnover.

To be effective in any business leadership position, many qualities are essential for success. At the same time, entrepreneurs must know that you don't have to possess every quality. Many people might wonder every day how they could start their own business. Just remember that if you don't have a particular quality, it's essential to surround yourself with others who have that quality you may lack.

For example, I happen to be blessed with being detail oriented, but people also say I have a strong creative side. Most people don't have both of those in balance. The one area in which I am relatively weak is in technology. But I do type fast. One of the most important things I learned in school was that my mother forced me to take typing. Typing quickly is a great skill and has been arguably more useful than any other skill I learned in school. But I never have been technologically astute or interested, so I always surround myself with those types of talented people. You have to know how to surround yourself with the right people.

Regarding our own company culture, one of the essential parts of our culture has to do with customer service and communication. I always tell my team that when a customer asks a question, you don't even have to let them finish! Just tell them the answer is "Yes!" Then we ask, "What's your question?" because it's all about customer service. We've grown from nothing to a customer list email database of more than fifty thousand in a relatively small niche market.

With ten employees, we are now celebrating our twenty-fifth year in business. While your in-house culture is super important, and everyone must get on the same page, it goes beyond your employees, I think it's crucial that if you outsource to a CPA, investment person, banker, computer tech, website designer, or a search-engine-optimization person, you need to make sure they too buy into the heart and soul of your company culture.

It's all about creating a synergy. To me, it's like being on a train that has two tracks, and you want to add cars to the train. You don't want to have one of the partners you outsource to be on a separate train or separate track because they could be going in a different direction. Synergy is essential. That compounds the positive energy that someone can create with their own entrepreneurial effort.

I have five key messages to share.

One, find the passion you believe in and love to share. Two, create a small and informal advisory team you can trust. Three, be honest about your strengths. Four, be honest about your weaknesses. Five, without a doubt, make a 100 percent commitment to excellent communication.

One of my favorite quotes is, "To be responsible means to respond." I'm not sure about the exact source, but it's a proverb from India. In today's culture, reliable communications and responsiveness are not that common. So it's easier to stand out if people have excellent communication skills. I believe it's a part of respecting the other person so they don't have to follow up with you or wonder whether or not you even received their email, text, or voice message in the first place.

I've written nine books now and am a part-time musician. I've also been writing poetry for decades. I published my first two illustrated books of poems. The first is called *A Father's Love*. The second is *Words, Wisdom, and Whimsy*. The series is called *Poems from the Heart* and is available on our website and Amazon.

I'm hoping to do three or four more in this particular series, poetry dealing with life challenges, joys, coping with pain, illness, relationships, and feelings, all sorts of relatively light topics.

Rob Lobreglio
Great Dane Pub & Brewing
Greatdanepub.com

We are a GroupHub group, so we have five brewery restaurants. When we were first planning to open our restaurant, we realized that we had brewing experience via me. I was already a trained and educated brewer, but getting into the GroupHub industry was a completely different game as we needed to be well honed as a bar restaurant.

We ended up contacting a GroupHub group from Colorado, although we're in Wisconsin, and our people went to train at their facility. During our opening, their people came to work alongside our people during the first few weeks in business. It enabled us to open as if we were a restaurant group that had been operating for ten or fifteen years and avoid mistakes that newly opened restaurants encounter or commit.

A particular person helped me in my journey, a brewer in Wisconsin named Kirby Nelson. He's the brewmaster from Wisconsin Brewing Company. I was a good brewer when we first opened, but Kirby was well versed in all the varieties of raw materials out there. He expanded my horizons as to the different types of malt and hops that could be used in the brewing process. He got me a lot more focused on exploring the differences between the different kinds of raw materials the average consumer wouldn't recognize. But as a brewer, it made me appreciate the nuances in these raw materials.

Our industry is not so young anymore. The craft brewing industry is approaching forty years old. There were a lot of pioneers out there, and there still are. The hallmark of American craft brewing is experimenting with unique ingredients, as well as unique combinations and traditional ingredients. We've come a long way from replicating the conventional European beer styles.

Many of those guys who started this industry are the ones who are pushing the envelope right now. The craft brewers are continually learning from each other. I would hope I've helped teach others along the way, but I have to admit I've learned from a lot of others as well.

There's a series of books by the Brewer's Association, and one of them is called *Brewing Great Beer Stout*, and that was a beneficial book for me. There are a couple of books in the *Brewing Great Beer* series, which each focuses on one particular beer style. How to brew a great Belgian beer, how to brew a great pilsner, and some of those books were helpful. When I was starting, those books weren't available. It was much a learn-by-doing situation back then.

We have a lot of guys come through here, as well as a couple of gals, which I have trained to become brewers. I've had some of them contact me and tell me how much they appreciated education and the hands-on experience I gave them, so I would like to think I've been an excellent mentor to the next generation of master brewers.

To become a master brewer requires a combination of education and experience; there's no formal licensing or degree you can get. Well, some schools will offer a degree in brewing, but it's not necessarily accepted in the industry. It's a good indication of this person who graduated from this institute or this university, but education alone is not enough to make you a master brewer or brewmaster.

You have to have hands-on experience and be exposed to the industry for a while. No one comes out of school and immediately gets a job as the head brewer of the brewery. Well, I should say it usually doesn't happen.

I think a lot of entrepreneurs are coming to the market with usually some type of innovative idea, and I think they need to figure out how to shape their plan into the traditional structure of the markets. That could accomplish a lot of different aspects. Whether it's the employees that I'm going to look for, what their skill sets are, and how I am going to market my product. Just a good idea alone is not enough. It's okay to be new and different, but you have to bridge the gap between what's currently going on in the marketplace and your business model. Unfortunately, a lot of new ideas end up dying on the vine because they were not executed properly.

New entrepreneurs have one chance to make a good impression. We're tackling a broad topic here, and the entrepreneurs who are reading this are going to be in many different shapes and forms. With that in mind, you only have one chance to make a good impression, so you want to realize that no entrepreneur is an island. Team building is, in my book, one of the most challenging and vital things you could do.

Don't try to do everything yourself. Build a good team. Make sure the individuals in that team have the proper skill set for the function they're going to perform for the business. It comes down to team building, and for us, that's become a personal mission. We want to empower people to take control of their divisions, whatever that might be. If we recognize that they might have the potential, but not the experience or ability, we give them the opportunity to either receive ongoing education or training to get to that point. We do whatever it takes to build a good team.

Of course, that plays into rewarding everyone. Part of that core is financial, but a lot of it is just letting them know they've got the opportunity to run their section of the business as they see fit and see how that can change over time with great discussion. No one likes to have someone looking over their shoulder every minute of the day. We're about empowering our employees.

It's funny because I got into this job as a brewer, so I made my first book proposal last year to the Brewer's Association. It's supposedly still in the running. They usually choose one new book every year or two. It's just a proposal at this point, so if it gets the green light, then I do the writing.

The working title was *From the Vault: Recipes from America's Favorite Craft Breweries*. There are a lot of recipes written by professional brewers for homebrewers, but there was never a book written by brewers for brewers. I had a lot of breweries make tentative commitments to share their award-winning recipes. So I want to get all the participating breweries to provide one of their top recipes, and it would be shared with other professional brewers. It would include a lot of pertinent thoughts on the style and the raw materials, and we would give the nod to them by adding their social media contacts, websites, locations, and a little history on them to make it have more appeal. I plan to include the homebrew version as well, but the priority is recipes from one brewer to another.

Rochelle Kopp
Japan Intercultural Consulting
Japanintercultural.com

One strategy I've employed in my firm is to have many team members who are significantly older and wiser than me. One of my earliest team members was a woman named Susan Doctors, who I'd met while I was starting my firm. Someone had introduced her to me with the idea that since I was pretty young, it would be helpful if I had someone with more experience to give me some perspective. Susan is about twenty years older than me and had more executive experience, so she was an excellent resource for me.

I didn't have anyone around me who had experience starting a business or doing consulting or doing any of the things that I was trying to do, so it was invaluable to have someone who could offer that perspective. Susan's still a member of our team, but I've had others on our team who are older and wiser than me.

Misako was the person in charge of our Japan branch when we started. She's about fifteen years older than me, and she was a great mentor—particularly on how to get things done effectively in Japan.

It's essential to get that other cultural perspective when you're doing intercultural work. We always say in the intercultural field you need what's called a native informant. Someone who is from that culture and immersed in that culture can share their perspective on how something might be viewed. There are some things that you can't see the way someone from that culture would.

One example of something I would not have realized without your mentor in Japan is when I asked Misako to give me a report of what she was doing every week. We managed long-distance, so I didn't know what she was doing. I'm going to date myself, but this was before you could easily send files by email. Since we conduct training seminars, the set of participant materials might be a hundred pages long. Before you could send things of that size easily by email, we used to send them by Federal Express to people, and then they would use that to make copies for the participants. I noticed on Misako's reports that she was spending a lot of time running around Tokyo, bringing that copy master document to clients.

In Tokyo, you can kill a lot of time going from place to place because it's fairly spread out. I said, "Misako, I'm not paying you to be a deli person. Why aren't you putting that in the Japanese equivalent of FedEx and sending it to people? Why are you running around all over the place?"

She said, "Rochelle, I am doing that on purpose. This is a traditional Japanese sales technique to show up at your client's place as frequently as possible. When you do that in Japan, they don't say, 'Thanks for the document, goodbye.' At the door, they say, 'Come in, sit down, have a cup of tea.' And every time that happened, I would find out some interesting new information. I would be introduced to somebody else. I would get a new lead for another way we could help the client. I make every excuse to show up, and this is a perfect one."

So that was not something I would have known myself. The people who take the time to visit in person gain an advantage. It becomes a calling card or a positive difference you can offer.

One book I liked was *Take Time for Your Life* by Cheryl Richardson. She's become a celebrity coach, and I think that book was one of her early books. I still recommend it to people because it honed in on the idea of not trying to do everything yourself and thinking carefully about what you can outsource to other people, both in your professional life and your personal life. She recommends that you focus on where you're adding the most value.

We do a lot of mentoring among our team members, and I'll use Misako as an example. She does a lot of mentoring for our facilitators in Japan to ensure the quality of their methodologies. One thing we found that's interesting is for some of the people we've worked with in Japan: they might not have gotten as much feedback about their work as you might expect if they were, for example, in the United States. Sometimes the Japanese are reluctant to give a lot of feedback because they don't want to be rude or hurt someone's feelings.

Meanwhile, Misako, for a Japanese person, is reasonably straightforward, and she has spent nine years out of Japan, and they were all indirect cultures like the US, Korea, and Belgium. So she's got into a more direct mode. Sometimes it's startling for people that she's on point in giving negative feedback, and then maybe people don't get that so much from Japanese. But it's all done nicely, of course. But we found that her detailed hands-on work with people when giving them a lot of feedback makes a significant impact.

We do a lot of work with Japanese managers who are managing non-Japanese people. One of the key messages we give them is that more timely feedback is helpful because people do want to improve. The Japanese are, in many cases, not sure how to deliver that feedback, so it sounds like you end up getting the input from another westerner.

We work with the Japanese to help them be more comfortable giving that feedback themselves and knowing they can give negative feedback in a way that is not going to damage a relationship but instead will constructively help someone. People would rather know sooner if there are some things that they need to change. This issue comes up frequently.

I'm excited to tell you about this fantastic program wherein I've been mentoring since 2012 called Tech Woman at techwoman.org. Tech Woman is a program from the US Department of State that brings emerging female technical leaders from the Middle East, Africa, and Central Asia to Silicon Valley, where they offer internships for one month every year. So you might get a structural engineer from Tunisia, a physicist from Yemen, an architect from Nigeria, an intellectual property expert from Zimbabwe, and an entrepreneur from Morocco, creating a new online company.

You get all these talented, amazing women from parts of the world where it's challenging for women to pursue STEM (science, technology, engineering, and mathematics) careers. They get the opportunity to work at Silicon Valley companies, such as Autodesk, Twitter, and Juniper Networks—and all these places offer fabulous internships.

Then there's another program that goes around that to help them develop their leadership skills. I've been serving as a mentor at Tech Woman since 2012. My first mentor role was as a cultural mentor. Since I'm not a STEM person, I'm not one of the professional mentors.

The other mentor category is where the professional mentors from the companies hosting the women work with them. The cultural mentors spend time with them outside of work to help them get to know the culture and the way things are done and also to have some fun here in Silicon Valley. I did that for several years, and then in the last couple of years, I've been in a new category that they've developed, which is an impact coach.

One element they've added to the program is since there are between two and five girls who come here, they become a team for their country.

These women didn't know each other before they joined this program, and together, they're asked to come up with an idea for something they can do in their country to pass along knowledge or address issues. They each come up with a business plan and a proposal, and they do a Silicon Valley–style pitch contest, and the best ones get seed funding for their project when they return home.

The impact coaches work with each of the teams to help them get ready for that pitch contest. I've been volunteering in that capacity for the last couple of years, and that's been fun.

I was with a team from Algeria this past session. In Algeria, people will learn their native language, which is Arabic, and they tend to learn French in school, but they don't get a lot of practice. In the workforce, a lot of the technical jobs are dealing with multinationals who somehow acquire English, which a lot of Algerians don't get a chance to learn. Some might learn on their own. One of the girls in the group Salma was always asking me if her English was okay. I thought her English was terrific, so I said, "Yes, it's great. I understand you quite well."

She said, "Well, this is my first time using English in a professional context."

I asked, "How did you learn?"

She said she taught herself.

When I asked how, she told me she learned English by watching *TED Talks*. I think that requires some base talent there; not everyone can learn English via TED Talks.

The group's idea was to have summer camps for high school students to help them improve both their French and English so they can position themselves for the job market. They had to have a business plan that included all the aspects of how their idea would work, and they had to have a Silicon Valley–style pitch. So we helped them put it together, and it was lots of fun.

When I consider the area that most entrepreneurs seem to need mentoring in, I think of the different people with whom I've worked.

One person I mentored had to start networking, although he had not needed to do so in his career before he started his firm. One time, I said to him, "You have to come out with me—you're networking." I dragged him out to an event. Now he's a master networker and thriving, mainly because he's done networking with a lot of diverse groups. He was an architect, but he works with a lot of different communities. He always says, "Rochelle, you taught me how to network."

If networking is not something that you've done before, it's not something that comes naturally to you. You have to get a little bit of a mentoring nudge on that. I've also mentored other entrepreneurs on how to promote themselves—whether by social media or blogging or speaking or writing—to get people to know about them and what they're doing. Again, that's something that doesn't necessarily come naturally to everyone, but I think it's critical now to get exposure.

I write a lot of books, but mentoring is not a general topic of mine. I write a lot of books for Japanese on how to work effectively in a global market. I also have a book that's helpful for entrepreneurs who want to get funding. It's a book about Silicon Valley buzzwords called *Valley Speak: Deciphering the Jargon of Silicon Valley*. So if you're trying to get funding, you need to know the lingo.

I'm a little bit doubtful I could contribute something on the mentoring topic that's not already out there because there are a lot of good entrepreneurship books out there. If I were going to advise an entrepreneur, it would be about realizing that you have various roles to play, and you have to decide how much time to spend on each and to get the balance there. Realize what you can have other people do, and don't do everything yourself.

Thinking strategically about what you are going to do and what you aren't going to do is the critical thing and an essential skill to build.

Lynne Waymon
Contacts Count
Contactscount.com

Contacts Count is an international training company, and we focus on one topic only, and that's business networking—a skill needed by almost everybody, in nearly every job type, at virtually every level. Our clients cover a wide range, from librarians, IT people, CPAs, lawyers, plastic surgeons, to people at the CIA.

A unique way that our company and I have been affected by mentoring is the idea to start this company came from Don, one of my mentors.

He said, "Why don't you teach a course about small talk?" We laughed about the idea at first, but I recalled that it had been a challenge for me as a teenager and in my twenties, so I thought I should do some research.

I looked into what had been written and said about how to make the best connections in small talk, and I didn't find anything helpful. I began interviewing people and eavesdropping on conversations at conferences, in airports, and when I was with my friends. While my mentor Don gave me the idea for the business, he was also mentoring and teaching me a lot of strategies for working with groups and teaching classes.

I've been in a lot of Mastermind groups. When we decided about ten or twenty years ago to train other people to teach our material, that idea came from a mentor by the name of Sam, and I noticed that with her training topics, she was also in the whole general field of communications. She trained other people to go out and teach. I was getting tired of getting on an airplane, and so was my partner, my sister. She lived in Kansas City and handled the West Coast stuff, and I tended to stay on the East Coast. But we were both tired of the airplane thing, so we decided to get other people to teach our material.

Another mentor has been my husband, Todd, who joined the business about thirteen or fourteen years ago. He'd previously worked for IBM and was a college professor of computer science, so he brings a whole new skill set. Todd has an organized and technical mind, while I have a more creative, extroverted mind, so he's been a great help.

One fellow who's a guru in the speaking and training and coaching field is Dan Sullivan, and he coaches entrepreneurs. But he says that what you need to be an entrepreneur are courage and ignorance, and that is so true. Every day, there's a new challenge, so you better say I'm ignorant, then know how to learn, have a lot of courage, and have a lot of good people around you. Dan encourages entrepreneurs to hang out with other entrepreneurs or, in my case, hang out with other trainers and other speakers.

Another guru in terms of a book is Jill Konrath, who wrote *Selling to Big Companies*. Another one is Daniel Pink, who has written a book called *Drive*, as well as a whole lot of other publications. Another one is *What Great Salespeople Do: The Science of Selling Through Emotional Connection and the Power of Story* by Michael T. Bosworth.

All those books have been helpful to me. As an entrepreneur, you can feel a little lonely sometimes. I have, even though I've had my sister as a partner and my husband on board. But you have to be willing to be a learner every single day.

Another mentor is Andre, our partner in Sydney, Australia, who has taught me a lot because his background is different than mine. He has a consulting organizational development background and international expertise too, and he has come to Washington a couple of times to meet with us.

When we decided twelve or thirteen years ago to train other trainers to teach our material, I mentored them. We have seven of them now around the US, and then one in Australia. And almost every day, I'm on the phone with one or two of them, and additionally, we have a quarterly phone meeting for all of them.

I teach them several things, such as our content, because we have a unique approach to building business relationships. Then I'm also training them to be trainers. They know a lot about training when they come on with us, but I find that as I can always learn something from them, they can learn something from me too.

The area that I feel most entrepreneurs need mentoring in is what to do to bump it up to the next level.

Somebody might have a fine business, but it's not growing. It's the same thing over and over again. Partly, it's likely to be money management and money growth, but it could also be perceiving or imagining what the business could be. Now we decided around eighteen years ago that we wanted to be a lifestyle business, that we wanted to manage our business, and we didn't want it to control us.

As my business grew, I saw other trainers who would be working seventy hours a week and tied to their business. I did not want that, and neither did my sister nor my husband. That's one reason we chose to stay in the niche into one topic—business networking. We decided to grow by certifying other people to teach our material.

About fifteen years ago, we decided we wanted to live in Nova Scotia every summer for about three months. That was another reason why we chose a lifestyle business so we could have a life more important than our company. The business has been extremely important, and I love it, and although it's endlessly fascinating to me, I didn't want to have a huge company.

Another area entrepreneurs need to consider is this: What do I imagine for myself down the road?

It's hard to predict what's going to happen tomorrow—even more so what's going to happen in five years. What do I want? What do I want in ten years? As we looked at our business fifteen years ago, we didn't want to be getting on an airplane. We didn't want to be tied to something that was all about us, so that's why we got other trainers.

Over the last twenty-eight years, we've seen the business evolve quite a bit. People want you to teach time management in fifteen minutes, and don't take people away from their job, which is ridiculous.

We teach face-to-face networking skills. We don't teach anything about LinkedIn as our niche is the face-to-face people. It's weird to think of teaching face-to-face strategies for connecting, conversing, and collaborating through a webinar. But we found a few ways around that.

We ask that the client try to put all the people in one room. If they have three offices, Chicago, Seattle, and Atlanta, they get a room there, and they put all the people in those sites in one place so that there can be some interactive, participatory activities during the webinar.

If I were to write another book, I would advise people to create what we call a keynet. A keynet is a strategically chosen, special-purpose, short-term network of people who can help you do one particular thing. Maybe you have decided you want to train other trainers, so who would be the ones that could advise you and support you and ask you the hard questions about that?

Suppose you want to open an office in Dallas, who would be a keynet for that project? Suppose you want to write a book, who are the people you know that would be a keynet for that project?

Whatever you want to do, build a network of key supporters and advisors around you, and then you're always creating new keynets. They might last a month, six months, a year, depending on the size of the project.

David Merrell
AOO
Aooevents.com

One unique way AOO Events has been impacted by mentoring is by bringing in a business coach. About three or four years ago, we were looking for our direction and our way, so I found him. I would consider him to be the best mentor I've ever had. He mostly helped with the framework of management and how to look at things and deal with things.

He helped me identify what was holding the company back and correcting that and then realizing there's going to be something new right afterward. That was probably the most pertinent information I got that's helped us move forward in managing our company better.

He told me a story about this boy scout troop. The troop was going up the mountain, and there was one boy named Herbie. He was a little overweight and not quite as in shape as the other boys. Herbie had a heavy backpack on as he was going uphill, and the entire troop had to slow down to accommodate Herbie. They realized Herbie was the one holding the group back, so they decided to take the backpack off him and lighten him up so he could go faster. Sure enough, he started going more quickly and getting into the pack. Later they found another boy holding the pack back. They had to lighten his load and get him going, only to discover another slow boy.

The management style that we work with now is we identify our Herbie. We concentrate on fixing that situation, whether it's a person, a procedure, or a client. We find the thing that's holding us back, correct it, and know there's another one after that. That's how we manage our system now, and it was probably the most significant thing that I've learned in my career.

When I started my business in 1989, there was nobody in my industry you could rely on. There were no hospitality management programs, no schooling, nothing. It's mostly been people who have helped me along the way. I've always relied on the advice of people I respected in the industry to help me see my solutions to problems and issues. My first mentor was my father's good friend, who was very good at running his own business. By watching him, I learned a lot about how to run a business.

I reach out to different people in the industry all the time to ask questions and get advice. Because I don't have the answers, I know that even if other people don't have the answers, they may steer me in the right way and give me clues. So if I don't have the full answer, I'll ask somebody else. I run my business by going to mentors and asking for what I need.

I regularly mentor, and I just won a leadership award for mentorship. I haven't even shown it to my employees yet. I've always been one to give back, and I won't refuse any conversation unless I'm busy. I feel that it's essential to give back. If I'm taking from the industry by getting advice from people, then I need to give back just as much.

Currently, we have fourteen full-time employees and another thirty who work part-time. I don't know if we formally call our program a mentor program, but we do major orientation. The way we work in our company is all through teamwork. It comes from my background in playing college football. Everything we do is teamwork. Everyone uses the same procedures, so if anybody gets behind, anyone else can jump in, know exactly where they are, and help them. So we're continually mentoring each other. It's a large part of the DNA of the company.

If I didn't have a degree in accounting, I know that I would need much mentoring in the profit and loss and the financials of a corporation. You cannot survive and make money unless you understand them or hire someone who understands them. So the most important thing you can know is how to run, know the back of your own house and what your books look like. What it means and how to leverage that with banks. The only way you're going to make money and have longevity in the business is if you understand what your break-even point is, where you make money, and understand your profit-and-loss statements like the back of your hands. You can't get any clearer than that.

I always wanted to run my own business. Out of college, I was recruited by a couple of companies, and I stayed with one long enough for them to transfer me from Ohio to California—knowing full well that I was going to run my own business eventually. I went through phone sales, literally selling phone systems, and I went into the career business for a while. Every job gave me clues as to what my skill set is, which is marketing and administration. At a company similar to mine, I became friends with the owner and told him I was unhappy.

He asked, "You want to be vice president of sales and marketing for me?"

I agreed, but I had no idea what I was getting into as in 1989, there wasn't much known about the special events industry. It was during the first job I did with him that I realized that this is where I wanted to stay. I loved the industry, and it was also in that first job that I realized I didn't want to work for this guy. So I went on a crash course.

There were two magazines, *Special Event Magazine* and *Event Solutions*, which were the only things that gave me clues. I subscribed to them both and read them cover to cover. I took every single job the guy could give me. I worked through the day and tended bar during the night to make money but also learned. I went on an intense study program, so nine months later, I started my own business.

I used to publish an online magazine. Because I just realized it was a blog at first, it was called *Design Docs*. I'm also an industry speaker, and I speak all over the country for the special events and hospitality industries, so I amassed a following. We realized that many people were reading this blog, and I was looking for an exit strategy. I decided to start a magazine so I can take over everything, and it can run on its own. Little did I know that magazines were more work than what I'm doing now.

There was a whole set of rules I didn't understand, and it was taking away from what I was doing. So gaining much speed, I think we had a tremendous following per month. But after ten years of doing it, I realized that this magazine would eventually outgrow my reputation. All it did was make my reputation as an individual even bigger. So it was clear that *Design Docs* was never going to surpass David Merrell or the AOO Events brand. So we decided to drop it and turn all that energy back towards myself and the company.

Now we're going to be coming out with a podcast and a few other things because we still have the audience. However, it can't stray too far from the business because that dilutes the energy and effort, and that's what *Design Docs* was doing—diluting the energy and effort.

Mark Moses
CEO Coaching International
Ceocoachinginternational.com

My company is called CEO Coaching International. We impact CEOs and leaders all over the world by coaching and mentoring them through what they want to achieve.

First of all, I have a coach, and we have a mentoring program that lasts for a year for all our new coaches. Then we have an ongoing mentoring program for all our coaches in the company that goes on indefinitely.

The biggest mentor I've had in my life has been Richard Carr, the former CEO of Vistage International. He was also on my board for ten years and my coach during that period.

I learned five things from him about being the ultimate CEO. One is vision: where's the company going? Two is cash: as the CEO, you're the ultimate responsibility for the cash. Three is to have the right people in the right jobs. Four is around key relationships: who are the most important relationships to the company, such that if they were to go away, you'd be in deep trouble? The CEO needs to own those key relationships. Lastly, five is the process to continue to learn.

I read many books or listen to many books while I'm running. My favorite book of all time is *Good to Great* by Jim Collins. What I like about his book is that it's about having the right people in the right seats. For example, if you have cancer in your arm, you must have the courage to cut off your arm. The only way to deliver to the people achieving is not to burden them with the people who aren't performing.

I believe it's up to the leader to ensure they have the right people in the right seats, and Jim Collins makes a great point. You must make sure you're lean and cut the chaff throughout the company to ensure everyone is playing at the top of their game.

I spoke a year ago in Singapore to a couple of hundred CEOs. I asked, "How many of you would rate every person on your leadership team an A?"

No hands went up. I was shocked, so I asked, "Why not?"

They had all commented reasons as to why. Then we got on this topic called "Is Good Good Enough?" So many people are satisfied with the people that they have yet also recognize that those people aren't the people who will take them where they want to go.

For many of them, they afraid that these people have been with them since the beginning. They say, "What will everybody think about me if I let them go? We're family. We're all friends. Our spouses hang out together. Our kids go to the same school. What impact would it have on our customers? Our vendors? Our culture, if I were to make it a change?" The general way of thinking is, "Go with the person that you know because the person you know may be better than the unknown person that you'll bring on board."

If you want to build a great company, hire the best people in the world, and you will build a great company. Many of our clients have sold their businesses for over $100 million, and you don't create a $100-million valuation without hiring the absolute best people. Most of those people will not come from within, because if you're an entrepreneur—who built your firm and had those people from the beginning—they most likely have not walked down that road.

When your business goes from 0 to 10, there's a different set of people that get you from 0 to 10, and then there's a different leadership that will take you from 10 to 30, 40, or 50, then 50 to 100, and 100 to 250. It's a different skill set.

The biggest mistake I've made in my career is not having the courage to act on people sooner, and by not acting on it sooner and bringing in the absolute best people, it slowed down the growth and hurt our culture. I've learned as I've gotten older. I always ask audiences, "How many people have you fired too soon?" The answer is a short list—as a matter of fact, there's nobody on the list.

I have a coaching company, and we coach 185 CEOs around the world in twenty-eight countries, representing about $11 billion in annual revenue, and over 70,000 employees. So the mentoring that we do is within our firm. I've been a member of YPO for almost twenty years, so I've done all kinds of volunteer work for YPO and EEO.

I also volunteer to mentor any of my friends' or clients' high school or college kids to help them figure out the next step in their journey.

It makes me feel good, and I know it has an impact on people I'm mentoring. Sometimes it's hard for the parent to give advice and for the child to accept that advice, but when it comes from a third party, it's credible. People tend to resonate more with that. I have that same issue with my kids, even though I run a world-class coaching company. My kids would rather listen to my friends and other CEOs and leaders than listen to Dad.

I believe most entrepreneurs need mentoring in figuring out what they want and then how they're going to get it.

A third point would be if you asked me, "Mark, tell me about all the companies that your clients that have sold their businesses between $100 million dollars and $550 million dollars?"

I would tell you it's all about putting the right people in the right seats. Most entrepreneurs need help with that. It's about navigating the conundrum between fear and courage to act.

To bridge that gap, design what your organizational chart looks like three years from now. Who would you have in what roles? How many of the people that you have today would serve in those roles if your company was twice or three times the size it is today? If that's what your work chart would look like then, why does it not work now? It usually does.

I don't think I've ever met anybody that went through that exercise that didn't get it. If I asked them to draw what their org chart would look like at the end of this year, they'd likely draw the same org chart.

If I pushed them out two or three years, they'd draw a different org chart. By implementing that org chart right now, they'll be able to execute on their vision. They can keep the people they have today that may be over their skis in their role. I'm not saying you need to get rid of those people, but you can bring in leaders, the C-suite, that can help drive, inspire, teach, and bring out the best in those people.

In some cases, if you have a weak chief operating officer or chief financial officer who may have worked well at a $20-million company, that doesn't mean they'll work well at a $100 or $200-million company.

I'm the friend of Marshall Goldsmith and enjoyed his book *What Got You Here Won't Get You There*. I often use this example. Even though he doesn't directly talk about that issue in his book, I love the title, and I like to say the people and the processes that got you to where you are today are not the people and the processes that will take you to where you want to go. Marshall's book is excellent. It's one of my favorite books about leadership.

I wrote an Amazon bestseller in the US and Canada called *Make Big Happen: How to Live, Work, and Give Big*. The book is about building the business and the life that you want to experience by asking four questions.

Where do you want to go?

What do you have to do to get where you want to go?

What's going to stand in the way?

What is the process to hold yourself accountable to get what you want?

Throughout the book, we tell stories and provide examples of others who have built businesses. We discuss their journey and struggles. By defining what they wanted and figuring out what would drive what they wanted, they recognized the obstacles they had to deal with, built a systematized process and accountability, and that enabled them to achieve a lot more than they could in their past.

Jacopo Bracco
Scale Capital
Scale.capital

Scale Capital is an investment and management company, so we participate in other companies. We have a portfolio of six startups in which we have invested, and we're helping them grow. Eventually, we will continue looking for other opportunities to invest and improve companies while generating value for the companies as well as Scale Capital.

I joined Scale Capital about a year ago after I'd spent eleven years as president of DirecTV Latin America LLC. The idea is that a company, such as DirectTV as well as Scale Capital, performs better and at their best when people are fully engaged with and committed to the company's mission. To me, mentoring is all about personal development.

Most professionals get in companies with the aspiration to not only generate value but also to improve themselves as executives, professionals, and leaders.

When I joined Scale Capital, the idea was that we would use a lot of the things I had helped to develop at DirectTV. My former career was centered around creating an environment where people could aspire to give the best of themselves, and for that, they need to be able to interact with leaders who could be mentors.

I think mentoring should not be structured as pure mentoring but should be part of the day-to-day life of every leader. Each leader should be thinking about how to make the work of the people who work for them more engaging. How can they learn how to do what they do better to be faster and be more effective?

Of course, there's a human component providing an area of comfort where people can bring up their concerns. They can make mistakes, and they can be coached. They can continue to improve their performance.

The concept of an open door is that it's only an open door if you find a constructive environment when you go inside the door. Let's say your job on the line. If you meet with somebody, and you know that if you fail, you're going to be scolded or your compensation is going to be affected, then you're not going to be able to help people develop themselves.

If people know that if they've made a mistake or made a decision that didn't deliver the expected results, then they could bring it up collectively, and the company can improve. Then we apply the same things with our portfolio companies at Scale Capital.

When I finished my MBA at UCLA in 1999, I joined 20th Century Fox, a company owned by Rupert Murdoch. Right from the beginning, I was exposed to the work of some senior executives.

Murdoch himself wasn't a mentor, but his leadership in the company had an impact on me, particularly his lieutenants Peter Chernin and Trace Carey and my first boss Ken. He was generous with the people who worked for him and exposed them to his mentorship right from the beginning. He allowed them to learn at the highest levels of the industry. And that's where I relate my mentoring, which is about learning and improving oneself. Much of it has to do with my experience with Ken.

Ken was a significant influence on me. I didn't know that style of leadership before I met him, and I found it genuinely inspiring. It was an open style of leadership with frank, challenging conversations and always striving to deliver the best as a team. Ken was not about each individual; but he was about a strong collective or organizational cohesion that would provide the best mutual outcome for the team and the company.

That was eye-opening. It was something I intuitively related to, but I had not seen it before in action. Since then, I've been working to improve myself when I had opportunities to lead larger organizations like DirecTV Latin America, where we had twenty thousand direct and indirect employees. With the fund, we create that opportunity within our investment firm and the portfolio companies to recreate those learnings.

Entrepreneurs don't come in one typology. There are a lot of different personalities out there, a lot of different things that drive a person to pursue an entrepreneurship endeavor. The one thing that tends to be a recurring theme is the transition from being an entrepreneur where the entire company depends on your decision making towards becoming a leader that guides and inspires the company. Let the decision making occur at the lower levels, at the people that report to that person— developing trust and the ability to delegate tasks, which goes with trust. You cannot delegate if you don't trust.

The open door is essential, and it comes more naturally for some people than for others. Whether in an entrepreneurial company or a large company, many times, senior leaders are intimidated by the capabilities of people who work for them. They hesitate to provide mentoring, guidance, and teamwork that go with it.

I've also attempted at DirecTV to do a more formal mentoring program. However, I did not find that to be effective because it does not deal with the real issues that a person has in developing their career. It becomes a check-the-box exercise. It typically happens again in larger companies, not in entrepreneurial environments.

I like to turn the problem on its head. It's about helping people develop themselves to their fullest potential. If you do that, the results are going to be better for the team and the company. The open door is fundamental to creating that level of trust because I, as a leader, still need to measure people's performance. You have this obligation, but your need to measure performance is different than giving people everything they need to perform at their best.

My advice is to find the best people and trust them. Work with people collaboratively and cohesively so that you're not only mentoring and helping them, but they're also helping you improve yourself. Those relationships are the best ones where you can have that level of trust, and the mentoring goes both ways.

I may be a senior executive, and I may have a thirty-year career. Still, if I'm working with somebody smart, just out of college, or with some different experience in a technology startup, I can learn a lot from that person. There's a lot that I will get from that relationship if I allow myself to be open and not feel that that relationship could be threatening to me.

Michael Heinrich
Oh My Green
Ohmygreen.com

I've been trying to create this new model of leadership.

I've observed that often entrepreneurs—and leaders in general—foster this culture of burnout. People are highly stressed at work. I recently read that stress accounts for more deaths than any other unhealthy factor.

It's mesmerizing to me that in today's world, that's still the case. So I want to create something different and be a role model for change. There are three components for how I think about leadership:

One is I am anchored on purpose. That means I have been clear from the beginning. One of the first things I did when starting my company was to precisely explain what the mission statement was, and why I'm doing this. There is a whole story around why I started the company, but the mission was clear—to empower people to live healthy, blissful lives.

Two is wanting to make sure that no matter how tough it got during the journey, I always maintained personal wellness. To me, wellness is for endurance because entrepreneurship is more of a marathon than a sprint. As an entrepreneur, you have to stay healthy in mind, body, and environment, which is what I think of as the three factors.

My nonnegotiable things are that I sleep seven hours a day, meditate twice a day for one to two hours each time, do kung fu three times a week, eat healthy organic food daily, and make sure I have meaningful relationships inside and outside of work.

During meetings, I make sure that we can go on walks in nature, and that is how I nourish my perspective mind, body, and environment. I maintain that wellness, no matter the situation. Sometimes you will have sticky people situations to deal with or difficult customer situations. But you should never lose your wellness.

The third piece is around the relentless focus. One of the things that I believe I have done relatively well is to make sure that at any stage of the company, I am deeply, intensely focused on what matters. There are a lot of things that we can do, like answering emails all the time and responding to every inbound request that comes in versus thinking strategically and asking what the core metric that matters for me at this stage is.

For example, at the beginning stages of entrepreneurship—and that goes a little bit into the second point where I mentioned general entrepreneurial advice—all that matters is product-market fit. If you do not have a product-market fit, then it doesn't matter what all the other activities are. You might be trying to sell as much as possible; you might be trying to spend as much as possible on marketing. All that does not matter unless you have tailored the right product to the right user base.

One of my key messages to being a good entrepreneur is to do whatever it takes to get the product-market fit. Once you have a post-product-market fit, then it's much more about building the company, making your next product, building a strong distribution pipeline, and so on.

I became who I am through two components: one is through my experiences in the corporate world, then two is by having influential mentors alongside me. There are too many examples to list the type of mentorship I have received over time.

My experiences have shaped me, as I've been fortunate to work in various fields. I've worked in tech product management at Microsoft, being a management consultant at Bain and Company, working at a hedge fund called Bridgewater Associates, then moving into an entrepreneurial journey. I learned about the different types of environments of which I wanted to be a part. Sometimes the settings pushed me toward a bit of a burnout stage.

I also learned that specific environments do not think about wellness. For example, companies might claim to support the idea that work-life balance is essential. But then you'd go into the kitchen and see ultra-processed ingredients and sugary drinks, and that's not entirely congruent. Some of these experiences then shaped me into figuring out what is meaningful to me in a particular work environment.

That's how I ended up starting my dream. While I was enjoying the people, the problem was that when I was working in these environments, I found all them to lack meaning. When I went through this search of meaning, health and wellness came up strongly for me. I recognized that I grew up with a grandmother in Germany, who is a medical doctor.

But instead of giving me medicine every time I had some health issues, she had a much more preventative health mindset. She would tell me to eat directly from her garden, and then I wouldn't get sick. She said not to drink too many sugary beverages and get regular exercise.

When I look back at my past, I realize that she was way ahead of her time in teaching me this preventative mindset. I said I could bring this wellness-thinking to corporations in the U.S. and create a company around it.

So that was the first ah-ha moment for me. But then I had to figure out how to do that. How do I build a business model? How do I create a company around this whole concept? That's when I went back to graduate school. I went to Stanford and took a class called the Lean LaunchPad with a professor named Steve Blank.

He was probably one of my biggest mentors early on in this whole process of getting to product-market fit. He had a few interesting core messages. One was that startups are not a smaller version of a big company; they are in a search process for a scalable business model.

Until you have a product-market fit, you're still in a search process. To determine what your business model will look like, you have to get out of the building and speak to about a hundred people in the industry to understand whether your idea works, how to shape it from different angles from having the right product for the right customer demographics to having the right channel and having the right operational model.

That has profoundly shaped me as an entrepreneur and changed my journey over time. So I feel fortunate to have had him as a mentor along this journey.

There are a few different types of mentorship I'm currently engaged in with my company. First, there's a type of leadership mentoring. For example, if I see a behavior that's maybe not fully aligned with the company culture, I can do some mentoring around that and do some correcting around behavior.

Then I would say there's a general managership that I provide to other peers and startups. I've joined an organization called YPO, and there are a lot of ad hoc opportunities there. It could be on a specific business or personal problem somebody is facing. I love giving back because I felt fortunate to have had mentors like Steve Blank.

In this last quarter, I was a mentor for the Lead LaunchPad class, and so it came full circle. I helped the team with their ideas and thinking through that and helping with their business model creation.

I am going to be super biased and say that my favorite model is my team's model. They created a gym for the mind, and they called it the neurocognitive gym. Initially, they had this idea that they were going to work super well, and then the moment they tried to execute on it, they met with a lot of resistance from the initial target market they were targeting. They didn't see other models taking off with that concept.

But as they made more discover, they figured out that other models in other locations were not focused on specific aspects and specific target demographics. They innovated on that with their business model by going after what they called body hackers—people who want rigorous training for their minds so that they can be the best athletes possible.

And so, when they ran a test, they had a thirty or so NPS score, and then over a few sessions, I think the NPS score improved to almost sixty or so. That ended up driving a substantial amount of revenue for the cost as well after having done a few test sessions. So I was very proud and happy to see the team succeed in that way.

My way of thinking tends to be more systematic. It's how I digest information and then structure it for myself.

If I were to write a book, I would talk about this new model of leadership that I am trying to build and then add some of the general advice that I mentioned around being an influential entrepreneur. I would write about being anchored on purpose, who inspired me, and what the backgrounds of my story have been.

I would discuss how had I not worked for Bridgewater, for example, I would not have gotten exposed to transcendental meditation, which has been such a joy to have incorporated that into my life. It has helped me maintain a healthy balance along my wellness journey as well.

I would discuss how I maintain wellness and what some of the models are. As part of that component, I would talk about having a learning mindset. Many times, things do not quite go as you had planned. It's easy to blame oneself in that type of situation when you say we have lost this customer or this key employee left, so I must have done something fundamentally wrong.

But if you have more of a learning mindset, you can ask what you can learn from this situation to improve this type of situation the next time around. It's a much healthier relationship with yourself. I would have a component under wellness that talks about that as well.

The final piece would be about how you focus on things that matter. That relentless focus piece is part of that new model of leadership. I was able to go to grad school, have a full class load, start a company, work as a teaching assistant; meditate two to three hours a day, get the right amount of sleep, have good social relationships, and still have rest time on the weekends, and be able to take vacations and so on.

That schedule requires a robust, relentless focus on the things that matter, so I would write about these components.

In summary, with this new model of leadership, I want others to embrace something around life and leadership and building enlightened companies.

Ofer Hubar
Aviv Service Today
Avivservicetoday.com

One particular way that I have been affected by mentoring would be how my mentors taught me to think outside the box.

My line of work is in appliance repair, so I had one mentor who taught me the appliance business, then a couple of others who were entrepreneurs. Each of them taught me that the key to success was not to follow the steps that everybody else does. They taught me to come up with new ideas and do something different that other companies don't do. Providing better service allowed us to access the higher end of the market, which is the more profitable part. Sometimes those mentors can be books that we read and other people.

We learned through our mistakes as well as from mentors. One of the more significant errors I've made was trusting people too much. I also learned over the years not to micromanage, as that practice can suck up all your time and energy. I also learned the hard way that even if you do assign something to someone, you still have to follow up to some extent and make sure that things are done.

I had to learn to strike that balance between finding trustworthy people to work with and not micromanaging them. It wasn't easy, and it took time. It was a matter of sitting down and asking myself if I wanted to spend extra time micromanaging.

Did I want to spend 24/7 doing everything, or was I willing to let go at a certain point?

I concentrated on finding better people that I could trust. One of the things we realized was that to get better people, we had to pay them more. We decided to increase our entry pay, then we were able to attract better workers.

A significant mentor to me was a guy who primarily got me into the business, who has gone on to open a franchise and other enterprises. We're still close friends, so even now, when I have questions, I can call him, and we'll talk. He's been a significant influence on me in helping develop the company.

I don't know if I would consider them mentors, but I've read books on successful people such as Bill Gates. I enjoy learning from people who have been successful in business. I can get their point of view as to what they thought and what they did that made a difference. There was a great book that I read about the banking industry called *Good to Great: Why Some Companies Make the Leap and Others Don't* by Jim Collins.

When I read biographies by some of these prominent businessmen like Bill Gates, their example inspires me in my business. It inspires me to see what they did and what they were following and which systems they implemented. They talked about how to do things and what were the decisions that they decided to change something and how that impacted their companies.

Over the years, I've met people who I mentored who were starting new businesses. There's a guy in my town, a one-person operation. He's starting a garage door business, so he often will stop by and ask me questions because I started on my own. He'll ask me questions about how to grow the company, so I will try to give him advice on things to do or not to do and so forth.

I mentor new employees all the time as we do hands-on training. We used to train people from zero knowledge, so that's one of the things we've started doing differently. My wife is a great help in the company as well, and she came up with the idea to import people from other states with some experience and then teach them to do things the way we do, and it worked.

After the first couple that didn't work out, we learned from our mistakes, and it has been a successful change for us. Whether they come with experience or none, I mentor them regularly.

I mentor for the entire company. During our meetings, we go over the protocol to help improve performance. I mostly mentor on how to do repairs and deal with customers. I don't mentor so much on how to run a business, although we do share some things with our employees because we want them to understand what it takes to run a business. I found that when I started as an employee, it was hard to grasp the big picture of how a company was run. But our employees are usually not interested in becoming a business owner, so it's not something on which I tend to mentor them.

Probably most entrepreneurs need mentoring to have a vision for the future and look at the big picture. When we start in the business, we tend to get so wrapped up with the daily operation and the small things that we don't give ourselves the time to develop the company.

There has to be a good balance, especially if you put in the actual labor, but also come up with ideas and ways to do things in the company. My advice is to hire good people to help you out or take some of the daily work from you, which gives you more time to work on the company. I think that's a big thing, especially when people start up a company. Many people need guidance in delegating parts of their business.

If I were to write a book, I would advise new entrepreneurs to find ways to be different. Don't follow the road that everybody else did, because you become monotonous. You'll be just another person in the industry, and that isn't going to give you the greatest success—if you're looking for that, which I assume most people are.

Also, learn to find balance. I did not take a vacation for many, many years in the beginning, and I realized that I probably should have. Make sure to get away for a few days now and then. That's one of the things I learned, and I make up for it now. Making sure you have that downtime to refresh is essential.

We've developed strategies to help our company stand out from the rest and do things differently. For instance, most appliance repair businesses provide a warranty on the repairs that they do, which usually vary anywhere from thirty to ninety days to one year. We decided to give warranties for up to five years on the parts, at least. Nobody else does that in our market, which puts us in the upper level. When people consider their repairs, they look at it and say, "Well, I get a five-year warranty on this part, so let's go with their repair."

The company is continually evolving based on how things change and are different from twenty-five to thirty years ago.

For instance, cell phones were not around twenty-five years ago, so we evolved into using texting a lot, which helps tremendously because it takes a lot of time to trade phone calls back and forth with our customers. We are continually trying to change for the better.

When we decided to offer five years warranty on some parts, there's a give-and-take you have to do to determine the cost to your business versus the potential new customers that you might attract.

There's always a chance that the changes you make won't be successful. But that's how you learn from your mistakes. We had a computer program we were using for many years, and we realized that it was getting to the point that it was not the right program for us, though a lot of people in the industry were using it.

So we did our research and found another company with another program, and it was a major hassle for the first couple of months, and a lot of people resist it because it was hard for people to make changes. In the long run, it turned out to be a good move for us. We always try to take into consideration everything we do what the impact will be if we can foresee it. We always try to make things better.

My message for new entrepreneurs who are just starting is not to give up. Even if it looks like there will be hard times. There've been times when my employees got a paycheck, and I didn't. If you stick with it and believe in what you do, you will get there. It's not a microwave thing, but a slow cooker. You've got to give yourself the time, and it may take time as it did in my case, but the rewards will be there at the end.

Persistence is key.

Cory Capoccia
Womply
Womply.com

At Womply, mentoring is super critical to the development and ultimate success of our employees. We're firm believers in the concept that one of the most significant inputs into an employee's happiness and success is ultimately heavily influenced directly by their manager.

Employees generally don't leave companies; they leave managers. Or they stay with companies because of the relationship they have with their manager. So one of the things that we focus on is deploying mentoring across a bunch of different dimensions of our business, with a particular focus and emphasis on training our managers.

By investing in management first and giving them the skills and resources they need to motivate, develop, and manage their teams, that, in turn, will help provide broader mentorship across the organization in a one-to-many approach.

What I think has made a big difference is having our people operations team regularly meet with every manager, to understand what their approach is. There are all kinds of different levels of management, and most people don't wake up one day and at once have all the tools they need to become excellent managers and mentors for their team.

The role of the manager is to mentor staff and help develop their careers, understand what motivates them, know the goals they're working toward, understand the constraints, and know who they are as people. The human element is a massive part of management.

We spend a lot of time with our managers to develop them as mentors. We want them to understand who their team is and avoid falling immediately into the transactional-tactical discussions so easy to do.

Rather than have a conversation like, "Let's go through the checklist of what you did last week, and let's focus on what's coming up next week," we want them to spend more time understanding who their mentees are as a person and the things that make them tick.

They should ask, "How can I play a role in helping you develop you personally? How can I help you achieve your success in the office and then ultimately beyond that?"

Many times, we'll see our mentor managers encourage their team to take advantage of our educational-credit subsidies that we provide for those who want to do continued education to develop their skill sets. Based on what we've put in, mentoring has helped us develop a much happier and more productive workforce. Now they're better equipped—not only to perform in their role and manage their career but also to balance all the challenges that life brings to the table.

There are other things that we'll continue to do to mentor and develop our team members. Do we look at our role as to how do we make our people succeed in life since they spend so much time with us in the office? There's a pretty significant role we can play in helping them balance all those different pieces.

I've read pretty much every classic business book out there, like *Invisible Influence*. You can go down the list, and there's a ton. *Don't Split the Difference* is a pretty cool book about how you think about negotiating and inspiring people through the process.

Many people have been influential in my life: parents, teachers, family, siblings, and friends. They've all been mentors in different senses. They've helped me along the way and to reflect on my path and help me learn and grow throughout life.

What's had a more significant impact on me than any book or person in my life is an organization that I sought out to become a part of called YPO, which stands for Young Presidents' Organization. I think that's a fantastic organization, and I've been involved in lots of them.

Why YPO has been the most influential mentor for me is because there's a strong focus on developing what's called the forum. A forum is a group of people that's a subgroup of one of the YPO chapters, typically about six to ten on the larger size. We meet every month. There are a couple of core norms or principles that you live by, like the highest level of trust and confidentiality, which enables you to be vulnerable and unpack what you're feeling and learn from the experience of other people in the group.

The other important piece is about active listening and not projecting your advice onto others. In response to what you hear, you can share the experiences that you've had, because no one can live your life in your shoes. But people might have had experiences from which that you can learn. They may feel on the surface that they're completely unrelated, but there are lots of different threads and lessons that you can pull from that.

The other piece that had the most significant impact is the extreme focus on maintaining a balance between three critical pillars of life, which are your personal life, family life, and professional life and how you allocate time and investment on each. The belief is that if any one of those gets out of balance, then it impacts the other two.

We've read all the books. We've got lots of experiences from others that come naturally. But what's impactful is finding your tribe, or a group, that you can trust. You go in with a deliberate purpose to focus on working on yourself. It's too easy for too many people to spend the time getting caught up in the day to day.

Instead, what I've found is a select group of people where I've got five or six other mentors who are always there to inspire and motivate me. They help me understand the ways they've approached different problems and overcome various obstacles and how they prioritize the different things in life.

By far, those relationships have had a much bigger impact than taking more of an academic route of, "Okay, read this in a book and then go apply it in your life."

I do not deny that I've done that, but I think there are a lot of examples of groups that you can find where you can be a part of something like that and build that type of your relationship and mentorship that becomes bidirectional.

YPO is an international organization with over twenty thousand members. There is an international group that you can tap into. You've got a region, which is typically like the Pacific Northwest or different parts of the world. Then you've got chapters, then finally your forum. That's the smallest group that you work with.

What's neat about it is because everyone comes from that core, base forum, there is already an understanding and a bond when you meet any of those twenty thousand members. No matter where they're from, their age, the type of business they're in, or the background they have, there's this core understanding and openness that's incredibly refreshing in a world where people tend to be pretty guarded and don't open themselves up to others.

I tend to break up my mentoring into two camps in my life: the preprofessional years and the professional years.

The preprofessional years include the time being a child on up through early education and then ultimately college at UCLA. I sought out every opportunity I had to spend time with people. I was a camp counselor for one of UCLA's camps, UniCamp, where we brought underprivileged children out for a week in the wilderness and let them be kids and talk about a lot of different aspects of life. That had a considerable role in shaping how you think about the world and how you can help others understand that there's a lot of options in life, and you have a choice. You're controlling your destination and future.

Then I tutored, working more in the academic framework, helping to provide general guidance, then also giving career guidance to individuals in my fraternity. As an alum, I helped undergrads explore career options.

In the professional years, I've been a member of a bunch of professional organizations. Entrepreneurs' organization is another one that I was involved with for some time. There are some local groups in Utah in which I'm involved as well. It's good to find those types of organizations where you can have that shared mentorship, and some are more active and focused on pairing you one to one in a more formal setting as being a mentor. Others are a little bit less formal, where you have collective mentorship in a more casual environment.

At our company, I try to spend a lot of time, not only with my direct reports, but also with other peers and colleagues. The primary thing I focus on is connecting with them as a person, trying to understand who they are as a human. I want to know what motivates them.

What are the things that might impact their ability to come in and perform? What are the ways that I can help them?

Once we get past the basics, then we can spend more time learning what they want to get out of their time with us while we can help support them. Beyond their time with us, whenever that time may come, we want to know what we can do to help set them up.

I bring the YPO principles of understanding to people on our team. For example, I like to help them explore the balance between personal investment, professional investment, and investment in the company. I want to help them understand whether they are balanced or needing some help in bringing them back into balance. There have been many different examples across the company where I've been able to play that mentoring role, and it's been a fantastic experience.

The two areas that I feel most entrepreneurs need mentoring in are primarily vulnerability and empathy.

I've interacted with many entrepreneurs, and I am an entrepreneur. It's easy to have a clear motivation and drive toward what you're trying to achieve and forget to bring people along with you. You can be so charged that you're blindly going ahead, and everything else can feel like it's more of an anchor slowing you down.

I think the biggest thing that's important is recognizing that you need to, again, going back to some of the previous commentaries, be willing to be vulnerable to your team. They need to understand that while you're the one providing the strategy, inspiration, and motivation for people to show up at work every day and work toward innovation, they need to understand that you are human too.

Putting up a false shield that projects that everything is perfect in your life and you have everything under control kills credibility, because everyone knows that isn't true. There's always something that impacts you, whether it's something that's out of your control, like having a relative or a loved one unexpectedly pass away, or things that are in your control, like decisions you've made where the outcome wasn't what you expected.

It's important to be vulnerable with your team and let them know that you make mistakes too, and you don't have all the answers, and you're on this journey with them as opposed to them trailing behind you. That's an essential characteristic that most entrepreneurs overlook because they feel like they need to be the bedrock for the organization.

Part of that is empathizing with the team because everyone in your company is going to come from different perspectives and backgrounds; they're going to have different objectives. Get good at putting yourself in their shoes to understand their point of view. Even if you don't necessarily have the same background or experiences to sympathize with them, you need to empathize with them at a minimum.

If I were to write a book, my key message to entrepreneurs would be to explain the three components. I typically break this down and ask, "What are the three things that we need to get right?"

I've touched on them throughout the conversation.

Seeking to understand deeply is the first component. Seek general guidance to deeply know before you try to jump in and solve or arrive at any conclusion. Understand your customers, employees, shareholders, and investors, if that relates to your company. Make sure—before you form any of your own opinions—that you understand what motivates and inspires them, what constraints they're operating within.

Because if you don't know what and who you're dealing with and how to correctly engage with them because you haven't taken that step, then you're projecting your expectations. There are going to be mismatches there—guaranteed.

The second is to be honest about your limitations. You've got to hire people that address your gaps and can fill in what those limitations are. Then what's most important beyond that is how you ramp them up and empower them to be as successful as possible in their role.

Ultimately, you must trust that once you've made that hiring decision that they'll be successful because without doing that, you can't scale. It's impossible for any single person to build these thriving companies. There will be multiple limiting factors stunting your growth. But it would be your own headstrong decision there, so you got to know where you have limitations, and then hire to solve that area.

The third component is that balance is essential. Take a checkpoint regularly and understand your balance between three areas (personal, professional, and family).

On the personal side, are you taking care of yourself? Are you eating well? Are you exercising? Are you taking time to exercise yourself, not just physically but also mentally? Are you spending too much time filling up your day with the tasks of running the business?

On the family side, are your relationships suffering as a result of what you're doing? Whether you recognize it or not, that's going to impact you, and something unlikely for anyone to be worth it over the long run. Make sure you don't give up everything for what you're building, but recognize that there needs to be a balance there, because your family, in particular, the ones that helped you get to where you are and will support you through it, should be a part of that journey with you.

Then finally on the professional side, make sure that you keep it in balance. I think it's easy to feel, especially in the early days of building a company, like every waking second need to be spent on the company, and if you're not spending a second on the company, it's going to fail. But if you don't balance your judgment or maintain that balance between all those areas, ultimately, your judgment is going to be hindered, and you're going to impede your ability to be successful.

I like the phrase that you need to take time to step back and work on the business, on yourself, on your relationships and not be lost working in the company on a day-to-day basis. So I think that the third component of maintaining that balance between those three areas is supercritical.

Joshua Hebert
Magellan Jets
Magellanjets.com

I'm the CEO of Magellan Jets, which I founded eleven years ago with my business partners, Anthony Pivnen and Greg Belzarian. Magellan is my second company. I sold my first company after eight years, retired, then started Magellan Jets.

What we do is sell twenty-five, fifty, and one-hundred-hour increments in nine different private jets. On one side of the scope, let's say we have a customer who owns a private plane, a Gulfstream 450. If the aircraft is down for maintenance 25 percent of the year, or their spouse or business partner is using it, they can call us and say they want to go from point A to point B, such as Pittsburgh to Florida. We'll send over the itinerary, and the plane will be there within eight hours of the request.

The other service we offer is for people who don't want to purchase planes. Instead, they can buy twenty-five, fifty, and one-hundred hours on one of our aircraft, or whatever they're going to use, and that's their entire commitment for the year.

I've been in this business for twenty years, and I remember when we had no technology in this space and did everything by fax. I was in this space before we even were using faxes, and I have witnessed how times have changed. Now you can go to your app and book straight from your phone.

As a mentor, I've been able to fine-tune my business and see what my issues are. I mentor students at Bridgewater State College, Harvard University, and high school kids who want experience in the workplace. I also have many people who I mentor at WeWork. Mentoring has been a positive experience for me, as I've mentored people who are much smarter and have much larger companies than I have.

When mentoring, you have the opportunity to become aware of what you're not doing: that whole "practice what you preach" thing. When you're talking, as you've probably done with a relative or child, you tell them what they should be doing in life, then you might look at yourself and realize you're not taking your advice.

Let's say you're mentoring in marketing or search engine optimization or pay per click, and in one segment of a business, you're helping your mentee improve their marketing strategies. You might walk away from your meeting and realize that you're not doing half of what you just advised. So I find mentoring educational for me while it helps others at the same time, which is why I believe that everyone should mentor and be mentored.

One of the most challenging things is mentoring family members or your children because they usually like to learn their lessons on their own or learn from other people. I feel that the essential thing when mentoring is to give less advice and provide more experience sharing. It seems as if everybody has information to offer, and of course, advice can be helpful. But if you look back at your best learning experiences in life, it's usually around experience sharing.

You can explain how specific actions affected your business or a friend's business. Perhaps a CFO was stealing from your mentee. You can say to call the police or punch him in the nose, but that's your advice. Maybe you've never experienced a situation like that, but a colleague of yours has, so you can tell the story of how they handled it and how the situation was resolved. I'm a huge advocate of experience sharing. We learn by mistakes, so when mentoring, I advise less advice and more experience sharing.

There's a gentleman by the name of J. Ira Harris, who was the CEO and chairman of many organizations such as Manpower, William Blair & Company, LLC., Salomon Brothers, and Lazard Freres and Company. Ira has built a worldwide reputation for himself as a gentleman of extremely high integrity. Fifteen years ago, Ira took me under his wing and explained the importance of integrity. Ira has been an invaluable mentor to me.

One of the things Ira explained to me was the duck test: if it looks like a duck, swims like a duck, and quacks like a duck, it's a duck. There are a lot of opportunities presented in life and business that you know is too good to be true. If you go down the paths you know are too good to be true, you waste time and sometimes hinder your ethics meter.

I also have a business/personal coach, Eric Cruz. In the beginning, I met with Eric monthly and then quarterly, and now I meet with him twice a year. Having a paid business/personal coach gets you through some of the personal and business weeds because the coach isn't in your line of business, so they tend to look at things differently.

One of the books I've enjoyed and learned from was Ray Dalio's book about principles, which has been instrumental for me. The book has influenced me in how I make decisions and help grow the company based on processes and principles and not repeating the same mistakes. There's nothing wrong with making mistakes. But if you continue to repeat them, it becomes an ongoing problem that sometimes can't be solved, so it's crucial to develop processes and principles to avoid mistake repetition.

There's another EOS management style book I enjoyed called *Traction* by Gino Wickman. It discusses how you manage yourself and your managers and how to identify issues in your company. It urges you to ask questions such as how you address those issues, how you solve those issues, based on a detailed process.

We learn through our mistakes with mentors, but when I got into the business, I thought you built a business plan and then started your business. Everybody always asks, "Do you have a business plan?" I believe you need a direction instead. You need to know where your business is headed.

Today, you probably don't write a business plan but make a deck about where your company and your industry are going and provide examples of who your competitors are. Having a proper deck is invaluable. I read many books on this subject, but the most recent book that *Harvard Business Review* put out is called *Get Backed* by Evan

Baehr and Evan Loomis, in which they provide great examples on how to build a deck, which is the new version of a business plan.

You need to know your direction and build a proper deck, whether you're going out for funding, to raise money, or sell your business because when you're building a company, you're making it sell. Not enough people know their direction. You hear the question, "What are your one, three, five, and ten-year business plans?"

Well, all you have to do is determine your direction and write the deck to explain your end goal. Think about your end goal and know the route to get there. Whether you can get there or not, that's a different thing.

Get Backed is an excellent book, and I recommend that everybody read it. It's one of the easier reads, especially if you want to understand how to build a good deck. I think depending on if it's B to B or B to C, everyone wants to understand how to market their product/company.

There are many challenges with people, culture, and core values, and people often discount culture and core values. They might think they have culture, and they might think they lead with their core values, but when you look at yourself, you've got to practice what you preach. When you're talking about the core values of your company—and it's happened many times when I've been mentoring people, and they explain their core values—I'd say, "But hey, I just saw you do the opposite the other day."

Whoops.

When mentoring, I found out that businesses have a lot of issues with handling their people. There are many studies on why companies lose customers, and usually, it's an internal cause. It's a disgruntled employee. It's someone having a bad day within an organization who's speaking to a customer. Think about the expression "Happy wife, happy life." If you can have a happy culture and happy employees, then you will have happy customers, which creates retention and lifetime value of a customer.

I think millennials are the best thing that's ever happened to business, but a lot of people have issues with millennials. I'm older, so I was brought up with the saying, "work smart, not hard," but guess what? I worked hard and did not work smart.

But today, the millennials and Gen Zs are working smart, and they're incredibly efficient, and they use technology to their benefit.

I asked my EA, "Could you please hire someone to fix my excel spreadsheet pivot tables? They've been broken for the last six months." She came back twenty minutes later and said, "All right, it's fixed."

I asked, "You already hired someone?"

She said, "No, I Googled it and read a little bit, and I fixed the pivot tables."

Back in the day, someone was hired to fix it. I'm incredibly impressed with the efficient nature of millennials. We built a great organization here with millennials. Many people want to know how to mentor millennials. They think everybody wants not to work or work from home, and that's not true. Millennials enjoy being in a work environment because they do so much on their tablets and phones, and they don't meet as many people at bars the way we used to, so they love great culture in a company.

We used to meet people at school and in bars and restaurants, and now they don't meet people that way. A big part of their socialization is coming into a great culture company. They genuinely appreciate the mentorship one-on-one, in person.

If I were to write a book, my key message to entrepreneurs for them to replicate my success would be that when things are easy for you, that's the time to give those job descriptions and problems to other people.

The only issues you should be dealing with within your organization are the things that you're having a hard time fixing. You shouldn't be wasting your time when you recognize a problem and know exactly how to fix it. That probably means there are probably five other people in your company that can fix it equally or better than you.

Be honest with yourself as a CEO, owner, president, or entrepreneur and know that if it's easy for you, then let somebody else do it. You deal with the hard issues because that's why you're there.

My other advice would be to get comfortable with monkeys on your back. If you want to be a good entrepreneur, you will have problems coming your way. It needs to be a "sort of high" for you. It needs to be your drug of choice for people to put monkeys on your back, and then you fix and solve those problems. You need to be able to delegate the easy issues.

Sherry Orel
Scentered
Scentered.com

We have a couple of seasoned vets at the top of our company. Lara Morgan, my business partner and the founder of Scentered, and I have thirty years of experience in the agency side of the business. We've both had our fair share of opportunity to mentor people over the years, and being in a scrappy startup entrepreneurial environment, now we employ the 80-for-the-20 principle.

We don't have a formalized mentoring program like some larger companies do. Ours is more hands-on, on-the-fly, and the expectation is that when somebody needs mentoring or coaching, they can get it directly from whomever they might be dealing.

Once they get it, there's a level of expectation for accountability and empowerment. That's why we deploy the 80-for-the-20 rule: 80 percent of the time they're making one of the right decisions. The expectation is that they're always making the decision we would make, but if their rationale and decision-making process are sound, then you cut them loose and let them go. One of the most critical elements of growth and learning is making mistakes.

I've found that when someone has been let loose, and they make a mistake, it serves as an essential learning experience for them. They do a lot of self-analysis and Monday morning quarterbacking to make sure they don't repeat that same mistake. What you want in most of your employees is for them to hold themselves to a higher level of accountability than you would so that they're continuously improving on their game. That's the approach that we take here.

It helps the people naturally that are poised to rise within an organization. It gives them a platform to do so. Those who are content to stay where they are can float or coast as long as the organization can sustain them, and it works for them. It also helps shine a spotlight on those who aren't right for the organization—either because they're not applying what they've learned from their mistakes to the next situation, or they don't take the accountability and are quick to point out why nothing is ever their fault. It allows us to figure out who you want to invest in for the future and who might be passing through.

We all make mistakes. One of mine was assuming that if you do a good job, then eventually, you'll get whatever you "deserve." I wouldn't say I like to use that word often because I don't think earning, deserving, and receiving are equally aligned. However, early in my career, I was involved in private sector businesses that grew quickly and then ended up in exits. I was always very much a team player, so I assumed that either I didn't deserve to be a part of any exit upside, or that if I did, it would automatically and naturally come to me. While I've been given some nice parting gifts in terms of checks and things like that at the exit of individual businesses, they were disproportionate to my contribution to the company.

Those experiences taught me to learn more about equity and what you're entitled to and what you could potentially request. I learned that by not asking, you don't receive. Women tend to want to play nice in the sandbox and assume that our excellent work and our efforts will be noticed—we'll get that raise, and we'll get that promotion. When I was ready to move into the C-suite and run a company, I'd been with another company for about six or seven years. It had sold, so the founder/CEO was quite content sitting in the corner office.

He'd taken his millions and millions and millions of tens of millions off the table and was coasting through the earn-out period while I was ultimately running the company. At that point, I got brave and said that I was ready to run the company and if that was not an opportunity for me in the short-term, I'd go elsewhere, which ultimately resulted in a promotion to my first CEO position.

That experience helped me understand that I needed to seek counsel. At the next transaction I was involved in, I made sure I was personally protected. I sought advice from people who had been there before, some of whom knew me and some of whom, through other professional networks, were friends of friends. I was able to ask point-blank questions and found that if you ask a succinct question, you can be respectful of somebody's time. Then they're often willing to share insights with you so you don't have to learn everything the hard way.

One of my first mentors during the early stage of my career was a woman named Gail Sharp. We worked for what is now a division news corporation, and she was quite a bit senior to me, and she was the only woman in the company. She stood out with her stilettos and flashy style, and she was, by far, the top producer in a company surrounded by a bunch of men. Being placed under her early on gave me a star to shoot for, and I quickly rose up from more administrative roles into revenue-generation roles.

I had this great opportunity to give this presentation in New York, and since I lived in Chicago, I flew in a day early to cobble together the presentation. I'm dating myself, but it was pre-PowerPoint, and I had all these slides to place in a round slide projector. I had to make sure they weren't upside down or backward. If I wanted to move the order, I had to physically take the slides out of the carousel and move them around, and all the materials were produced over various periods for various reasons, so there was no cohesive layout.

Gail was coming in the next day to run the slide with me, but she'd made it clear that it was my show, my stage, and it was mine to win. We got together on the morning of the event, and I started to take her through the presentation.

It was a disaster. She was frustrated, and I could tell she was getting angry with me. However, we got through it and practiced a couple of times. We went to the meeting, and since we were one of several companies presenting, we had the opportunity to see a few others perform before us. They had put together elegant presentations, unlike our approach to the meeting, and I could feel myself shrinking as these other great presenters went before me.

I could see Gail beginning to sweat, as I was already doing. Then it was our turn. Gail put her hand on my knee and stood up, and she swung at it, and it was fine, but it was not like anything I had seen her present in the past. I waited for my lashing after the meeting for having put her in that awkward position. One of the greatest lessons I had already learned is the importance of preparation.

Gail didn't lash out at me. Instead, she apologized and said, "I'm sorry for putting you in that position. I now realize that I should've prepared better and understood what you were walking into. I didn't ask enough questions. I didn't realize the audience that we were going to face. I didn't realize the caliber of whom we were presenting to, and if I would've done my work as your manager, I never would've put you in that position."

So that was a dual-ended lesson on the importance of understanding what you're walking into for any meeting and preparing and over-preparing.

I've spent a lot of time reading books that are more neurological in basis, such as *How the Mind Learns*, *Mindset*, *Mind State*, or *The Power of Habit*. Those types of books helped me understand what makes people tick. Whether you're in sales, managerial, or mentoring role, everybody makes decisions based on emotion. If you can figure out how to anticipate emotions in advance, react to them in real-time, and manage them properly after the fact, that's the key to any personal engagement, no matter your role in the company.

I've had upwards of 350 people reporting to me at different times. Over the years, many of them were young women, so I tried to be a role model, as I think that's the first step to mentoring. People have to see themselves, or some version of themselves, in you and want to follow in your footsteps. One of the things I've employed that has been a contagious element in any organization I've run has been one question, "What did you learn?" So I ask this after every meeting we have, primarily with those with external partners.

If we've had a sales or partnership meeting, and I've got people traveling with me, everyone takes their notes, and they expect to recap the next steps, and I put somebody on the spot and ask, "What was your key takeaway? What did you learn from that meeting?"

They will first answer, "Hm, well…this is their budget, and this is their timing."

I say, "No, those are facts. What did you learn? What did you observe? What did they ask? What didn't they ask? Why do you think I answered the question this way? Why do you think I asked them this?"

My questions force them to get into the guts of the meeting's psychology. Over time, people learned that after every single session, I was going to ask them what they learned. They went into meetings preparing to listen for things so they could answer my question with some intelligence at the end. They wanted to sound much better than they did the first time I asked them that question, but it also forced them to listen differently. Maybe they would get out of the PowerPoint presentation deck that they were so enthralled by in going slide by slide. They'd get out of the deck and come into the room.

I might ask them, "Did you notice when they wrote down something on slide 27? What do you think caught their eye? Did you slow down enough to ask, 'Is there something there that interests you?'" It makes them explain to you what's in their heads so that you can understand what might be driving their emotional or logical decision-making process.

People who work with me start to anticipate and get much better at listening, and then virally, they would give a shortcut to the new people. "Hey, by the way, when you travel with Sherry, she's going to ask you what you learn, and this is how you need to be able to answer her questions." It started to have a pay-it-forward benefit throughout the whole organization.

The area that most needs mentoring is an interesting concept, as it depends on what entrepreneurs don't know. So many entrepreneurs—and entrepreneurs are a special breed—come at an opportunity because they have some areas of strength, whether it's product development, manufacturing, finance, branding, or innovation. They'll have a set of strengths that makes them believe that this could work, but then there's a whole completely different set of weaknesses that could potentially derail their ability to be successful. The most important thing for them is to figure out what they don't know and then figure out how to fill those gaps.

What don't you know? What you don't know can hurt you.

It's important to seek the counsel of other mentors and networks proactively. Some people might be willing to have coffee with you if they've run in the same shoes as you did in the past. So many entrepreneurs fall in love with their idea so passionately that they're afraid to talk to too many people. They're worried that somebody might suggest that their design has some flaws, so they tend to get defensive. They love their idea to death—literally to death.

It's essential to remain open-minded and stay true to your vision but understand that the strategy and tactics along the way might need to change once you're presented with more information. You can reserve the right to change your mind when the facts represent themselves, and I have met many entrepreneurs of the year who do so.

I was meeting with an entrepreneur who had an exciting idea—a concept of a world lottery for good. He presented to me, and his idea was riddled with flaws, but his passion was unmatched, and he was young. When you're a busy professional, you have to limit yourself when investing in staff. You can be spread too thin, so you want to make sure if there's someone that you've chosen to mentor, that it's going to be a worthwhile proposition. It must be somebody who's going to benefit from the experience.

At the end of the presentation that he gave with all his passion and crazy numbers that didn't add up, my first question to him was, "Do you consider yourself teachable?"

He immediately and passionately said, "No." Then he said, "Well, I take that back. I've had some professors that I felt like I could learn from, but never from my father."

For me, that was a red flag, and that probably wasn't the place where I was going to choose to invest my time. My advice is to be somebody who is teachable and who craves learning because you're much more likely to attract mentors who can do just that.

I think everybody has something to share. I think the word *mentor* is a little boxed in. There was an article in Cheryl Sandberg's book *Lean In*, and I think it was called "Would You Be My Mentor?" It was about people being advised to get a mentor and how you go about getting somebody to mentor you. Understand that everybody has something to share and could potentially give an ounce or a pound of themselves to somebody else. It's a bit of a pay-it-forward situation.

I have often had junior-level or mid-level people come into the organization and my office and say, "So-and-so just got a promotion. What do I need to do? Because I've been here for ten years. It's time for me to have a promotion. I haven't had a change in my LinkedIn in a year and a half, and it's time."

Typically, that involves the discussion of, "Well, what exactly is it that you want to be doing more of? What do you want to be doing less of? Because to move up in the organization, we need to identify the skills that you need to learn. We also need to identify the skills that you've mastered, and you need to be able to hand them off to new people, some of whom may already be in the organization. Who within the organization do you feel would benefit from learning some of the skills that you've mastered? What specifically do we need to do to put you in a position where you can teach them and off-load some of those skills that maybe aren't where you want to go?

That right there is mentoring; whether they are being called "the mentor" or not, and once you do that a lot and do it at scale, then you've probably earned the mentor label. Folks need to be teachable, particularly if they want to move on and flourish in the business world. You should approach the world as if everyone you meet and every situation you encounter can teach you something.

If I were to write a book, my key message would be about my approach to business and life in general as calculated fearlessness. People have asked me, "What made you think that you could do that?"

I was in high school, and I was a bouncy athlete, gymnast-type kid, and it was the first day of freshman year track. The high-jump pit was set up, and the junior, beautiful, long-legged gazelle that went to state was ready to jump over the bar. I had never done it before, and I was silly, so I cut her off, ran in front of her, flipped over the bar, and got off the mat. The coach was yelling at me, and I assumed, through my head, it was because I had cut her off and was wasting time. Then I heard him ask, "Why did you do that?"

When I slowed down, I said, "Oh, I'm sorry. I was goofing around." Then I realized what he asked was, "What made you think that you could do that?" I didn't understand the question, and apparently, the height that the bar was set at the time was the state-qualifying height for a girl in the high jump, and I had never jumped over a bar before yet was able to do it.

His question "What made you think that you could do that?" stuck with me my whole life. Because I didn't know I shouldn't be able to, and so my philosophy in life and business is, "How hard could that be? Eh, I'll try."

There have definitely been things that I've tried and stopped that would be designated as a failure. It sounds cliché, but there's a series of cinder blocks or stepping-stones or whatever visual works for you that led to me being educated in one way or another.

At one point, I dabbled with the idea of multilevel marketing and working for myself by selling Mary Kay, which was entirely not who I am as a person, but I wanted the experience. I wanted to learn about how multilevel marketing worked and how that particular industry played, so I bought some products and tried to sell it and eventually got rid of a lot of it on eBay.

Years later, I was able to consult a friend of mine who was starting a new business that was going to be based on multilevel marketing. I was able to share with him and consult him and help him along the way, so what was a failure to me was a mentoring experience for someone else later.

The idea of taking risks and being fearless but not crazy is called calculated fearlessness. So educate yourself as much as you can, even if sometimes that's just a quick Google search, but then jump fearlessly and know that, most of the time, there's a way to course correct (or adjust) along the way. Be open to those opportunities until you nail it.

I've been asked if it's been a trickier field to navigate in business because I'm a woman. The truth is probably, but quite honestly, I'd have to put all the trickiness aside. The fact that I didn't go to a traditional university was also a challenge. I was a woman, and I was younger than most of my peers because I was starting in the same roles as they were without having the four years of fun back at the state school. My parents didn't have the pedigree and the background. I grew up blue-collar and didn't have anybody to aspire to be until I found myself in professional situations and then started to try to align.

I think there were certain situations where being a woman was helpful. Some people took me under their wings and wanted to help me be successful because I was a bit of an underdog. There were certain situations where I had to get myself out of uncomfortable situations that were close in line to the whole #MeToo experience of the '80s and '90s. Fortunately, I didn't have any devastating encounters.

I find in today's investment environment, though the percentages of women entrepreneurs are fewer, the portion of financial investments that go toward women entrepreneurs is lower.

When you've prepared, sought out all the mentors, positioned your product the way that you should have placed it, I think that there are many people out there looking to back the right women. For a company that's interested in gaining some financing and escalating our business, we think we have a competitive advantage in the marketplace today.

I've been involved with three previous significant exits, not billion-dollar exits, but a-hundred-plus-million-dollar exits where I was on the sidelines and have literally made a handful of men the aggregate amount of a half-billion dollars of personal wealth. I saw how that was not spread across the people that potentially "deserved" a share, so I set out to do something unique with the next ten years.

We sold our last company to a private equity. We were private equity–held, and I'd run it for fourteen years, and I knew I was ready for a change. I talked to guys who had had exits of their companies and tried to figure out, "How did you even go about figuring out what your next gig was going to be?"

All the men all looked at it linearly, like, "This is the industry I want to run. This is the company I want to start. This is the business vertical that I want to be in." It was all direct, and I felt like I needed to step back and ask myself some different questions. I came up with two that were the guiding post that ultimately led me here, and one was, "What evidence do I want for the next ten years of my career?" Because that's about how much time I want to be crushing it.

That doesn't mean I'm ever going to retire. Then I asked myself how I want to feel about that time. So I concluded that the evidence that I want is the capitalist trophy. I want a significant exit that has the opportunity to bring me considerable personal wealth, not so that there could be generational wealth for our family, but because I think that the amount of good that my husband and I could do in the world with a significant exit would be a fantastic way to spend the last twenty or twenty-five years of my life.

I want to go out, saying, "I made a stab at it. I took a run for it and want to sell a company for a hundred-plus million dollars." That meant I wasn't going to work at Google and run a business unit or anywhere that my mother would know. I needed to be entrepreneurial in a fast-growth sector, so that helps narrow down many things.

The second question was, How did I want to feel? While I can talk about lots of different professional successes over the years, many of them involved doing things like selling more Pantene shampoo or Cheerios. I wanted to be a part of something that could change people's lives for the better.

Where I'm at now is a mindful aromatherapy brand that's teaching people a wellness ritual using the science behind your sense of smell and the part of your brain where habits and memories are formed to try to shortcut habit development and ultimately make people happier. When I can say that worked, I'll be ready to write a book.

Tyson McDowell
Lead Wingman
Leadwingman.com

One unique way our company has been improved upon by mentoring is improving upon the core methodology to ensure that we get the best talents, and ultimately, the best way to fixing the business problems we're trying to solve aligns with the passions of all the employees.

The best way to create value in the world is for people to find purpose in what they do, and it's hard to do that without talking to someone who has been there before. Experience sharing is critical.

I assume everybody is a fully capable mentor. Put any two people together, and they're each qualified to mentor each other in one way or another. It's not a senior/junior, hierarchical relationship. It's where you as the mentor—in terms of the topic, experience, or passion—find the one that wants to be mentored in those areas. But the roles can reverse in the same conversation on a different topic.

We're in the venture capital business, so we create lots of teams for companies and lots of products. Some of the products are dynamic mentoring-facilitation services. Imagine LinkedIn for mentoring, if you will, and cross coaching. There are lots of examples where we've built actual systems that understand where someone is strong and where they're ambitious. We match where they're strong with where they're ambitious, and that's an electronic capability. The converse holds true as well: where someone is ambitious, we find someone strong placed there.

We do it with software solutions that are sold to big companies. We also do it internally, in terms of mentoring our company. So as an executive chairman in a company, the job is to be there for the CEO, but not usurp their power. Oftentimes, we're in a sales situation, so being able to hold the role in a sales situation—where neither the CEO nor the executive chairman can speak on behalf of the company—is critical because it opens the opportunity for that CEO to see the experience in action. It's much easier to observe by doing than it is to just teach, so that's another important role.

We want to be able to put people in a position where they can see the master work—in real-time in the real world—on their problem, and then they partner up on it. So those are two formal ways that we handle it.

We address self-reporting, so employees enter their strengths, but it goes a little bit further. People imagine where they're strong, and they give you an answer, burt that's usually not the true answer. Humans are amazing. They're like onions, with so many layers to peel back. To know the real answers, a process of self-discovery and peer review would be needed.

I can tell you that my greatest value is mentorship, and I ask my peers, "What do you think about my opinion of my own greatest value?"

They say, "Yes, mentorship, sure, but you also value equality. You also value empowerment."

By having group feedback on each other, there's an important prerequisite in that the peers have to opt in this way. They have to say, "I'm going to help you, you're going to help me, and this is a safe place," and that's very important. From here, we have a better belief than what was reported as the person's underlying values, skills, or passions. That gives the algorithms that information then match people up the ability to work much better. Any algorithm can match. The question is this: Are the labels attached to the people truly aligned with their core? Or is it just something superficial they thought at the time?

I've been a pilot since I was a little kid, and my biggest mentors were my flight instructors. As a twelve-year-old flying an airplane, I did not only look up to my flight instructors because they were doing the things I was so excited to do myself, but also because I had a life incentive to listen to them as they were teaching me accountability and responsibility.

My parents have been amazing for putting me in that kind of learning environment. With me being responsible for flying an airplane before I could even drive a car. I saw not only the mastery of skills of those who captained the aircraft but also their sense of responsibility for the whole flight. The way they mitigated safety concerns and negotiated with other air traffic.

They were incredible mentors, and all those lessons I learned that time applied through all my life and impacted the way I lead.

As far as the books go, I found science fiction incredibly instructive, though it does not have so much mentoring in it. But science-fiction stories play out our patterns. So many of these books written by Arthur C. Clarke, Larry Niven, and those kinds of folk are playing out these stories which are moral tales, but they're built on, "If this is how we are now, imagine an enormous scale, and look at how all the goodness and the badness scale up too, and see what happens." Science fiction had brought so much of the consequences—good and bad—forward.

Those books have always shaped me, and I've developed many business concepts, mentoring concepts, and team design ideas straight out of the lessons of science fiction, particularly Arthur C. Clarke's short story "Childhood Zen."

I deal a lot with artificial intelligence, and the idea of humans and AI coming together fascinates me. Facebook has demonstrated that hyper-connectivity is a double-edged sword. How do you fix that? How do you take one of those edges off? How do you turn that into good?

Well, you only have to look as far as "Childhood Zen" to see what's going on, and you can also look at other examples of how to fix it. That story is just so instructive and inspirational.

Mistakes for me include looking up to others prematurely and underplaying my own value. I'm so obsessed with creating value for others first, and I think that's my greatest strength and my greatest weakness. I've given to the wrong people in the past, and they didn't return it. In various business dealings over time, even personal dealings, I've given too much, and I've cared too much when it wasn't of service to me.

I felt at the time like I was giving up a piece of myself, and I've learned that if I'm being overly kind, and it hits me in my gut a little bit wrong, I know how to stop, come back, and analyze the situation.

The only way to overcome that is to seek mentorship. I go to my mentors, and I say, "Here's my transaction. I don't know why I'm not totally feeling good about this. I know I'm valuable, but I'm not that confident. I'm giving too much opinion to their value," and they help me reconcile that. That third-party voice that comes from experience is everything, and the negotiations are fixed, so lots of mistakes around negotiating against myself is how that could play out if I'm not careful. You must learn to trust yourself or at least know when your gut is telling you that something's wrong. Then you seek mentorship and guidance.

I started a software business in healthcare eons ago, and right away, I was going around and doing entrepreneur and resident services for other software startups through a wonderful organization in San Diego called Connect. I'd mentored companies through Connect. Additionally, I taught at the Founders Institute, which is also a service for entrepreneurs. They come in, and we mentor them to find their business and opportunity.

That mentorship activity paid off in droves in my core business. I saw so many of my mistakes played out. But I also got to see so many new techniques and tools and new pricing models. I also got to see the way that the world was starting to think, and this was all the way through dot.com one and two. Lots and lots of change in tech and business models, and I'm so proud of that mentorship. I wanted to support them because it gave me the opportunity to return the favor since I was mentored as a young kid, but I learned so much that it made my business that much easier to execute.

Teaching is an absolute requirement. You haven't learned anything until you've taught it. I've noticed that most entrepreneurs need mentoring in everyday deal-making: raising capital, selling to the first client, doing a strategic business deal, making that hire, how much equity to give away, acquiring advisors, and acquiring board members. Each of these things, to an entrepreneur, seems extreme and possibly scary.

There are two things going on. One, they're giving up a piece of their baby, and two, they're taking a huge financial risk, because all them are looking at burn rate and don't have much capital. So these are hard and scary decisions to make. On the one hand, this person can transform us. But then, on the other hand, I might run out of money, so I'll give up more so I'm not giving up the risk of near-term money.

All those decisions can be made through mentorship, in particular, if you go to someone who's been there before. These are nonissue decisions. These are a no-brainer, standard, templated, cookie-cutter, no question, done, dusted, get it out, don't even worry about it type of decisions. There are so many decisions that are obvious to anyone who's done it before. Once an entrepreneur has gone through each phase, they become good at making those decisions. But they experience unnecessary heartache and waste too much equity in that early phase and give away too much control to people who don't deserve it. If they would have gone after a long-time, well-versed entrepreneur and clued them into the hardcore terms of these critical transactions, fifteen minutes of input would have transformed their lives.

That's all it takes. Give me a contract between a company and a strategic entity such as a big customer who wants to pay an advance for some stuff, but they're asking for exclusivities, big cybersecurity insurance, and other stuff that you can't afford.

I'll look through that contract and quickly tell you where the centerpieces are and how it's going to settle out. Then you can go back and ask for that, get your champion to call legal, and tell them you have got to get to the second layer of audit, but just tell them no, and it'll be fine. You're not going to lose the deal.

Only experience gets you through that process. You can look at comps all day long, but experience does it. For businesses that don't have access to a mentor, the biggest book that I can recommend for anybody, for anything, is called *Thinking Fast and Slow* by Daniel

Kahneman. The author breaks down how humans are bad at making decisions and why and how they're manipulated.

Other books address how to do a start-up, how to grow fast, or how to market a book, create narrow content, and people take it as gospel. You end up with a flavor of the week of strategy, and the books are written to make each one sound so special, and so different, that it undoes the lessons of the last one you read.

I love *Thinking Fast and Slow* because it talks about understanding how you think, and it points out your blind spots, generally and naturally. So that's where I send people. Businesses are all pretty unique, so I don't have a whole lot of books that I've read that have blown me away, in the self-help or business-help space.

Thinking Fast and Slow literally blows up your mind and points it right back at you and says, "See? You've been manipulated. Even by yourself, and here are the specific ways in which it's done, and here's how you can tell that it's happened." It's an absolutely fabulous book.

I am writing a book, but it's not on entrepreneurship. It's on AI and humanity partnering. If I were to write a book on entrepreneurship, it would have to be about the value of picking partners and how to find your core early, so you know what you should be passionate about. The act of entrepreneurship is going out and getting a thousand noes from investors, friends, family—everybody is saying no all the time. Most entrepreneurs, or most human beings, take that as rejection when that's just information.

The act of entrepreneurship is about getting more noes than the next person. Because that means that person has more real information about reality than the others, so one company finally finds a business model that works, because in six months, they've gotten over a hundred noes, whereas the other person gave up at ninety.

It's the passion and persistence that happen. When someone's saying no, you must not necessarily agree with them right away or don't defend yourself, but you want to state your case. I'd write a book about how to find your soul and stick with it, so that you can be much more resilient to those noes, then also how to reframe noes into opportunities and realize what the game is.

You want more noes on the leaderboard, because it means you got more information. If you're getting yeses, and you're not getting closes, that means that you're not pushing the envelope hard enough. You got to be more aggressive in starting a more aggressive position. You've got to tell them what you want the terms to be so that they can react. You don't want to say maybe this, maybe that, because the other side won't say. It's about presenting a case and letting people react to that so you know how they're going to react.

COWORKER

A mentoring relationship often and usually develops naturally within the workplace. These types of relationships can grow organically due to proximity, teamwork, and easy access through connection and communication. Some leaders choose to set up formally structured and ongoing mentorship for their new hires.

Other coworking mentors can develop haphazardly with great success. Workplace mentors are often in a pivotal position to help others due to their experience at the company. In a loosely structured organization, those seeking mentorship are free to develop their own unique and beneficial relationships.

David Dangle
Joan Rivers
Joanrivers.com

I began working with Joan Rivers after experiencing the typical TV and film career schedule. I'm very driven. I love hard work. I love being focused. I love pushing ahead, and my frustration with my previous very successful career as a designer was the nine-months-on, three-months-off schedule. I would feel as if I was finally building momentum and then suddenly would be waiting to see if the show I was working on was picked up for the next season. Or waiting for the next season to start.

When Joan and I started working together, I finally had this fifty-two-weeks-per-year, seven-days-a-week-sometimes commitment. It gave me the opportunity to shift my focus and do something dramatically different. That new challenge would be building a business, building a brand, really, from the ground up, which is an extraordinary opportunity on any level to say, "Okay, we're going to start a business. Let's go."

I was not only building a brand and business but also doing it with an equally driven, equally loving-of-hard-work kind of famous person who had the same passion I did!

The two of us had this attitude of "Just get out of our way." Her mentorship changed everything for me. Before I knew it, I'm traveling the world with Joan Rivers, and we're creating beautiful products and building this incredibly strong brand in a new medium. We kind of take home shopping for granted now.

In 1990, when we started this company, nobody really knew what it was. It was, really, kind of a bold step for Joan and I to take in a medium a lot of people are not familiar with. So that was a huge leap. We both said, "Hey, let's try it. Let's believe in it." Joan believed in it from the very first day. I think a lot of people give her credit for putting much of the home-shopping experience on the map.

It's funny because our original business was not going to be necessarily focused on fashion. The original thought that Joan had was to enter into the beauty business and skincare and color cosmetics niche because she felt very strongly about that. I will give QVC credit for saying, "Hmm, we can't see that, that's not a good space for us. We see an opportunity for our fashion brands." QVC was gently saying, "No, don't do that, do this." It clicked instantly because we both had a passion for fashion and for jewelry and all those types of products. A huge light bulb went off for us, and I remember that moment where we said, "OK, that's a better fit, and that's something we will get very excited about."

The first offering we brought to QVC was a capsule collection of fashion jewelry. The very first item was a little bee pin, and it was based on a pin that Joan's husband had made for her. There was a whole story and history behind it. She felt very much that it signified who she was in life. She was breaking barriers and achieving the impossible. What happened next was absolutely incredible. I don't think happens very often anymore.

We sold everything we had! We literally found ourselves in a position where we ran out of inventory and had nothing left to sell.

I wish I could say we struggled and we had a few years there while we kind of found our way, but it really was kind of a magic moment where, right out of the box, we knew we had something very, very powerful.

So we started asking. What else did Joan love? She was a collector of fine art, antique furniture, and Russian Fabergé objects and jewelry. Her collection had been exhibited at the Metropolitan Museum of Art and had gone to Saint Petersburg with the famous Fabergé exhibit. So she had the authority in that space. That's how we launched the Fabergé egg offerings on QVC. We were asking ourselves, "Can we take these items that Joan is so in love with and introduce that world to our customers?"

The answer was a resounding yes! It was a perfectly natural fit. To this day, we do a lot of Fabergé-inspired pieces. She mentored me and groomed me to know and love this world of beautiful furniture and fine art—the world of Fabergé and Russian art, which is so beautiful.

We were probably about fifteen years into our business at QVC, and just like many businesses, in order to really be effective and grow, you must be hands-on. I was commuting back and forth from New York. I was occasionally staying at a hotel down there. We realized that if we were going to really kind of blow that business up, I was going to need to be there more often. So I built this crazy modern house in Pennsylvania. The first time Joan saw it, she was like, "Oh, okay." Haha. It wasn't necessarily her taste in a home, but she understood. She totally understood. It's funny to think about now.

I had some other fantastic people that put me under their wing and really kind of nurtured and mentored me. In my early days, it was theater designers that were very successful and further along in their careers. I also worked for some of the greats on Broadway and in film. During those days, it wasn't mentoring; it was probably more like slave labor. But I was indeed learning and paying my dues.

I then started really working mostly in television, and I had a very strong mentor who became a very close friend. She was a big producer with Procter & Gamble, and ultimately with CBS television, and she kind of gave me one of my first big breaks. I'm grateful to her.

She said, "Gee, you've never done this before, but I want to hire you to do it."

So I often look back and think my whole career really is owed to some of the early people in my life who had faith in me, who saw something and said, "Come on board." That's why I think as someone that can mentor someone today, I want to give that back. I think I was very fortunate.

I always say to younger people that paying your dues may not be what you thought you went to school for, but it's what truly makes the difference and gets you opportunities. I sometimes see younger people in an interview asking questions about benefits and other items they haven't really earned yet. They haven't even seen the meal and they want to know what the dessert is going to be. I do think that I paid my dues, and I don't know if people see that as part of the equation today. I'm sounding like my dad.

Joan and I got our PhDs in hard work. I feel like I got a degree in the School of Hard Knocks before I worked with her, and it paid off.

Books that have inspired me include, of course, Joan's very, very successful book called *Enter Talking*. It was just fantastic. She describes how she became Joan Rivers and the hard work that she put in and the dues she paid. She experienced struggles. I read the book before I met her, and then we started working together, and I went back and read it again. It's not a traditional success in business kind of a book. It really is a life story, but it is about how to push your life forward and how to be successful if you kind of read between the lines. So that's a book that I very often give to friends to read.

Then the other one, it's going to sound so corny, but I really think Dale Carnegie wrote something amazing with *How to Win Friends and Influence People*. There's a message there that's very timeless and very much about how to have a life that you feel good about.

I think my approach to mentoring would be a more hands-on experience. I ask, "How can I help you?" I've had the experience twice now in the last five or six years where I help a person who I see has enormous potential. They are in a situation where they're not going to be able to shine and not going to be able to thrive.

An example is this young guy in Pennsylvania. I met him through his parents—or actually, his uncle and aunt. He really needed some direction and guidance to get out of his current situation and go toward what he really wanted. I think that's what mentoring is.

I'm very proud to say that I helped him pick out his college. I helped him apply to college. I had him in my office here as a summer intern for two summers in a row. This kid—I can't call him a kid anymore—is finishing college now, but he has a full-time job with an enormously successful fashion house here in New York. They hired him from the internship he did last summer. He hasn't even graduated from college, and he's already on his career path. I took somebody who had no direction and helped him. Who knows where he would have ended up, but I stepped in and said, "There's a fantastic school in New York called LIM, it's for the business of fashion. You need to apply there. You need to talk to them."

Mentoring is paying it forward, and I find it enormously rewarding. I also find part of the mentoring process is having a very good company culture. We have a program that Joan and I put in place many years ago of paying for education for our employees. So our current controller is a CPA now because we as a company paid for her education to become a CPA.

Investing in your employees, investing in your company culture, will pay back tenfold. I've been to both places. If it's a crummy place to work where you don't feel valued, you won't give the performance that you would in a place where you feel celebrated.

If I were talking to executives, it would probably be what we just discussed—the company culture, the keep managing your people, hiring the right mix of people, keeping your finger on the pulse of all that.

If I were talking to maybe a younger generation who were just starting in business, I would tell them that listening is one of the most important things you can do. We all talk a lot, but do we really listen all the time? I think it's a learned skill to actually hear what people are talking about. I think that's something we don't do very well.

I don't know of a single successful executive, CEO, president, who hasn't worked very, very hard and hasn't sacrificed. You have to try to keep a balance between your private life and working life. But there will be times when you have to give extra. You're going to work way more hours than you thought you were going to. Some of it is just being in the right place, right time, and having the smarts and the listening skills to know that you're in the right place at the right time.

I did not leave art school thinking I was going to be a businessman. I knew I would be creative in my life, but I look back and think, well, what if I met Joan and didn't like her, and I just decided to stay working in film and working in theater and would have had a very different life. I would still be very happy. But I saw something, something completely new. I loved the idea of being in a business that was kind of not too traditional.

It makes me think again of this young man I mentored from Pennsylvania who's now working for Calvin Klein. I wish someone had said to me, "Don't apply there. That's not the place you need to be. If you're interested in the business of fashion, you need to be here. That's the school for designers. You don't need to go to Parsons, you need to go here."

It really was simply guiding him into choices that turned out to be the right ones. Mentoring helps us do that. On your own sometimes, you wouldn't make the right choice. It's about how you can help people become more successful than they might have been.

Kathy Stack
Grafx Design of Tampa
Grafxtampa.com

It all began on April Fools' Day 1991. Grafx Design of Tampa opened its doors with a five-hundred-square-foot office. It housed two artists and myself. I had a Mac classic that looked like an eight-inch black-and-white TV and a kitchen table for a desk. The only mentor I had was a previous employer. I learned how not to succeed.

I remember being twenty-nine years younger, ready to chase my dream. I was hungry for success.

Obtaining new clients without much of a track record in the industry was going to be tough, but I was up for the challenge.

I had no new business development experience, so I ran with my passion and gut instincts.

My break finally came a few months into this hunt for new business when a friend of a friend mentioned that Busch Gardens Tampa was opening a new area called Myombe Reserve, a gorilla exhibit. I bugged the marketing department until someone agreed to see me. An appointment was set up with the director of sales.

We worked night and day on all kinds of marketing materials. Such as billboard designs, brochures, magazine ads you name it! All related to the new gorilla exhibit.

The day of my appointment arrived, and one of my artists was wearing the gorilla costume I had rented, and I was wearing my very first navy-blue power suit, and we loaded my minivan (I had two small children) with our precious cargo. We sat in the lobby with a basket of bananas until we were escorted into a conference room. I guess the sight of a gorilla ignited the entire departments interest! My presentation was not for just the director of sales but also for the entire department. Wow, my first pitch, I was nervous, to say the least.

This began a nineteen-year relationship with Anheuser Busch Theme Parks. We had to move to larger office space in an old cigar factory and hire more designers. This relationship leads to other referrals, more pitches, and more clients.

I needed help managing the assignments pouring in. Mentoring new employees was hard for me in the beginning. I had my arms around everything and found it hard to let go.

I had no choice. My style of mentoring is fairly simple—here's your desk, show me what you got, come see me with questions or issues you are unable to solve.

I am not a micromanager. I believe it is important to have good relationship with your employees. Give them freedom. The employees hired are always younger than me, so you can see the hunger to excel. Like I had twenty-nine years ago. I must see that in the interview process.

As the business grew, the company needed more staff. Staff meetings are important, as allowing the employees to have a voice provides them with confidence and a feeling they have just as much blood and guts on the wall as I do.

Mentoring for me is allowing employees to run, ensuring they develop great relationships with coworkers and, most importantly, with their clients.

All employers have different methods of mentoring, and also, each employee may need different styles of mentoring. For me, a strong relationship do not, by any means, suggest a "friendship" but rather listening and encouraging them to think for themselves, using their hunger to succeed and doing that without micromanaging.

The work environment that develops with my method, I believe, gives the staff a feeling of empowerment and ownership.

Lauren Asghari
Alderson Loop
Aldersonloop.com

Mentoring helps when people can see clear paths. So we're focused on scaling, and part of scaling is moving quickly. I think that teams move quicker when everyone is candid with one another and share a common goal.

I also believe it is essential when following a mentor that you also pick up bits and pieces from different people and adopt what works best for you, because I think authenticity is important. What we've done well as an organization is being able to learn from each other.

A common misperception, especially for people early in their career, is that you have to follow the exact path of your mentor. My perspective is that you should take bits and pieces from different people and find what works for you to define and create your unique style.

This has had a considerable effect on the way I run businesses. I believe people are more comfortable at work when they can be themselves. People don't want to feel like they have to wear one hat when they're outside of the office and a different persona in the office. The more people can be themselves and work in an authentic environment and understand that everybody has strengths and weaknesses but working together, the more efficient teams work. That's been a huge part of our growth.

Thinking of a book perspective on mentoring, what comes to mind is *Fierce Conversations: Achieving Success at Work and in Life One Conversation at a Time* by Susan Scott. Early in my career, I was very much the type of person who had an opinion and a clear train of thought on what I thought was the best next step, but I was sometimes hesitant about vocalizing my opinion.

What I learned from *Fierce Conversations* is the ability to have a direct conversation with people. Even if it doesn't always come out right or how you planned, it's going to be a thousand times more beneficial than either not saying anything at all or trying to be too wordsmith-y when crafting a message.

I've learned that if you can be direct, even if you're overly direct, you can always claw it back a little bit and say, "I don't know if that came out wrong, I didn't mean for it to come out that way, but that's what I was thinking." Speak up, as opposed to dancing around a subject too much, or else your point is watered down and less impactful. That book had a tremendous effect on me. It's applicable in leadership, interacting with customers and clients, and in business and life in general.

My learning style has been based on bits and pieces from people I've worked with throughout my career. No one person that jumps out to me that I could say changed the course of my career. But there are undoubtedly different pieces that I've pulled from people.

I learned two things in particular from one of my former bosses. From others, you learn what you like about what they're doing, and then there are some things that you think, "I'm not going to do that." It's equally valuable to discover that you should be doing something differently or approach something differently than how others chose.

It's equally valuable to understand, "This is what I like to do, and I want to continue down this path," versus the pieces that aren't important or you don't like, or that type of work that you don't enjoy doing, to steer away from that and continue focusing on the stuff that you get passionate and energized about.

From my previous boss, I learned to overvalue and appreciate customers. In any services business, you're there to provide a service for your customers. That doesn't mean that the customer is always right and that you roll over or agree to whatever they're saying, but to always have an appreciation for the opportunity to sit at the table and do business. I think it's essential not to take for granted the work that it takes to earn the opportunity to even able to ask for a sale or a piece of business.

What stuck with me from working for him was his ability to say, "You shouldn't take for granted the fact that you're able to be in the room to ask for the opportunity, because not everybody gets that chance." Whether it is a chance that you created for yourself or the opportunity fell into your lap, it doesn't matter. If you're in a room, and you have the chance for an opportunity, you have to reach out and grab it.

Of course, I've made more than a couple of mistakes. The one that jumps out at me was a contract negotiation. I went into a meeting, knowing the purpose was negotiating terms, and without giving any inclination of what my objections were or business reasons why, I went in and said, "These are the things that I have a problem with. This is not going to work for us." My view going into the conversation was that it was "win or lose." That is how I saw negotiations, which I now believe is not true. Negotiating is about making it work for both parties.

After that meeting, the person I met with was gracious enough to say, "Hey, let me tell you how I think you could have handled this negotiation better." I appreciated it because the advice that they gave me was "to give a little heads up, in terms of what your issues are, give me some time to think about it. We're all moving in the same direction to get this deal done. It doesn't have to be a win-lose scenario. It's okay if it's a little uncomfortable for everybody, and you feel like you gave some." That has stuck with me in all facets of business, even if the negotiation gets a little uncomfortable, meaning you had to give more than you wanted to. If both sides leave feeling that way, that's okay.

Inside the business, I try to set an example for the organization. I believe that leadership and direction come from the top. So whatever you allow in your organization is what's going to be filtered throughout. It's okay to say to somebody, "You did a great job," and it's also okay to say to somebody, "I think that we need to work on this area, and let's talk about how we do that."

I believe that admitting you're not good at everything is a good thing because it's a universal truth. Especially early in your career, it's a little bit harder to admit that, and some of our egos get in the way. I am constantly striving to set an example and set my ego aside. We're all in the boat rowing in the same direction, so let's work together to get there quickly as a team.

Outside of the office, people have asked me for help when they're thinking of starting a business or engaged in the early stages of their business. Even some established companies are trying to catch up with technology changes and trends or adapt their business as their industry is evolving.

I do my best to ensure that I connect with everybody in the company and that I understand their personal and professional goals. I don't know that I would say that it was necessarily formal mentoring, but I try to set the tone that I'm open to talking with anybody. Whether they want to work for a company that I own or run for the rest of their lives, or if they wish to work here for five years, and then go on to fulfill a different set of ambitions, that does not really matter to me. I want to support our employees' ambitions, and I appreciate the transparency of what they're trying to accomplish. We haven't had a formal way of doing that, but that's something that I think is important from a corporate culture standpoint.

I believe the area that most entrepreneurs need mentoring in is cash-flow management and delegation. When you start a business, usually, you're wearing multiple hats. As that business grows, you have to understand and accept that everybody's not necessarily going to do it your way. But if they're carrying the torch in the same direction, and they're supporting the company values or what you as the entrepreneur have set as the company values, it's okay. Ours are customer experience and integrity, hands down. Of course, we are a business, so revenue generation is important. It is not the most important, but it is a key factor. As long as our team upholds those values, I'm less concerned with the specifics on an individual's style.

I think it's an adjustment for people when you have an idea of perfection for your business, and that concept, exactly as you envisioned, becomes difficult to scale. The people you're hiring might have a unique flair and often end up doing something better than what you were doing as the owner or entrepreneur. So I think giving people the reins—and say, "Hey, do it your way, but make sure that we're constantly moving in this direction and not compromise on the things these values or factors that are critical to our business"—is essential. I think that's challenging for all entrepreneurs to do because they're so tightly holding on to perceived perfection.

Cash-flow management is one where we can all get a little bit stuck. The biggest thing for me when I started the business was to make personal adjustments, which might have been viewed as sacrifices up-front, to make sure that every dollar was going into the business, and I was not hamstringing the business early on to support my lifestyle choices. If you're not good at cash flow or if you're not good at cash management, you have to be conscious enough, and you have to get a basic understanding of it; that is not something you can outsource.

I have two pieces of advice when starting a business. Stay true to yourself and use your sweat equity. Staying true to yourself is essential, as there are probably a million different ways to get from point A to point B, and you've got to do it in a way that feels authentic to you. Pretending to be somebody else—such as operating in a way only because you saw somebody else do it—is going to be stressful and wearying over time. I think it limits a person's ability to get energized and sustain that energy over time.

You are going to get knocked down a bunch. If you're not doing it in a way where at least you can fall on your sword and say, "That's the way that I thought best," I think it is harder to stay motivated. So be true to yourself.

When I started my business, I made significant adjustments to my finance side. I cut back on expenses, whether it was simple things like grocery shopping or how often I would get a haircut. I cut back on my costs so that for the business, I could always make the right decisions for the company, not short-term financial decisions.

People can get in trouble if they're focused on making short-term financial decisions instead of making the decisions right for your business over the long haul. Most of the time, that comes from financial constraints. The more you can minimize those before you get started, the better off you're going to be. Use your sweat equity and work to get things done versus outsourcing, particularly early on.

Of course, it depends on the type of business that you have. My experience is with a services business, so upfront cash out was limited, but it was a lot of actual work. The business then grew to a point where, "The business can afford extra help, but at what point, if for example, there is a dip in revenue, can I still afford that person?" So you have to get back to that cash-management piece and be thoughtful about your plan so that you're not always reactionary to highs and lows in business.

I feel that it's crucial to put in as much work as you can. From the outside, some people think entrepreneurship is all glory. Make no mistake, it's a grind. It's always a grind. Even when you reach that first milestone and think you've accomplished something, your bar gets raised again, so you never get that rest. It's important to be thoughtful about your planning and growth strategy, whether you're going from yourself to three people or three people to a hundred people.

There's a delicate balance between being too thoughtful and procrastinating. I started the business when our daughter was maybe four and a half months at the time, so my husband and I had to make adjustments—not only because we had a four-and-a-half-month-old, but also because we were no longer living on two salaries.

As an example, I went quickly to, "Okay, let's get to the worst-case scenario that we end up living in our parents' basement for two months, and I have to get another job in the corporate world." In the grand scheme of things, we'd still be fine. I was trying to go to a place of, "If this doesn't work, what's going to happen?" That for me has been super helpful because I'm not afraid of failing, but I'm afraid of the regret of not trying.

Even today, when negotiating a contract, I think, "Okay, if we don't move on this term, what's the worst case that's going to happen? Or if we move on it, what's the risk? What's the worst-case scenario?"

Then I get comfortable with that and operate from a place of what I perceive as control. You don't feel like somebody else is in control of what you're doing, you feel like you're deciding from a place of power.

Gordon Gronkowski
G&G Fitness Equipment
Livefit.com

Once a year, I shut down our fourteen stores and four warehouses, rent a resort, and bring everybody in for two full days to do team-building exercises. I have about one hundred people who work for me, so it's incredible to see how everybody interacts with each other during those periods. Otherwise, they could be working for me and never know the coworker, who is two states away. Because I'm in eight different states, when I bring everybody together, it's an unbelievable experience for us all.

I get up in front and speak to the whole group. Then all the leaders and managers get up in front. Then everybody else can address the group if they choose. We hand out awards and recognize the people who did a great job during the year. It's a great team-building time and very useful.

Every year, I do a survey afterward to see how it went down. Everybody loves the experience and asks that we keep the tradition going. We make sure we introduce all the new people. We explain our philosophy and talk about where we're going, what we accomplish, and where we're going this next year so everybody understands our trajectory. They have the focus of what our company is trying to do.

We also invite our vendors for the experience. The vendors say no one ever includes them, and that this is one of the greatest things. They love to see how close our company is. We let our vendors have the floor too and listen to what they have to share. We bring in the presidents of the companies we do business with and pick up a ton of information from everybody.

I would say our average employee has probably been with us for eight years, so it means a lot to employees and vendors to be able to see the faces. I interact with everybody, and it's a good time for me because I can't get around to eight different states and eighteen different locations to see everybody. I sit down with many of my employees at these events and have some one-on-one time with them.

I'm always learning. My philosophy is such that when I hire somebody, I always try to hire somebody smarter than me. Then I can feed off them, and they can feed off me. It's essential to put great people around you so you can feed off each other.

I create this positive loop that keeps building everybody up. It's a big team thing, so everybody feels like a part of it. You don't feel like that guy who is left out all the time—you're part of it. If you want to say anything up in front, you can, and if you had a great year, you could get recognized.

I played division 1 football, so I learned a lot through that experience, such as how to compete, how to work as a team, and how to work with other people. Because when you play football, to get one play done, everybody has to do their assignment. You can't be one person, and you realize that when you play sports. No matter how good you are, if you don't have a team around you, you're not going anywhere.

I got a lot of my intuition from my football experience. Once I got into the business, I ended up doing Dale Carnegie courses. I took the management course, the public-speaking course, the sales course, and I followed the principles.

The book that I got a lot out of is *How to Win Friends and Influence People*. I have every one of my employees read that book when they come on. It's a classic, and it teaches you how, if you treat people right, smile, do all the right things, that it's all going to come back to you. I read a lot. I like ripping apart and reading books about why companies didn't make it and learn why they didn't make it, so I don't make the same mistakes.

I learned a lot by making mistakes. I learned the hard way that you've always got to fine-tune everything and watch everything. You have to watch your expenses always, especially with retail. My central core of people gets together every single month. The P&L

is done by the second week of the month, so we review the month before. We go through every single line item and examine what's being spent and why it's being spent to keep a tight grip on those expenses.

Another major mistake I've made is around not picking an excellent location in retail. I have fourteen retail locations, and if I mess that up and sign a five-year lease, I'm stuck with that thing for the duration. I was stuck with a couple of dogs that beat me up down the line a little bit. You have to be careful and make sure you know what you're doing in those aspects.

As a mentor, I give everybody the benefit of the doubt. I'm a great motivator, but I always let people know where I stand. The day you come in and you can't look at that employee anymore, that person must go. You can't wait around for change; you need to bring the person in and let them know how you're feeling. As a mentor, as a leader of a company, you can't hold back. You have to let it out so you can keep on moving along and thinking straight and moving forward.

You always know where you stand with me. If things aren't going well, or I don't think that you're the right fit, I'll bring you to my office, and I'll talk to you. We work it out. I'm neither nor yelling. I'll say, "Hey, this is my viewpoint. This is our company's philosophy: either you get it, or you're not going to be here."

I love getting people excited. I love what I do every day, so I come in with a big smile on my face. When there's a big sale around the horn, I'm watching on the computer. I'm on the phone saying, "Hey, great job."

Entrepreneurs have to know finances. Many people think they're entrepreneurs and want to start a business, but they don't have the funds. They get it going, then they realize there are many expenses, such as insurance, leases, wages, and all the taxes on top of the salaries. The list goes on and on.

Before an entrepreneur gets into business, I recommend that you do your homework and know your expenses inside and out because if you don't, you can get eaten up quickly. That's why out of a hundred businesses that start today, only two will make it past two years. That is because they didn't do their homework and didn't set aside enough funds for long-term staying power.

They thought they were entrepreneurs, but they're not. They have a good idea, but they don't know how to go about making it happen. My best advice is to make sure your finances are in line before you go out there and spend all that money. If you run through your life's savings, the next thing you know, you don't have enough money, and you won't have anything.

Entrepreneurs can educate themselves on that part of the business before they get started by doing their homework. I'm in the specialty business, so before I got started, I went around to three different stores in different states, looking at and shopping on, asking questions, and finding out the whole business before I attempted to get into the market.

As an entrepreneur, you have to be willing to work. It's not going to happen by working forty hours. If you think you're going to get rich and work forty hours a week, it's not going to happen. You're going to have to put in seventy or eighty hours a week if you want this to happen. Even today—and I've been doing this for almost thirty years—I'm still putting in sixty to sixty-five hours a week.

An entrepreneur has to have a passion for the business. If you don't have that passion, if you don't come in every day ready to kick some butt, it's not for you. There's a lot that goes behind it. Again, you have to watch every single penny. Go in there, make sure you're financially okay, and then watch every single penny, know it all, then hire the right people around you.

You get great people around you, and you're going to be great. If you get so-so people, you'll be so-so. If you get bad people, you're going to be bad. Know how to read people as quickly as possible, and make sure they're the right people for that perfect fit. You've got to make sure you can read people so you can put them in the right place.

I have five very athletic kids who play pro baseball or play in the NFL. I wrote a book about how we got there called *Growing Up*

Gronk. There's a chapter about how I motivated my kids and what I did with them, as well as how my business all came about. The biggest thing, as I said, is that you have to be willing to work and make sacrifices. I could have gone out every weekend; I could have gone to every single party. But I didn't. I went to work at weekends. I missed spending more time with my kids as they grew up because I was working to get my business off the ground. You've got to be willing to do whatever it takes; people don't realize the time it takes to put into something to make it worthwhile.

But at the end of the game, I feel fulfilled in life, and I couldn't ask for anything better either. My kids are doing well, and my business is booming, and it just keeps on growing every year. Two of my sons are now working with me. They have the passion, and they put in the time.

If you want a normal life, an eight-to-five, where you go home at five, don't expect to open your own business because you need to be on call 24/7. You've got to be willing to accept the craziest things you're ever going to see in life. It's going to come, especially when working with one hundred different employees, where everybody has problems. You must sort through it all and keep everybody motivated and moving. When you do get thrown a curveball, you have to know how to handle it. One of Dale Carnegie's principles is you always have to think, "What's the worst thing that can happen? The worst thing that can happen is that you die."

Once you put it that way, everything else isn't that bad.

Ernest Freeland
Crofton Bike Doctor
Croftonbikedoctor.com

I haven't had a structured mentor per se, but I have had many relationships with businesspeople from different industries. What's been unique is that I've gotten perspectives from people who are not only in retail like myself but also those who own boat dealerships, jewelry stores, or beauty stores.

Having different owners to talk to that have had different experiences has been valuable along the way. I've never had one mentor that I've worked with, and I've never been coached either.

One of the things I most enjoy about what I do is that there's a twenty-year age gap between many of the employees and me. Many employees are high-school kids or college students. To be able to work with them and help them develop the skills they need as they progress through their careers and their schooling has been where I've gotten much satisfaction. I always tell the new employees, "I realize that this is a retail job, and for most of you, you're not making a career here." Hopefully, some of them fall in love with retail, like I did and progress, but that's realistically not the case.

So I tell them, "If you do a good job with me, and I'll help you, I'm more than happy to reach out to my customer base on your behalf." Pretty much any career that they want to participate in, I will have relationships with customers where I can say, for example, "Marissa is doing a great job for me, and she's looking for a job in your field. Can you help her?" I've done that with some success over the years, which allowed my employees to get jobs in other fields.

I probably have an MBA from reading all the business books I enjoy. I'm a big fan of Michael Gerber and his whole *E-Myth* series. Those are books I would recommend every new business owner and entrepreneur read. I'm a big fan of *Getting Things Done* by Dave

Allen. That's helped me structure my day and my thinking about how I group stuff to be productive and complete my goals.

I also like *Work the System* by Sam Carpenter. He talks about the importance of putting processes and systems in place early on in your business so that as you go to scale and develop your business, you can easily do so. Looking back, I wish I had started a lot earlier to complete that consistency for my business.

I think most mentors need to realize we're not superheroes. We can only go so far on our own, and we need help to go further. Many of us have a hard time asking for help, though it's not in our nature because we're so used to doing it all on our own. But learning to ask for help—whether it's because something is not going right or something is going well, and we want to grow—will make us all better businesspeople and allow our businesses to grow and develop faster. But for a lot of type-A personalities, that's a tough pill to swallow.

I think it's easy to get stuck in the day-to-day grind of doing the work. I feel it's essential that we take time to look at our business from an outsider's perspective. We should look down the road several months or years at a time and work toward those goals. I know it's a struggle. You've got to spend much time getting the day-to-day stuff done.

But you have to look down the road and push your boundaries of what makes you feel comfortable and take educated risks. If you want to grow as a person and business, that's what you need to be doing. Nowadays, with change happening so fast, it's essential not to be so focused on today, but thinking, "What's this going to look like in six months? What's this going to look like in a year? What is this going to look like in three years?"

Fifteen years ago, when I started, this is not exactly how I thought things would look. Retail is changing so fast nowadays. I'm not surprised by online selling. I think the biggest surprise for me has been the decline in the entry-level availability of employees. High-school kids seem to have no interest in working, and neither do college students. They're so focused on schooling and extracurricular activities that that section of the workforce is gone. That's come as a bit of a surprise as a kid who grew up working part-time while I was in school. It's been a significant change to find that entry-level employee.

Also, I'm working a lot more than I envisioned fifteen years ago. From the beginning, I didn't want to be one of those owners that had to work on the sales floor every day or had to work in the business. I wanted to be more out of the business, working on it, and networking, and I haven't entirely made it there yet. My big focus right now is getting out of the business, networking, working with customers at events, and allowing the team to do more of the day-to-day stuff.

It's related to not being able to get the entry-level employees. I think that's a big part of it. We now have a smaller team that still wants much flexibility. Many people who work in our industry are doing it for a lifestyle because the pay isn't as competitive as it could be in other places, and that's a real challenge. So they're willing to trade the dollars in salary for flexibility. But you can only have so many payroll dollars in staff. So juggling full-time folks with enough part-time people that you can give them hours is one of my biggest challenges.

I live on a busy street in this neighborhood between two schools. We've lived in this house for eighteen years, and I haven't once had a kid come to my door or approach me while we're outside removing snow to ask, "Hey, would you like me to shovel your driveway, or would you like me to rake your leaves for you?"

Parents are so focused on school being the kids' full-time job that they don't want them to do anything else. I think that's sad because you learn many skills in a part-time job, whether it's washing dishes or raking leaves. You learn how to interact with people you don't know as well as the value of a dollar.

Many young adults still live with their parents, which is the norm up into your mid to late twenties from what I've read. That's a big challenge for our economy because all these kids graduate college but don't spend money. Back in the day, you would graduate college, you would rent an apartment, you'd have a job, you'd buy furniture, maybe buy a car, get married, and you and your spouse would buy a house together, and you would spend all this money in the economy. Nowadays, that segment is not what it used to be.

I'm writing a story right now about a boy coming of age and learning from his parents how to be a good person and how to negotiate adult relationships—some of those life skills we need to learn as kids. I've started writing that, but I've always wanted to write a business book of some kind. I think there is not a lot out there for a smaller business like myself. I love to read business books, as they're fascinating to me. But everything is usually designed for a much larger scale.

It's not geared toward that maybe sub-fifty-person business or even sub-twenty-person business. Many mentors you see online are hawking their wares, and it's all about electronics companies and how to sell a white paper or a course. If you look at their history, many of them don't have personal experience. They haven't been in the trenches working with a brick-and-mortar business or industry where you're facing people, whether it's insurance, retail, or whatever.

I have to deal with the issue of being unable to get kids to work in my store. Most of them are geared toward corporations or more significant entrepreneurial things or not the meat and potatoes of the everyday businessmen, entrepreneurs, small business.

If I wrote a book, I would talk about setting up systems in your business early and documenting them so that you don't have to go back and do it after the fact. A huge mistake I made running a family-type atmosphere, where I've been a little lax sometimes with some of my requirements with my employees. So I have to reign that back. But it's also about developing a marketing plan and how to utilize Google, Facebook, and Instagram, and my email funnel.

I would also discuss sales training techniques and teaching people about customer service, as that's something I'm very passionate about. I like to read cues from customers when they come in so I can see how they're feeling and know what to do. I want to write a small business manual with a little bit of everything to get that small businessperson started.

Lawrence Farrar
Resodyn
Resodyn.com

We started the company on a garage floor through a program called the Small Business Innovation Research. We didn't have a mentor for beginning a business but decided to do so because of the goals I wanted to achieve. I've had people whom I've looked upon as mentors in the past as examples of how to conduct myself technically, ethically, and business-wise. But I haven't followed in their footsteps or worked closely with anyone along the lines of mentorship in my career.

I guess I'm more of an independent. I don't read business books, because I've found that generally there is too much fluff in them. If I read anything, it's technical stuff because I'm an engineer. I believe you should just roll up your sleeves and do things yourself—things that make sense.

I live in southwest Montana in a town of thirty-four thousand people. The reason I'm here is that nothing is going on, and there's not a lot of entrepreneurship happening in the area where I live. There's retail, but I don't get involved in that as I'm more in the industrial sector. I'm pretty busy, so I don't have a lot of time to spend mentoring. I'm growing the business, developing things, and we're moving rapidly. So I keep somewhat consumed with what I do.

We now have thirty-five employees, so I teach people how to go through some fairly rigorous technical processes. But that's just a matter of our protocols in terms of design reviews and bill books and the way we manufacture and market things. We have a worldwide market, and we're in about thirty different countries. This is due to the fact that we have some unique equipment that nobody else in the world makes, which we've patented and developed successfully.

Resodyn makes a couple of products. One is a machine called an acoustic mixer that uses sound energy for mixing instead of blades, which is used in about twenty different industries. The acoustic mixer is our value proposition as it's a device that allows people to make things they can't make any other way. It helps our customers make things faster, better, and cheaper, so we've been pushing those machines pretty hard.

We have a Resodyn Europe office in the UK, which markets and sells in Europe. Additionally, we have trading partners in South Korea and Japan, which is how you do business over there because of the culture. We're becoming the mixer of choice in areas of energetics, which includes propellants, explosives, military pyrotechnics, pharmaceuticals, and battery materials.

We have another product, which is a coating device, a thermal spray system. First, you put powder coatings on materials without putting them in the booth. You cure the powder coating with this machine. Again, that's a unique system that's patented, and we're the only guys in the world that do that. This set of products goes through a separate company called Resodyn Engineered Polymer Systems while the mixers go through Resodyn Acoustic Mixers. Then we have the Resonant Corporation, which does all the development, manufacturing, and engineering work for those other two companies.

Resodyn has some other R&D projects going on to keep people out of the streets, make them busy, and keep them from being bored. Things are going well, so we're looking to hire another five or eight people at this point as we're experiencing dramatic increases in demand for new products. We're developing new continuous mixers, as well as using the same platform to develop a continuous chemical reactor.

Coming from a technical background and being an inventor, I believe the most important thing an entrepreneur can do is focus. You can't chase everything all the time—you have to focus on specific areas as we do. We have teams that focus on certain areas with blinders on. They don't look to other areas so that they can continue to be successful without getting distracted. It's easy to lose traction if you don't focus. There will always be another bird in the bush, so keep the bird in your hand—don't chase the pretty parrot.

I'm not a big advice giver, but I know what I've done for us to be successful, which is to work hard, be focused, and be optimistic. As you're probably aware, most entrepreneurs are optimistic—to the point of foolishness sometimes.

I'm a risk-taker when it comes to technology and other things that I do in life, but when it comes to business, I'm very conservative. I suggest that if you want to be an entrepreneur, then keep a tight watch on your books. I don't borrow money, and I don't do investors. We bootstrapped, so we've been able to grow smartly with profitability every year. Although being bootstrapped slows you down, my philosophy is that I'd rather be healthy than big. People often get overstretched with financial commitments that they don't have control of, and I don't do that.

Because of the lifestyle I've chosen in the Rocky Mountains, geography limits my growth, so now I'm starting to develop strategic relationships with like-minded businesses. We have a profound technology that has a lot of interest with many folks across many industries. Beginning to create strategic alliances will help us grow the business through those relationships with like-minded, philosophical, international companies that are healthy and much larger than we are. Those relationships look to be moving along nicely.

Another thing that I believe is important is that you develop in growth by strategic relationships and not just get sucked into simple, one-way situations. My advice is to stay away from investors and investment bankers because they can be toxic to a business.

In terms of other locations for getting a competent workforce, I would suggest hiring from either of the two coasts. We're in a town of thirty-four thousand people in the Rocky Mountains on the Continental Divide, and we have cold winters and nothing going on here, which is not everybody's ideal lifestyle. Any place that could attract more talent might be easier. It seems like folks like to gravitate around miserable areas, such as big cities and traffic jams and so forth. I don't do that. I get enough of that when I travel.

I've lived throughout the United States. My father was career military, and I was in the military a bit, so I've lived all over the United States.

I've been here for about thirty-five years now, and it's the best place on earth as far as I'm concerned. We have a lot of outdoor activities. You have to like snow, winter, and blue skies if you want to live here. It's an absolutely beautiful place with a lot of mountains, game, rivers, creeks, and lakes—all the cool stuff.

I enjoy the technology, what we're doing, market development, business development, and coming up with new ideas. We're continuously putting in new patents for new things and developing new know-how and coming across new opportunities for our business. So that fully encompasses all my free time I do have.

Kevin Duncan
KDuncan & Company
Kduncan.com

I probably have not had what you would consider a traditional mentor. Maybe if I did, I'd be more successful.

I think about when I first started, and one of my first clients told me that although he understood I had other clients, as a consultant, my job was to make him feel like he was my only client. So that message permeated through us all. Even to this day, I think that probably a big part of our success is to make our clients know that we care about them.

I don't think there are any books I've read that have had a significant impact on the way that I do business. I'm an accountant, so even before I started my company, I always worked hand-in-hand with the owners of the company, and I learned a lot from that experience.

A big lesson I learned is that my experience has always been with a controller or a CFO, so when I started, I think that because of that experience, I knew everything the owner needed to know. What I didn't realize was that there are a whole lot of other things that come into running a business, such as handling employees and handling customers. So I gained great respect for the people whom I've worked with over the years that I don't think I appreciated when I first started my company.

The other thing that I think is important as a consultant is that my last boss told me that if he could impart me with any wisdom, it would be that I'd have to be willing to be whomever I had to be to get my point across. Whether it was to be a nice guy or a mean guy, I had to be willing to take on that role. So that was important to know as a consultant.

I've had other CPAs and other accountants who brought me along with the business that they're doing. My focus is on government contracting, so a big part of this industry is teaming with other companies. So I've had teammates—probably more experienced teammates—help me along in certain business lines, especially in the government contracting arena.

I've had a lot of peer mentorship that has happened along the way, so my mentoring comes in a lot of different ways.

First, I've done quite a bit of training for government contractors over the years. Second, again because of what I do for a living, mentoring my clients is part and parcel of what I do, and some clients I've had for over twenty years.

I believe my employees respect me because I take time to bring them along and to understand some of the challenges they're going through. They focus on what we do best, which is to help our clients through their problems.

I feel that most entrepreneurs need mentoring in accounting and finance, but that's my area of specialty. Most of the time, owners start companies understanding their particular expertis but not the whole business thing. Even our CPA clients don't understand the financial part of the business, such as how to price correctly, how to monitor the profitability of their projects and the profitability of the contract, and then to a certain extent, how to develop relationships with bankers.

You're always looking for somebody who's going to have money available when you need it. So a big thing about the industry that I'm in is that companies can grow quickly, so having that financing available when you get an opportunity to grow is essential. But also to understand what the bankers' focus will be so that you can keep that constituency happy.

My advice is to focus on what your market is, learn what is important to your customer base, and always work to match what you offer to what the customer base considers important. Then I'd say the other thing is to hang in there because there's going to be a lot of times when it's not easy.

Michael Allen
Lanson B Jones & CO
Lansonbjones.com

My background is in nonprofit work, and so mentorship, leadership, leadership development, professional development, and counseling are in my experience and wheelhouse. We incorporate those areas as much as possible by teaming our new employees with as many subject matter experts within the business as possible. If our employees are young or inexperienced, they'll have somebody they can talk to and work with to understand the ins and outs of their new or current role.

Every new employee is paired up with at least two different people. We look to pair them with somebody who's operationally minded, a technical expert, someone who understands the functions of the role, and that we have to have a lot of core cultural experience, construction experience, client-relationship experience, and accounting experience. Pairing them with a technical expert in their position is helpful if there's somebody that we feel has more experience than the person that's helping them with the operational side.

I encourage everybody on my executive team to have robust, in-depth one-on-ones with their teammates and team members. I do the same thing myself, but I have an executive coach. I mustn't be only giving but also receiving from somebody else who's more experienced than I am. The person I consult with is from an outside service. We have an advisory board, and one of the members of that advisory board is my executive coach.

We've seen great success with the informal mentoring practices we use in the business. We're such a fast-paced business. Probably for our industry, we're considered small by your general requirements for business size. But the informality gives it more flexibility of saying that you have to do these things. From time to time, we create a tailored or specific plan for somebody, but it still allows for flexibility.

About five and a half years ago, when I first came on board, I was a pretty big proponent of these informal mentoring practices, as that's one of my main things. Everybody knows that that's the case, and it's now become part of the culture, which is great because it's hard to tear that down.

It's not like if we don't watch or manage it for a couple of weeks or months, it's going to go away. We provide a high-end service, and it requires attention to detail for design as well as understanding living plant material and the conditions they need to thrive, then the nuanced relationship of client-relationship building. All those things require in-depth mentoring.

These robust mentorship practices provide a support structure for new team members and keep everyone on their feet. Because it's part of the culture, people seek it out even when they're not being told to do so. Also, we like to put people in positions before they're 100 percent ready—and by ready, I mean filled to the brim with knowledge or information about that role—which creates a thirst to be mentored. It's not a matter of requiring everybody to mentor somebody else, but the mentee may go and seek that knowledge. Everybody on our team is always willing to share information, so it becomes part of the culture.

The measurable difference for us has always been the retention of employees and the success we have with building in an industry that's not currently filled with qualified applicants. Where it comes into play is that most of our project managers have an architecture background, and they're working in landscape architecture and project management. You're not going to find a lot of architectural schools that teach project management. A lot of folks are left to their own devices when it comes to operational-type training. We looked for people with an architecture background because we have such a strong design quality.

We were able to take some of these architecture students and mold them into project managers. The measurable success is the retention of those employees and watching them get better in their role of being able to manage a million dollars in projects. That's the key because most of our management employees have not been in that role before at a different company. At least half of them were not even in that industry. So that's one of the ways that we measure it informally.

Many people make fun of me around here because my office is like a mini-library. I've got full bookshelves on my wall, and then whatever I find to be most valuable, I will share. I will have a new book handy, so I can say, "Oh, you should read this book."

Going back to the informality of training here, I do go through different books with different employees. Most times, with people who are being introduced to our culture, I'll read a book with them about transitioning from another existing company to this one. There's one called *The First 90 Days*, which is a good book for that transition.

There is another simple, straightforward book that deals more with leadership concepts by John C. Maxwell, *The 21 Irrefutable Laws of Leadership*. I've been through that book with about five employees, as it keeps the significant leadership concepts front and center so that we can work through it and talk through whether something is working or not. I've used that book many, many times.

I read a lot of books from Patrick Lencioni as well. Right now, I'm reading a book by Doris Kearns Goodwin called *Leadership in Turbulent Times*, which provides a peek into four great US presidents and some of the ups and downs that they went through in some of America's darkest times.

Around the office, we use the Patrick Lencioni series of books. We're currently using a book called *Measure What Matters* by John Doerr, a book about how YouTube and Google and other companies have been able to achieve great success.

We've also used books from Jim Collins and John Maxwell as well, as those are easily digestible books. They're not hugely complicated. Still, they do an excellent job of bringing in data when they need to while leaving it up to the reader to dig deeper to understand more about the subject they want to learn.

I had a great mentor when I was about twenty-three until I was twenty-seven. He was one of the elders at a church where I was working. He was a lot more wisdom based, and he carried a pocketful of axioms. Whatever leadership situation we were in, he was always able to pull that right nugget out to shape the situation so I could understand it better or at least know how to treat people.

He taught me to look for signs when people are maybe not the right fit for the job or role.

My last role before I was the CEO of this company was a senior consultant. The principal of the company was a tremendous mentor to me—not only from a practical day-to-day business application, but even further. He was great at change management, and he spent a lot of time with me.

In the beginning, he said, "Mike, you require a lot of time." But after he spent more time with me, I was able to take his concepts and run with them. He put me in charge of a couple of divisions within the company. He was a great mentor, and he invested the time, and I'm forever grateful. He is someone that I look back upon with a lot of fondness.

I've certainly made some mistakes, and I don't know if there was one mistake that I would say was the mistake that made a difference. I played competitive sports when I was in high school and junior high, and I continue to play competitive sports even now, as I'm a big basketball guy.

When you play competitively, you understand that you win and lose regularly. You don't keep track of your wins and losses in an informal setting like that. But you might go to the gym and play pickup games and play six or seven, and you lose five that day and only win one.

I've never been one to spend a lot of time counting wins and losses or dwell on them too much because I know that with every success, there's a loss around the corner, usually the next day or within the next week. Then with the subsequent failure, if you sit in that too long, you're going to miss out on the win that's right around the corner. It's hard for me to dwell because I understand the nature of competitive sports.

I went to see Simon Sinek speak at a leadership conference, and he talked a lot about the infinite game and business this year. Maybe that's the thing he's on right now. There is no end. It's hard to say if you win or lose when the game is infinite. But understand that in every loss, especially in business or relationships or day-to-day operations, that a door closed isn't the end of the story; you have to look for another way around the obstacle.

It's essential to keep that mindset and maybe not categorize everything into large lumps of winning or losing. When I have gotten too stuck on a loss, I spend more time trying to mitigate the damage instead of trying to move onto how to win to get past it.

One of the most recent mistakes that come to mind was a time when we added too much expense in a department. Because our team was at full capacity at the time, we felt like we needed to add some more. But in our business, if two clients walk in the door, there's a chance that one of the two will not make it entirely through the design construction phase. It could be because of the economy or our finances or the client realizing there's s a lot more to the project than they thought.

I determined after some time, maybe a year or so, that I shouldn't have added expenses to that department because I was treating capacity as the potential capacity and not necessarily what is signed and moving. Six months later, I was faced with the same thing, and I decided to take this bit of wisdom that I learned from the last round and cut expenses. It turned out that for this particular occasion, I was wrong. So I was wrong twice. But the loss is fluid unless you're asked to no longer be a part of the company. Maybe that's the ultimate loss.

Until about seven or eight years ago, I dwelt on those losses way too much. I thought they were permanent stains on my record. My mentor helped me to see that I didn't have time to sit there and grumble too long about my loss. I had to move on. I give credit to somebody else mentoring me and spending time with me to get me over my hump and a blind spot for me.

There have been times when the person I was mentoring didn't know what I was expecting, and the time I spent with him didn't come to fruition. But sometimes you'll find that maybe a few years later, they'll come back and say, "Thank you for spending time with me. It didn't help me at the time, but it's helping me in my current role." From time to time, people will share that with you, and that feels great.

Right now, I'm working with someone at our company who works in another department but is not my direct report. I asked her supervisor, who is my direct report, if it would be okay if I spent some time with her every two weeks for an hour to work through some issues.

We set the parameters up front that we would leave it open to whatever she wanted to discuss. We would not focus on tasks or activities that she needed to perform daily, as that was her supervisor's role, but helping her navigate things that didn't have such a formal structure to them. How do I lead my team? How do I overcome obstacles in my department?

I try to offer pointed advice on how that's going. We've been doing that for a while now, and it's been phenomenal. What I found is that it's encouraging to me too—not because I get to share things I've learned, but also because I learn things as I'm sharing them. There are problems that I can apply my wisdom or things I've learned over the years to the current situation that was different than what I've experienced. She's doing fantastic in her role, and she's taken on more responsibility. It's probably one of the most significant transitions in our business right now.

This particular individual, by the way, is holding a position in our company that is predominantly held by men. We're probably one of the few companies in the city where a female holds this position. So, of course, there are things I'm going to learn from that because there's not a lot of empirical data available. Mentorship is a two-way street, at least for anybody who's not just wanting to hear the sound of their own voice.

I feel the area most entrepreneurs need mentoring in is around the vetting of ideas. Entrepreneurs are risk-takers by nature, and they're often doing something that has not been done before. Or even if it's been done, it may not have been done exactly the way that they want to do it. The same strength that allows entrepreneurs to take that risk and chances can also be their blind spot. I don't know how many people I've seen where if they would have had that opportunity to talk to somebody and ask, "What do you think about this idea? What do you think I should do in this situation?" they would have listened to somebody else.

Even if entrepreneurs are skilled in any way, they still need mentors. There's a premium placed on entrepreneurs where they can do no wrong. They're told to go out there and get it started and get it done. I agree, but sometimes you can fast-track your way to failure. You can save yourself the trouble and heartache by being open. I don't think you need to be indecisive and take a hundred opinions, but when somebody is not attached to something, it's a lot easier for them to give you good advice as long as you trust them.

I was in a mentorship role when I served on the board of a symphony here in town, and a young woman who was the CEO was an entrepreneur, one of the few in this city. She asked for my advice about how we could raise more funds.

First, that was huge for her. Not saying here's what we need to do, but rather asking me for advice. I went back to our team and said, "Honestly, I don't think that you have a money problem, but a presentation problem. You have enough people showing up to your sites trying to get money, and they were deciding whether they should or shouldn't have the next set of concerts because of this."

If she would've gone headstrong and tried to make operational decisions based on the current cash position, she would have been in a lot of trouble. She would've stopped short, and because she asked me and I saw it entirely differently, she was able to take a different route. She got me involved, and we were able to raise a lot of money and keep the symphony funded for another couple of shows. The entire experience was a huge success, and it led to the next step for her.

One of the greatest joys I've had is when I brought somebody else into the situation before they were ready. If you're working on a team, your team does better with more information, not less. It's easy for the leader to think that their job is to be the gatekeeper between knowledge and success.

If you're going through a hard time as a business, do you want your company to have an opportunity to help you get out of it? Or do you want to go home and be the only one working on it? Everybody else is probably wondering why you're so frantic and so stressed out. Human beings are human beings because we show up at work. We might try to turn it off, but we can't.

Good leaders go through the trouble of humanizing things, even if that means that in the end, you have to let somebody go. Most people can understand that you can let somebody go if the company is failing. But if they have no idea whether you're failing or succeeding, and then suddenly, they get an empty box and are asked to clear out their desk, well, that hurts them for the next job.

Our industry is filled with individuals who have gone from business to business because each one has lied to them, or it wasn't the best conditions, or it was an excellent condition for a while, and then it went downhill.

Everybody pays for that as in any industry, you're sharing information and knowledge. Think about it like a more extensive system and organization, even if your company is trying to beat another one, and do so with the general dignity and respect that you'd want to be treated with as well.

I think that understanding the people side of the business and letting them follow based on sharing both wins and losses with your team will help you overcome.

Rob Hoyt
Tethers Unlimited
Tethers.com

I started my career in a mentoring relationship. When I was in graduate school, I got to meet one of my favorite science-fiction authors, a fellow named Dr. Robert L. Forward.

In the last part of his career, he spent about half his time writing science fiction, with the other half doing consulting for NASA and the DoD on advanced space propulsion and other crazy, far-out stuff.

We started talking and working together on a project he had. A few years later, as I was finishing up my PhD, we saw that there was an opportunity to submit a proposal to NASA on the technology that interested us. We ended up winning it and started the company based upon that initial contract.

I learned a great deal working with Bob, as he was a charismatic guy who was good at selling big-picture visions. From him, I learned how to approach unconventional ideas and technologies and figure out how to not only market them to potential customers but also how to chip away at the technical challenges. I was able to take ideas that started in the crazy science-fiction realm to move them steadily toward being practical and eventually turn them into products. I learned a lot from him on how to market unconventional ideas and how to bring in funding to perform the research and development and to not be afraid to tackle significant challenges and ideas.

Having a science-fiction author as a mentor is probably one of the best kinds of mentors you could have in certain aspects. He didn't have a whole lot of experience running a business. I had to learn the hard way myself because my background and degree was in aerospace engineering and plasma physics. Frankly, when we started, I had no idea what I was getting myself into and didn't know much about how to run a business.

I had a few other people help me out over the years. In terms of running a business, one of the more important ones was a fellow who we hired as a CFO. He only lasted a few months before he got disgusted and quit. But before he did, he taught me how to do cash-flow management and cash-flow forecasting, and that's been a critical tool for me to be able to manage the growth of the company over the years, get us through some rocky spots, and keep growing. That's another case where someone helped me learn some of the critical aspects of running and growing a business.

I've had several other mentors. Several of our board members have helped me out in many spots. One of our board members is a fellow named Art M. Dula. He is a space-patent attorney, and he's helped guide me through some of the stickier spots we've been in and helped us keep our noses clean and on the right side of the path. He also has been an essential mentor in many ways over the years.

I don't read business books, but I like to read science fiction. From my perspective, there are a handful of science-fiction books that have inspired me to try and pursue advanced space technologies and contribute to developing an off-world economy. Some of the books include *The Expanse* series by James S.A. Corey and other books by David Brin. Those are big-picture vision books, not how-to-run-a-company books.

I'm a big science-fiction and fantasy reader, and a book that I probably read too young and that has had an impact on me was *Dune* by Frank Herbert. So I do stuff like, I can't sit with my back to a door. Anytime I'm walking somewhere, I don't like to take the same path twice. This was comical when I was in junior high school and wanting my dad not to drive me to school the same way every day just because we don't want to let our "enemies" know. But my dad wasn't too keen on switching up his commutes just because of my weirdness.

Early on the company, in the first few years, Bob was our business leader, and I did all the technical work. In that period, he insisted that we stay laser-focused on one particular technology called space tethers, which is why we're called Tethers Unlimited.

It's an unconventional technology that, even before we got started, had a spotty success history, so it's a complicated technology to sell and progress, and we learned the hard way that it wasn't wise to focus on just one particular technology and one customer.

The funding for that technology has been inconsistent. It comes and goes and vanishes over roughly a ten-year cycle, so early on, we almost went out of business because our funding dried up. Fortunately, we found some other projects to work on, and over the past fifteen or seventeen years, we have focused and diversified our technology base and our customer base.

Most of our work is funded by the government, either directly or through a bigger prime contractor. Budgets and interest in a particular technology wax and wane, and we've found that by spreading our bets, we've been able to smooth out the ups and downs in the company's revenue and business. We've been able to keep growing over time and have the patience that, if a technology loses favor for a year or two, reasonably often, a few years later, there'll be a new interest in it. We remain in business, and we've increased our capabilities so we can continue progressing that technology towards being a viable product.

Another big lesson I've learned is that, early on, we were a technology-push company. We had some great ideas we were trying to push, but there wasn't a whole lot of existing market demand for it. An example when we did quite a lot of work on solutions for cleaning up space debris, which twenty-five years ago, we saw that as a looming problem. But we were twenty-five years ahead of the market. At that point, few people or customers saw the need to address that issue. Nobody had a requirement to do anything about it, so we were like Cassandra, proclaiming doom, and trying to sell a solution and not getting any traction.

Over the past twenty years or so, we've become more focused on figuring out what the customers need right now and how to leverage that to move us toward our longer-term goals and longer-term vision in a stepwise manner.

Now, twenty-five years later, orbital debris is becoming a hot topic, and we see renewed interest in that. We didn't have success twenty-five years ago, but we've stayed in business, and we've continued maturing technology, we've been maturing that approach to it over time, and now we're starting to get some traction with it.

We've learned how to balance our long-term technology vision and desire to push revolutionary technologies with the reality of addressing the existing markets and how to use existing customer needs to move along toward our long-term vision.

I've served as a mentor in a couple of ways. Internally, with my engineering and staff here, I'm trying to do what Bob Forward did with me, which is to instill in them the courage or the drive to pursue long-term visions and the significant challenges.

I'm a good writer, probably because of my liberal arts college background, so I've done a lot of work trying to teach engineers how to write good proposals and reports. Much of that is figuring out how to tell a story, not just reporting the facts, but telling a story so that we can sell our ideas as that's an area where I feel like I've provided some value within the company.

Since I managed to keep the business in operation and growing over twenty-five years, I've developed a reputation of being one of the more successful users of the small-business innovation research program, which is a particular funding vehicle that NASA and the DoD use.

I've interacted with several other startups and small companies and given them advice on how to get their business going. I've counseled them on how to grow and leverage that program when it's an excellent program for getting started, but it can also be a little dangerous and easy to get stuck on a hamster wheel of doing SBIR contracts. The trick to success there is learning how to leverage those initial R&D contracts to find customers and follow on contracts you need to get your product onto the market. I've talked with several other small business founders and innovators on how to use that program to grow their companies.

Within my industry, there are two different classes of entrepreneurs in the space industry.

Some people are highly technical, like I was, coming out of graduate school with a PhD in engineering, and those folks, like me, tend to be pretty obsessed with how impressive their particular technology is. They need a little help in taking a step back and looking at the market and the customer needs and figuring out how to sell their ideas within the industry. They need help around the customer-needs focus rather than on the cool new gizmo or idea that they have.

Then the other group of entrepreneurs in the space industry is people coming out with business degrees or business experience who want to get into the space industry. They have MBAs and know how to run and market a company. However, they often lack the battle scars and realism to know just how difficult it is to get a new technology or a new service developed and proven and established in the space industry.

In my experience, it takes a long time, because it's an industry that's slow to change, and you have to have a lot of patience, and you have to prepare for your stuff blowing up a few times before it works right. Those folks need a little bit of coaching on realism in terms of their timelines and what it will take to get the risk-averse industry to adopt a new idea.

If I were to write a book, it would be on the mixture of focusing on industry needs and mapping out a strategy for how to use the near-term industry needs to get your business started and get some initial products or services on the market and work toward your long-term goals. The success we've had has flown in the face of typical startup approaches. Usually, venture capitalists and investors want you to be laser-focused on one particular business opportunity, and you'll either become a billion-dollar unicorn, or you'll fail, and they're okay with that.

We've grown organically; we haven't had outside funding or venture funding. We've done it all by winning contacts, grants from the government, and from eventually winning purchases and orders from customers. We've been able to survive the ups and downs of the space industry by diversifying our technology, working in many different areas, so that we can build up our internal capabilities and experience and gain credibility to be able to tackle the hard, challenging things that we want to do. My experience is that the laser-focused approach to the space industry can work, but it's also risky. I prefer having multiple irons in the fire and hope that one or a few of them will hit it big.

I would title my book something like *Screaming in the Technology Valley of Death* or something like that. Because it's relatively easy to get funding to pursue an idea and develop an initial prototype, but the big hurdle and cost are getting your technology into space and getting it proven and validated in-flight.

Once you can do that, the doors start to open, and the purchase orders will begin to come in, and there has been a real lack of NASA and DoD funding to support that middle phase of getting your technology through that valley of death. There are some games and tricks that we've taken, and there are some significant risks and sacrifices we've made to get some of our technology on orbit whatever way we could. We've made some significant investments in that, but once we were able to get some of that on orbit and prove that it works, then the real customers have paid attention to us and have been willing to work with us.

I've given a few presentations on these things to a few NASA program meetings. There's a program that NASA has called the NASA Innovative Advanced Concepts Program, and they've asked me to come in a couple of times and give presentations to their current performers on how to develop and market their technology. I've been happy with how those presentations have gone.

Kevin Collins
Diversified
Diversifiedus.com

The name of my company is Diversified, and we've been in business for about thirty years. We're a technology company that provides services to customers to build complex media-based solutions. We design and build content, TV production, and content distribution for all the major television networks. We help new media companies, like Amazon, Google, or Facebook in developing content for marketing, producing content for internal training, corporate communications, all video based and production based.

We also work in the workplace technology, so we implement platforms and solutions for global multinationals to connect their employees in the conference room and the boardroom and platforms like Microsoft Teams or even Zoom. We build thousands of Zoomers a year.

It's been a fantastic journey, and the business we're in is maturing. I think video as communication, training, and marketing tool, plus retail, digital signage, and all those applications are all areas where we can provide expertise.

I've been with the company for twenty-seven years, and I was the eighth employee. Our founder's name is Alfred D'Alessandro. It's been an evolutionary journey of reinventing ourselves, our business plan, and our strategic direction by hyper-focusing on how technology and the markets around us were changing and how our customers' needs were changing. I think we've been successful because we've paid close attention to that, and we've evolved with our customers to develop into a new company.

Regarding mentoring, there's always room to improve; that's for sure. One of the critical ways for me to mentor the group is demonstrating consistency through my leadership style, ethics, and values to everyone around me. We also mentor through our corporate communications of being a north star for our company's direction and how we expect people to interact with each other and our customers.

I try to be a mentor and an example to others, and so does our founder, but we do it in different ways across the enterprise. Some methods are distinct, and some are not as obvious.

For example, we have a couple of categories of employees. With a new entry-level-position hire, we work with HR (which we call our people team) to align new employees with an existing employee. The established employee gives guidance on our overall mission and corporate culture and the process of their job function to ease them into our environment and explain our culture.

On the other side, we have vigorous internship programs because we're trying to create a pipeline of new hires. We do a lot of mentoring with interns because they're our potential team members of the future. Some interns will come and go and then move on to other things as they graduate from school. But when we identify interns that have a passion for what we're doing, and what we're doing seems to resonate with them, we try to build a closer relationship so they'll consider coming to Diversified upon graduation.

We've grown at an organic, exponential rate over the last five, six, or seven years. But we've also done it through mergers and acquisitions; we've acquired about eight or nine companies in the last four years. When we go into one of those mergers, mentoring and corporate communications become a big focus of ours. When you acquire a company, you acquire people, and those people need to understand your mission, organizational values, and goals. On those mergers, we assign mentors from our existing organization to these new employees to provide a high level of guidance for them.

As I've evolved through my career, there have been certain books I've read and certain people I've worked with that have resonated with me. My father was undoubtedly my first mentor. He was an inspiring leader with a healthy ego. I always joked that he looked inward for approval and that the people around him sensed that.

I haven't followed any of the books that I've read to the letter, but they've influenced my version of philosophy. Probably the first one I read that resonated with me was Stephen Covey's *Seven Habits of Highly Effective People*. Jim Collins's *Good to Great* is a book that I've implemented in my thinking.

Lincoln on Leadership is about how Abraham Lincoln was as a leader. He brought people on that would challenge his thinking. I think there's a book about him called *Team of Rivals*, where he built his executive team around him to be people who he knew didn't always agree with everything that he did. He wanted to have a vigorous debate and be challenged and make sure that whatever they did would be the best.

I follow those philosophies. As an entrepreneur, you can fall into a rut of thinking, "Hey, I made this company, and nobody knows it better than me." I think the reason we've been able to scale this company is that we've always been open to learning. We've always been open to listening to others and taking some of that outside input to heart. We're open to changing some of our go-forward strategies based on being open and thoughtful.

I am open, and I think we've been far more successful than I think we would have predicted when we started. Today we have 2400 employees, and we're approaching $1 billion in sales. It's hard to believe, but some of our core values and DNA haven't changed, and I think that's what resonates with the people who have joined our team.

It's refreshing to interface with us C-level executives and have us be so ready to listen and open to learning new things. It doesn't mean we always do what people think we should do or advise us to do, but everybody knows that they're heard, and their input is considered. At times, they'll see our direction change based on our ability to take a realistic view of things at the given moment.

I focus on mentoring the people who report directly to me or the leadership of any of the companies that we bring in during the diligence process. We mentor them during the diligence to explain who we are, what our mission is, where we're going, what our ethics are, and how we expect the company to evolve. I'm a leadership mentor; I think that's a fair comment.

I mentor positively and proactively as I think that always gets better results. People are typically anxiety-ridden or uncomfortable when they're coming into a new organization when they've been acquired. I try to be sensitive about that. I try to acknowledge the gifts they're bringing in, and I tell them we're excited to have them share their gifts with us and for us to share our gifts back to them.

The terminology I always use with an acquisition is that the DNA of the company changes every time we make an acquisition, and it changes for the better. We're not a monolithic organization that thinks we know best, and since they just joined the team, we'll tell them how to do it. We're experienced leaders, and we think we clearly understand our strategic goals and our direction. Still, we're open to a discussion and happy to have talented people to join our team and join the debate and help drive the course of the business. I call it the best of the breed.

One of the traps of gaining some success as an entrepreneur that can be a block is when you get to a certain level of success and then can't get past it. You're in an echo chamber of your own mind, and you're not open to listening to others. Maybe you're caught in an ego trap of saying, "Hey, I started this company from nothing, and I got us here. So what could you tell me that I don't know? What could you tell me that is of value?" You have to challenge yourself and say, "Maybe I do have something special that got me here, but to go forward, I have to learn."

Entrepreneurs should look at life as a lifelong learning experience. Thinking you're gifted through your DNA because you're smarter than everybody else is a false narrative.

If you're going to be the leader or start a business, you have to have an evident passion and a clear understanding of what your goals are, what you want your company to be, what your business plan is, and what kind of place you want it to be for people to work there. Be open to learning all the time, and don't be closed-minded. If you hire talented people, you probably should be listening to their contribution to your success. No successful entrepreneur did this alone. You have to do it as a team.

Maybe that's an innate thing to choose the right people. With our acquisitions and the people we've hired from day one, almost ten years ago, I'd say we've been lucky. When I would interview people twenty years ago, I would always wonder if I would enjoy working with this person every day. Have they said anything through the process that I think is looking at a problem from an angle I never considered before? Or maybe they have an enthusiasm I find exciting. I'm always open to how this person can make me better as a manager or leader and how they can make our company better.

It hasn't always worked out, but you can't be afraid. You can't be scared to fail, and I'll use the term others have used, but you need to *fail fast*. One of the things I've learned over the years is that when you have a terrible feeling, and you think something is not working out, hope is not a plan. You probably need to be pretty proactive in making a change.

If you're going to try new things, some of them aren't going to work out, but you don't need too many to work well to drive a lot of success.

Scott Swartz
Nexceris
Nexceris.com

The best thing we've done is to establish a strong internship program in our company. Young college engineering students in their second, third, and sometimes even fourth year come to work with us for either the summer or through the school year. It's been effective in helping us identify suitable candidates. Our leadership team in our company is at about eight right now. Three of them started as interns when they were in college, and then we hired them.

We only have one location in Columbus, Ohio, so we have a good pipeline with Ohio State University and also other universities in the state and national in our field. Most interns come from Ohio State. The coolest thing, in all honesty, is watching our employees grow. I don't have kids in my family. However, I have employees, and it's been an incredible joy to watch them grow as professionals and people.

I had two mentors. One was my dad, who was also an entrepreneur. He formed a company in 1968, which is still running to this day. I watched him for many years, and he has worked very hard. He'd work a full day at his day job and then work all night, getting the company started.

Then he dared to quit his job and take on full-time responsibility for his company. I got to see that happen, and that was extremely valuable to grow up watching him from my twelve-year timeline.

I always had work to do for the company when I was growing up. I guess you'd call it nepotism, but I called it motivation, because in that environment, you work hard and get accepted, or you are just the boss's kid. That had a significant impact on me growing up.

I've had several other mentors throughout my life who were very helpful to me, especially in graduate school. I met one during my college career who was four years older than me. He was finishing his PhD when I started mine, and then he stayed on as a postdoc. We did a lot of work together over the years and published a lot of papers. He was very valuable to me; he taught me the ropes.

There's another fellow, who has since passed, whom I was working with throughout my college years. He was in my dad's company, and then when my dad's company split into three others, he formed his own company. He hired me to do moonlighting work while I was in grad school, so I had another source of income that allowed me to live a little better than the average grad student. That was always very valuable. He'd take me places to do experiments and testing. That turned out to be a useful experience for me as well.

I grew up in Buffalo, so my early years through high school were in Buffalo. The company moved to Columbus, Ohio, when I started college, so my parents lived in Ohio when I attended college in New York State. When I went to graduate school at Penn State until the mid-'80s, and then at some point, I decided I better get a job.

It turned out that I randomly ended up picking up the hall phone at Penn State and talked to a guy here in Columbus, which became my first job. I was doing my postdoc at the time and having a lot of fun doing it. The only reason I took the interview was that my dad was in Columbus for that next weekend, and then he was moving his company to Tucson, Arizona. I said, "Well, I'll take the interview if we can have it on Monday."

I got there, had dinner with my dad, went to the interview, and ended up taking the job, which is the place where I worked and learned the ropes. There I met my future business partner, the co-founder of the company. That's how we met, and we worked together and ended up forming a company together that has lasted several years, so far.

Our management team has always been reading particular books about leadership, but I can't say that there was one book in particular that struck me. We've been practicing many things that we read. Books that tell you, "Stay focused on your sweet spot, and make sure that you're doing something that matters."

We learned that the hard way, then we started reading about it. The books didn't necessarily help me find a eureka moment but confirmed that the direction we were going is okay. We found little strategies here and there that would point you in the right direction or get you using the proper habits and things like that.

I consider myself a mentor throughout the company. I have many people whom I worked with, and many of them joined us straight from college. We're a technical company, so we have many engineers working for us. My approach has always been to treat them as equals and help them make decisions. If they're making a poor decision, I try to steer them in the direction I think they should be going. That seems to have worked well. Early on, when we had interns, most of them were reporting to me, so I like to think I helped out along the way.

One of the kids, probably the brightest intern by far that we ever had, was at school in Ohio State. He came in and hit the ground running. He was strong, intelligent, and about as smart as any engineer in our company. He interned twice, and even while he was finishing up his degree, he was working with us part-time. He came to me toward the end and asked, "Well, would you like to offer me a job?"

I said, "I would love to offer you a job, but I'm not going to until you tell me you're not going to graduate school." I knew he was thinking about graduate school, and it was crazy for him not to go to graduate school. I said, "I'm not going to give you a job offer until you decide you're not going to grad school."

He ended up going to graduate school at Ohio State. I gave him some advice as to who I thought was an excellent faculty person from a research perspective there in chemical engineering. He ended up going there and working in the area of fuel cells.

I set up a scholarship at Ohio State, and I talked to the professor. I defined it something like, "To a graduate student working in chemical engineering in the field of fuel cells," knowing that there was only one person that qualified for that particular approach. I gave him a scholarship for $2,000 a year for the four or five years that he was doing his work there. Of course, that allowed me to buy Ohio State football tickets, so I had an ulterior motive.

Then, we ended up hiring him. He was far more valuable to us as a PhD chemical engineer than he would have been if we just hired him directly out of school. Ultimately, he ended up leaving us and forming his own company that is reasonably successful now. I like to think I had a positive impact on his career as a mentor. He's probably the best example of successful mentoring that I've done.

I believe that most entrepreneurs need mentoring in learning the lessons. If we have learned them a little earlier, without learning them the hard way, it might have been easier for us. At a contract research and development firm, my partner and I worked there. Bill worked there for eleven years, and I was there for seven years, and we learned the R&D business.

We learned how to write proposals. We learned how to interact with customers. We learned a lot about the nuts and bolts of doing R&D as a business. The problem with R&D as a business is that it's not a business. The ultimate goal is you need to establish products, which we have done over the years, and that's, in essence, why we have survived.

When we were starting our R&D business, we looked at it as a means of making money, which we successfully did, but then you end up working on projects that have no future. You're not developing a product, you're just providing a service. Over the years, we got smarter and decided we're not going to do government projects unless they are right smack in our wheelhouse, something that we can effectively do and do well.

By doing that, you give yourself a far better chance of winning the proposal you're writing rather than just spending day and night for a week writing a proposal that goes nowhere. Then you have a better chance of getting to the next phase where you get more money.

Our win rate on these proposals is well above the norm based on the ability to focus on our core. We learned that the hard way.

Maybe if we had some guidance along the way or had a little bit of advice early on, we might've gotten to where we wanted to go faster.

Ultimately, it's learning to look ahead, to where you want to get to, and that helps you decide what to do in the first place. When we started the company, it was the wrong time to be looking for a job, and we said, "Let's try this." We didn't know until four or five years later that we had something going. We decided to see what we could do with it, and we got serious.

The mentor whom I worked with in college had an R&D business, and that was the model for where we wanted to go. However, that wasn't the right model, because after we got started, we realized we had something good. We had to sustain it, and that meant developing commercial products.

We formed the company in 1995, and we started a commercial business from the company in about 2000. It took us a few years to find our path. We were developing core technology at the time to have the product, but it took us a few years to get focused in the direction we needed to go with the company.

If I were to write a book, my advice would be to focus on what you do well as that gives you a chance to be successful. Also, understand what the customer wants, not what you want to do, and that will also help. I think the last thing would be to establish relationships with your customers.

Being a perfectionist is okay if you work hard. I am a perfectionist, and I work like a dog, but if I were a perfectionist and didn't work, I'd be stuck in the weeds. When I'm writing a proposal or a report, I consider it a legacy thing. That report is always going to be there. Someone is going to read it and say, 'This was a good bit of work that these guys did." They read the proposal, and say, "Wow, this is a good proposal, and I think we're going to fund it." I obsess over things like that. I can spend hours and hours and hours and hours writing proposals and reports.

In terms of what I do for the company, that's my product. I run the government business portion of what we do at Nexceris, and I leave the commercial stuff to the commercial guys.

My advice is to focus on what you're good at, and you'll be successful.

Steve Mersky
Hawkins Point Partners
Hawkinspointpartners.com

The leadership of our company has undoubtedly benefited from the mentoring we've received over the years as we've grown as leaders. We remember those people and their ways that helped us. I would say from my perspective, I've been inspired by leaders who led in an authentic, relevant, and effective manner. What stuck out for me about these people was that they were dedicated to helping others thrive.

When I think of mentoring, I want to help the people around me thrive in the work that they've chosen to do. I aspire to pay forward what people have done for me. In my organization, we're committed to a culture that enables lifelong learning. The mentoring is an essential part in terms of professional and personal development.

We seek to create that environment where we all learn from each other. In my organization, we're all senior, talented management consultants. So we listen and learn from everyone that we work with and dismiss hierarchy along the way. We're focused on how we behave, so I've been mentored in the way of "It's not just what you do but also how you do it." We emulate a lot of those qualities that our leadership has been the beneficiary of and pay that forward to the team that we've built around us.

Organizationally, we have a couple of structures. We're a consulting firm, so we're pretty much all about the client and the employee because we are a services organization. Our asset is our people. We have introduced roles we've developed over the last year, one we call Client Partner that focuses on the success of the client. Their role as a professional on the ground working for their clients is to understand their business challenges and their key initiatives. We seek to become a trusted advisor to help the client achieve success. That person's primary goal is client satisfaction.

We also have another role: each person in the field has a Colleague Advocate. Their job is to be an advocate between the person in the field and executive leadership. The Colleague Advocate and Client Partner play mentoring roles in not just helping people but also learning from each other.

As I said, we're all senior people, so those people, as a team hopefully, are helping each other be successful and do the things they need to achieve client success. It's been effective for us. As we've evolved as a company, we've grown very fast in the last couple of years. We've had to introduce this type of structure to make sure we are serving both our clients and our colleagues effectively.

There is one individual who helped me. He was a senior leader in a relatively big consulting firm where I worked. Ultimately, I came to report to him, and it came at a critical time in my career. I've had a good career, and I've had some pretty big jobs at pretty big companies before we started our firm here. I became increasingly disenchanted with the corporate environment, which I found to be mean-spirited, selfish, driven by the needs of the shareholder at the expense of the interest of the employee and the client. I started to think, "Boy, it's tough to get a big job without being a jerk."

Then this individual came along at a point when I was feeling that way. He reaffirmed for me at a critical time in my career that you can behave courteously and decently and still be successful in the corporate world. He stayed true to his principles in the face of all the adversity he faced along the way. He reminded me that you can be a good person and still make it happen. I learned from him that you couldn't go wrong if you play it straight. Today he's still a mentor, an advisor, and a part of our advisory board. Whenever I have a tough situation or have a problem, I call him, and he helps me talk through it.

Now concerning a book, I'd have to say that Dale Carnegie's *How to Win Friends And Influence People* was influential for me. I read it as a young person, and it was quite impactful. I was sensitive to the critical human element of how we interact in business. I learned a lot from that book, and I took some lessons from it. But I was a young man at the time, and now I would not describe myself in that way.

Within the last year, I reread it when we had a company-wide initiative where we felt as though people needed to read that book. Many of us read it before, but we all committed to rereading it. I was fascinated by the timeless concepts, as this book was written in the '30s. It was a later publication, but what was true ninety years ago is true today. As a services business, our asset is people, so that critical human element is just such an essential part of our success.

Rereading that book made me do a little bit of career analysis and reminded me of when I was younger and how I've evolved as a leader, as a mentor, as a coach, and as a person. It had a significant impact; that book probably has had more impact on me than any other book I've read. The fundamental ways in which we relate to people haven't changed. In our business, soft skills are critical.

I've been lucky in that I've never had the big tragic career-limiting blunder. I make mistakes every day as we all do. When things don't go well, I tend to have the attitude of not reacting too quickly or with emotion. I don't jump in and try to fix every problem right away. Often, things work themselves out.

But I've had a couple of instances where I probably had my head in the sand, which is something I now guard against. I had one situation pretty early in my career, where I was a project manager. I had an important project, and I left my head in the sand for too long, and the project went awry. This was before the days of email, so I waited to get a phone call from our executive vice president about this project that was a failure, and we were going to discuss how to get out of it.

I was expecting his call at 5:00 PM, so I waited until 8:00 PM. I wasn't going anywhere until I got that call. I was nervous waiting for it, but he was helpful about we talked through what I hadn't done right, what I needed to do, how we were going to fix it. It was a pretty big mistake on my part to not be on top of that, but I received excellent mentoring.

That particular individual mentored me a lot. He was gruff, matter-of-fact, not a lot of fun, but he was honest and direct, and I trusted him. He helped me through that and gave me some good advice along the way. There have been a few times when I haven't reacted fast enough and asserted myself soon enough, so that mistake was a good lesson.

I think about mentor versus coach, and I'm a natural-born coach. I was an athlete, and I've always been a leader. I think of a coach as more of a hierarchical position while a mentor is more of a peer position. I've served as a mentor by leading by example. I've had the benefit of a healthy upbringing, as I was influenced by my father, who taught me much about work ethic and integrity. He never cared what I did, but he did care that if I did it, I did it well. If I didn't do it well, I heard about it.

My father instilled in me a commitment to "play the game the right way" by doing things the right way. I try to lead by example in that way, always be straight, clear, transparent, great to work with, and do great work. I try to be a mentor by leading by example on what I would call a soft element of doing the best I can at the vocation I have chosen—being committed to doing great work and being great to work with.

I also try to be a mentor as there are certain areas where I am a subject matter expert. There are certain capabilities of our business where I can go broad and deep. I look forward to and enjoy sharing my knowledge and my expertise in those areas where people are looking to gain. I tend to try to treat each discussion as though I'm both giving and getting.

For me, learning is lifelong. I'm always learning. My company has transitioned into exclusively focusing on the life sciences industry, and it's an industry I didn't know as well as some others. I'm loving learning all about a new industry and service in this particular industry.

There are certain areas where I have deep expertise, so I have something to give. There are areas where I know I don't have as much knowledge, so there's a lot I can get. As a mentor, I treat each discussion as though I'm looking to give and get. Give something that can offer to the people, get something they can provide to me, and collectively become better at what we do.

I was a three-sport athlete, and my son was a three-sport athlete. I coached him up through Little League. I used to run the youth basketball program, Besides that, I was involved in the youth soccer program and was a very visible figure on the Little League Baseball diamonds. When I was a young adult, I coached baseball teams. I was a baseball player, so I've done a lot of sports coaching and managing teams. I love kids, so I've always been heavily involved in children's causes even before I had a child. I enjoy being around kids and working with them.

It has kept me sharp over the years. Every kid is different, and so you can apply that in business as well. The good coaches will say they treat every person differently because every person is different. Some people take criticism better than others. Some you can come down on harder than others.

I was taught by my father never to criticize anybody for a physical mistake. Everybody makes mistakes. You screw things up. When you're in the baseball world, you drop fly balls, and you make bad throws and strikeout. I would never come down on a kid or anybody, even at work, for making a physical mistake. What I distinguish is the mental mistakes, and those are the things I tried to teach the kids—helping people avoid those mental mistakes that can derail us.

I'm a little hesitant to assess others. I can't say I did a lot of evaluation, and I don't know a lot of people who have done that. But I would guess that others may need mentoring in surrounding ourselves with great talent who understood the things that we didn't know. An excellent example of that is when we three founders started our business, we did so, thinking, "We know our business."

We knew we were going to be successful because we'd been doing this our whole career, and we were ready to start doing it for ourselves. We know what to do, and we were confident. What we did is surrounded ourselves with an advisory board. It was an unpaid volunteer, group of executives who had been previous clients who agreed to become part of our advisory board.

Through that first year or so, we vetted everything about our business: the services we were going to provide, the language we were going to use to describe them, our business plan, our website, our marketing approach. We used these folks, and they indeed were mentors, so we surrounded ourselves with people who were smarter than us.

For anybody who's starting a business, I would certainly recommend that practice. We knew our strengths and weaknesses, we were willing to admit to them and accept them, and we sought help from those people we trusted. That's what I think I would recommend any entrepreneur to do.

If I were to write a business book, it would be on the soft side: culture. We're in a unique situation where our product is people, so we're very people-centric.

We're also in a position where the labor market in our industry is tight. Every night when an employee goes home, we need to give them a reason to come back tomorrow; otherwise, they can go somewhere else. The employee focus of our business has been critical in creating the type of environment that people want to join. I would write about the importance of a culture that is clear and that we're committed to.

The other thing I would write about would be—and this has been critical to our success—is focus. You're not all things to all people. We are focused on the services we provide, and we're focused on what we do and for whom we do it. From a services perspective, we do a few things, we do them exceptionally well, and we do not take on things that are not in our core competency.

We're focused on a particular industry, so we don't try to be all things to all people. The discipline of focus has been a significant key to our success, and I have seen it be a detriment to others who try to be all things to all people. And it's hard because we're competitive.

In our office, we have what we call a team "no." We didn't all use to do all life sciences, so we all have relationships outside of that industry. When our good friend from company X that's not a pharma company calls and says, "Steve, can you help me?" we take it to the group, and we do the assessment.

Is it something we should do? We laugh about it; it's a team "no." Sorry, it's no. We're not going to do this anymore. We joke about that as we have team "no" to keep us straight.

We refer to it as the discipline of focus. That would make an excellent title for a book: *Team No*, or *The Discipline of Focus*.

Steve Spain
Spain Commercial, Inc.
Spain-commercial.com

A few years ago, I joined a men's group called C12, a Christian CEO's men's group. From there, we started a company Bible study, and that process led to us mentoring subcontractors and employees, and it's changed the whole culture of my company.

We're in construction, so the guys can be a little rough. We've had them come in and express concerns that they have with life in general or about the business, so we mentored them. One of the things we do is advise the guys to dream big, think big, and have a passion for what they believe in. I always tell my guys to be the best that you can be. Always want to improve—have that spirit of excellence. That mindset has done a lot for my business here.

The program has 100 percent helped my workers be more invested in the business. We're really close, and I have a personal relationship with just about all my employees. One thing I do is speak with them one-on-one and ask how things are going—not only about their projects or work, but also about their family.

We have about forty employees, and since we have an open-door policy with my office, they'll come up whenever they want to talk. I stay positive with them and help them with the way they carry themselves and the way they speak.

One of the things I always say to my guys is, "Show me your friends, and I'll show you your future." I always tell them that what you are speaking is prophesying your future. Your life will move in the direction of your words. I try to instill ways of thinking like that in them, and I believe it has paid off. We do a lot of work in health care, so we're working around the public, and we want clean-cut guys who are polite people of excellence. We nurture positive, deliberate action in our employees.

This type of mentorial relationship has improved our employee's personal lives as well. I've had a few people who never dreamed of owning or building their own homes, and we've helped them achieve those goals. I tell them to dream big and believe big. They work hard, they play hard, but I've seen them change before my eyes. It's incredible what that positive belief does for a person.

One of the biggest mistakes I initially made was around delegating tasks—I wanted to control a lot of things. I learned that once you give that employee, project manager, or superintendent the responsibility, and you trust them, it makes them feel better when they do a great job. It was hard for me to delegate a lot of tasks. One of the hardest things for me was to learn to trust and let go. You've got to delegate; you've got to grow.

My biggest mentor was Ralph Mille in my C12 group, who was one of the guys who helped me change my business culture. Books have been great for leadership mentoring, such as those written by Dave Ramsey and Joel Olsteen.

I'm for positivity and believing big. I think the younger generation doesn't believe big enough or try hard enough and tend to have a lot of small dreams. When you push people to think big, and when they start to take those steps, they see it come true, and it's incredible to see what happens.

In our Bible study, we have the chief of police, surgeons, subcontractors, and, of course, my guys attend. I mentor not only my employees but also our subcontractors. We have a great relationship. That has helped my business and my relationships with our subcontractors.

Of course, I mentor my employees, and some of the stories I hear as I try to instill that excellence in them are incredible.

For example, we have one gentleman who has been here for about five years. He had a rough childhood, very rough, but he's a hard worker. I mentored him for the first year. One thing I do is ask the guys for their goals. What's your vision? What are your goals for the next year, for the next five years? What would you like to be in six months? Where would you want to be in six months or a year? I try to keep it simple.

This one guy had a five-year plan to own his own house. Well, within two years, he bought a home, and he was amazed. Then I said, "What's next?"

He said, "I don't know, Steve. This goal was big for me."

I said, "What about building your own house?" He was unsure about such a big goal. I said, "It's up to you. If you don't want to build one, that's fine, but let me know what your vision is."

Now that has become his five-year goal, and we're going toward that route. I can tell him about land for sale to help him and ask, "Where do you want to be? What area do you want to live in?"

I keep track of all my employee's goals and dreams. The hardest thing is getting them to give them to me in the first place. Many people are afraid to dream big. There are a few who are good with it, but there are a few that after a month goes by, they say, "I'm going to get them to you, I promise." I tell them that unless you write down your goals and put that in front of you, you forget what you're thinking about.

It's incredible when you have them put their goals in writing, but it can be tough to get them to write down their goals. I tell them they're not dreaming big enough. because a goal might be, "I want to be able to pay my bills." Once they write down their goals, they feel better. I say, "Put that vision in front of you and work toward it, and you will actually see it happening."

I have mentored people at my company who have left the company for a different opportunity. I mentored two gentlemen for a few years who left and went on to start their own business. They're doing quite well.

I feel that the area that most entrepreneurs need mentoring in is the ability to focus on their dreams. You've got to have a passion for what you do. We do a lot of health care, and we love what we do. I think it's a challenge, but I have a passion for helping people. I think they need to have excellence in everything they do. They should always be the best. They always want to improve. I tell my guys that if you have that spirit of excellence, you'll go places.

Another thing is we don't ever want to stop improving. We want to keep growing, keep learning, and be the best that we can be. If you're a plumber, be the best plumber you can be. Be the best electrician you can be. Be the best framer. Whether you're a truck driver or a deli guy, be the best one.

When you have that kind of excellence, it gives you a platform. When you're on that platform, it gets people's attention. You attract even more goodness to you, and people recognize that.

Some of the unique challenges or aspects of working in health care construction involve infectious control. We do a lot of training and containments, and there's a lot of night work. It's not your typical construction site. We use a lot of HEPA machines and air filters that filter out any dust or contaminants.

We've been doing health care construction work for twenty-seven years, so we have a lot of experience as well as a great team that does the specialty work from lead line rooms, cath labs, MRIs, and things like that. In the construction world, you want to be courteous, and you want to be great at what you do. We're around the public, and we're around sick people who don't feel well, so we want to be courteous and ask them how they're feeling. That goes a long way.

We do construction on previously existing health care buildings, so we're interacting with patients and the people who work there. We have a relationship with a lot of the staff, nurses, and administrators. Right now, we have about forty jobs going on in major health care centers. We have a lot of work going on: some are small projects, but some are quite large. We're working on government bases in health care as we have a passion for this type of work.

If I were to write a book, I would say to love your people, your organization, that you serve, and you'll become a great leader. Surround yourself with people who challenge you, inspire you, and push you. When I started my business, I was around some negative people. Once I got rid of that, things moved forward. Negativity can stifle your business growth.

Alan Barlis
Barlis Wedlick Architects
Barliswedlick.com

Any architect will tell you that collaboration is critical. It's certainly been a significant focus for our firm, as our tagline is that as a service industry, we make sure we meet our clients' needs. The whole concept of collaborating, communicating, learning from each other, and listening is fundamental to what we do, and it's become a part of how we run the firm. Mentoring goes hand in hand with how the company works. We designed our firm so that people who've been around longer work with newer people, which is not unique by any means.

One thing we focus on is to make sure that our people help each other by realizing that mentoring goes in all directions. Someone with more experience, and who has been with us longer, might mentor people who are gaining experience, but we're all being mentored at the same time. In some ways, we're all mentors and mentees, and we like to focus on the fact that you can't successfully impart information unless the person receiving it lets you know that it's hitting home and making sense for them.

The effective management and mentorship of others must be communicated based on what the receiver can understand. It's an equally important obligation for the receiver to inform the sender that the messages are being received. Sometimes things need to be explained differently or revisited. There has to be some feedback to make sure that the people who are teaching learn how to be better teachers. It's a multidirectional mentorship.

We learned a valuable lesson from a client who informed us that it's essential to get a receipt when you're communicating with someone and to be sure you've got confirmation that what you think you're saying is being received.

My business partner, Dennis Whitley, started the firm, and I joined him, and we've been partners for over twenty years. We've had an excellent back-and-forth mentorship from each other since we met. Dennis has been my most influential professional mentor, as he has a way of working with clients and a professional attitude about making sure that the crucial aspects of life, such as comfort, joy, enjoying yourself, finding the good in what you do, and how you can help others are followed. All these things spoke to me, and I recognized them in his practice right where we met.

Dennis has been the most influential mentor for me in those areas. We've been a successful pair for each other, partly because we're different. We have different ways of conducting ourselves and running the business, but we have been forced to see all the ways we could learn from each other. Our fundamental values are the same, but we approach them procedurally in different ways.

Several books influenced me in my career, including *Creating We*, which is about building a firm of people. There was another book called *On Leadership*. These two books were about how to think about practice and working together. There's a series of books specifically about the design field that Keith Granet has put together that's been helpful. Those books do an excellent job of thinking about what it means to do your best work, especially for the design world.

I naturally serve as a mentor for our staff at a minimum. We make that part of what we do daily. One of the things we focus on is understanding what everyone's goals are, thinking about their careers, helping them make the right choices for themselves. We believe strongly that the office is a group of people who are doing their highest and best work and enjoying themselves and on track toward their professional goals. That helps keep people around for a long time.

We have people who joined us out of grad school or college and have stayed with us for years and years, and it's been great to watch them grow, improve, and impress and teach us in return. That's been the most prominent venue for mentorship. Also, architects have a whole system of mentorship that's part of our licensure understanding, so we have to have guides when we apply to become registered architects. So I have done and continue to do that for some people. I teach, and some of the people whom I've taught have tapped me as a resource as they move into their careers. Mentoring is something that I enjoy taking time out to do.

Most entrepreneurs need mentoring in thinking about how we want the people in our design world—those who work with us and for us, or who I'm mentoring in other ways—to embrace their entrepreneurial side.

When it comes to people in the design field, what does it mean to think entrepreneurially? How do you feel about the business side of things? How do you make sure that you're giving yourself time and ability to strategize and come up with the team to help you develop ideas? Where will you want to take that? How do you have ownership and direction in your career? More so than thinking about mentoring entrepreneurs, mentoring people to become entrepreneurs is our focus.

It's essential to have a strong practice not only in the service of clients but also in the service of ourselves, our careers, working together, and how to prioritize having excitement and delight every day. That is this notion of collaboration and how much time it takes, how much organization it takes, how one needs to carve out systems that allow us to be able to collaborate. Not just to be sure you're not shortchanging those exchanges. That they are regular and organized, that people know when and how we're coming to the table and what we're trying to deliver. That we're always feeling respected, that we always appreciate how the results of all the group of people thinking are going to be better than any of our thinking left to itself.

We focus on collaboration and build systems that support it. Being aware of how much time that it takes to think things through, to test things and to start over, we take our time to come out with the best approach before jumping into all the action.

People tend to rush off to accomplishments and deliverables only to find later that they're undermined by aspects that could have been thought through and considered more efficiently with a team or a collaborative approach and, therefore, better success in the long run.

Everybody's quick to start doing assigned tasks so they can deliver their deliverables without thinking it through first and collaborating with their colleagues. We encourage raising your hand and asking a question if you're not sure of the mission. Take time to nurture that back and forth collaboration. It can't be fake. It can't be a bunch of meetings held only to say we held a bunch of meetings. They can't pretend to have buy-in from a community you say you're serving, but then you walk out of that meeting and say, "Well, at least, we got the meeting done."

Showing real, honest, sincere, and engaged collaboration is hopefully an order of the day.

A lot of our books are on the practice of architecture. The focus of our last book was about how much our work and belief in the idea of doing architecture is about engaging and collaborating with clients. That's always been significant.

But I think we also do a lot of work, especially now with thinking about energy efficiency and climate change, and so there's a lot of work on that. What we're doing, we think we'll be able to put into a book.

It would be nice to reflect more on the practice because we do spend a lot of time to feel like this and perform like this, thinking about the system and the work, and thinking about what it *means* to do the work, not just *doing* the work.

Tom Hillman
Lewis & Clark Ventures
Lewisandclarkventures.com

There are several ways our company has been affected by, or improved upon, by mentoring.

The first is that we have a mentorship program, so it's not fate that someone shows up as a summer intern. We have the infrastructure, support, and a process for mentoring. We've benefitted from the emerging insights from our mentors so much so that, in some cases, we shifted from being a mentor to the mentee.

For example, we were looking at developing apps and technology. We always think it's good to have the young Turks who are savvy with technology and applications around, and they came up with a novel way to reach audiences that increased our user base twofold.

We've been doing mentorships for over fifteen years, and we have people reporting at a director level so that they have excellent visibility. Our goal is that when our interns answer the question "How was your internship?" they have great things to say. We want to know that they felt engaged, that they contributed and learned, and that they were inspired. Our hidden agenda is that it's an excellent way to do our scouting and have a farm club. We have hired many people who have come through our internship programs.

I am a serial reader, and I follow several thought leaders as I love the newer science of collaboration. I give people articles and books to read all the time, and one I recommend is called *Smart Tribes: How Teams Become Brilliant Together* by Christine Comaford. It's a great read about how to collaborate to bring out the best of everyone in the room so that everyone feels having a voice. People have ground rules of respect, but there are opportunities to gain momentum from teamwork and learn new ways to approach things.

I've had many mentors in my life who were visionary leaders with management skills, but they didn't manage their way through things—they led their way through. I reach high and try to surround myself with people who are inspiring and have led a life of purpose and passion and made an impact. I've been active as a volunteer board member and trustee at a major private university, and the former chancellor has become a mentor to me. I find pearls and nuggets of information that are provocative for me and my critical thinking, and I learn lessons all the time from the people who have dug deep reservoirs in our community from which people like me have been drinking for quite a while. Part of a transition with mentorship is that you become a mentor yourself to someone else and that you dig your reservoirs as well.

I've probably made more mistakes than most people. You have to recognize and reflect and realize that you can fail. I say, "Let's fail fast, and let's fail forward." We are all about culture and people, and as a practical matter, I say, "The best thing about my work is the people, and the worst thing about my work is the people."

When I've made big mistakes, it's been while wearing rose-colored lenses and believing that everything is going to be great and wonderful because my cup is overflowing. I made some serious mistakes with some past partners who didn't pan out to be the people I wanted them to be. As Dickens said, "The greater the expectation, the bigger the disappointment if it didn't work out," and so I've made some "people mistakes" in the past.

I've found a way to see things more clearly as a result of these mistakes. One is that I surround myself with other people and get comparable perspectives with other people who would review and interview and understand the good, the bad, and ugly of people. We all have dark spots, and we have strengths, so I collaborate with other thought leaders in our business to be selective.

We say, "Hire slowly," but there's another side of this that's become ingrained in everything we do at a top leadership position. We work with industrial psychologists, and we want to be a little more scientific about hiring, more fact-based, when confirming. So we do behavioral tests, personal interviews, and seek to understand their leadership effectiveness. We have objective, independent third parties that help us make decisions about people now.

I've owned over sixty companies, and I've started over sixteen of them, and I have had a penchant for identifying younger people whom I believe in and have agreed to sponsor. I work with a stable of young entrepreneurs, and I do everything I can to determine what their best and unique gifts are.

Then I set them up in ways to be even better than what they think they may be able to be. It's about believing in them, empowering them, and being an aide and private ear and discussing every imaginable situation—professional or personal—while helping to navigate and guide them through life as they reach different decision points in their professional development.

The area that most entrepreneurs need mentoring in today is situational, but there's a gap between theory and book smarts and applied practical understandings. One of the crucial things for me is to help people understand that there's a difference. Smarts are not always going to deliver the value that businesses need, and therefore, that will hold them back in their careers.

I have the young MBA who knows everything about the business through cell number 12, role column F and has built this elaborate model and understands all the data. They complain, "I don't get it. My knowledge is so valuable, and this team doesn't recognize that if they pay attention to these details, they could do different things with outcomes in the business."

I say, "Let's step back a second. You believe that it's valuable, and I hear that loud and clear, but how valuable is it if it's not valued? What can you do to make this valuable and valued?"

My idea is that you get into the organization with the people who are producing the information and understand how they think, how they document things, what information they're working with, then you can build based on their understanding of what they're doing in their routines. You could help demonstrate what kind of information you could interpret based on where it becomes useful for them. If it becomes useful, then it becomes valued because you're going to have different kinds of outcomes.

Sitting on your perch with your MBA while saying you know more than the people in the field doesn't always work. If we want to be valuable to them, your test is not to say, "I'm a member of their team." Your test is for them to say, "I view you as a member of our management team because you're helping us rethink how we could take what we're doing and incorporate it in a way to lead to transformation."

Make the perspective of the people you're creating a product for your own. A lot of people have a lot of data, but they have no information. You have to be able to articulate the information on terms people understand; that front row analysis is essential.

If I were to write a book, I would say work smart, work hard, be a great listener, challenge yourself, and be a great communicator. You can learn to become a better communicator if you don't innately have that kind of talent.

There are many ways to communicate, and if you're a good listener, then you have more insights and wisdom based on what other people are thinking and saying. You're able to provide relevant information to them, and sometimes it's in writing, sometimes it's the spoken word. There are some things you must get through by true grit. I tell young people that communication is so vital, and I recommend that when you're taking your college classes, take some writing classes and be a great writer because that's a high form of communication.

I'll give you an example of how entrepreneurs should challenge themselves. I've had many mentors in my life, and when I'm faced with a situation, I challenge myself and ask, "How would my mentor handle this situation? What am I not doing? What am I not seeing? How can I gain additional insights to challenge myself to be better, based on how I would interpret someone else that I look up to and how they would handle this situation?"

You don't ask for someone to be a mentor and help you. I have people ask me all the time, "Oh, Tom, will you be my mentor?"

I say, "No. Do you want to do something? Get engaged with me, and as we're working on things, then you're going to learn," and that's how you develop those relationships. Part of that challenge is to approach people you're working with that you respect and learn from and ask for more.

Ask to be challenged, which ultimately makes you better if you do it productively.

CLIENTS

Clients can be prime candidates for a productive mentor relationship. As our next group of leaders proves, in many cases, working with clients can illuminate where you need to improve. Their field of expertise may be different than yours, but developing relationships with your clients can help you grow your strengths as well as see your weaknesses.

Particularly, working with experienced clients can put you in a fabulous position to pick up lots of valuable information. As you will see from the testimonies of the following entrepreneurs, when you help your clients, they are in a prime position to guide you as well. Keep reading to see how these leaders tapped a rich vein of instruction!

Bryon Beilman
Iuvo Technologies
Iuvotech.com

Iuvo is a Latin word that means "to help, assist, delight, or gratify," and we're an IT-managed service IT consulting company. We're an IT infrastructure for SMB and mid-market companies. We are the IT department for many companies that need it or that don't have one, or we are supplemental for larger companies that don't have the expertise on some of the technologies that we understand.

We're over twelve years old and delighting our customers every day. We have twenty-four employees at present. We're based outside of Boston in Westford, Ma.

Most of the people in our executive team belong to a peer group, and the peer groups are primarily from those companies in our industry that are not in our geography. So we're not competing with each other. We have NDAs, of course, so we share information and mentor each other. We can explain how we've done this and how we've solved particular problems. Then we collectively make each other better and stronger. We're active in these things, and everybody walks away with some accountability for what we're doing. Because when you're in a leadership role, we spend time mentoring the people around us who are in our company. But sometimes, finding that peer mentorship is sometimes harder to do.

We've embraced an open-book mentality where we share everything with the employees. The only things we don't share is maybe some HR-sensitive stuff or anything related to salary. We have some formal and informal mentorship. The formal one is when people start with the company, they get to shadow somebody for at least the first sixty days.

Being in an IT services company, they have to learn how we do business, and they have to learn our customers. It wouldn't serve our customers or us to throw people into situations where they're not ready. We want everybody to be successful because it's a relationship-based business, so they need to understand how to do that. Formally, it's probably about sixty days that somebody shadows another. Almost all positions are mentored and shadowed.

Our business can be tricky because we have a way that we do business. We have a set of tools, a set of processes, and various things, and new employees have to understand that. Because we serve many different customers, they have to become familiar with those customers and their uniqueness and their relationships. We call it "drinking from the firehose." We make sure to give new employees a chance to get a little sip at a time because otherwise, it'd be overwhelming. If you don't mentor and don't guide people along, then the employee is not doing their best work, and the customer is not getting the best service.

Throughout my career, I've had different managers who believed in me. I don't think I've had a formal mentor, but I do a lot of reading. I read about the same business leaders that most people read about, like Steve Jobs. One book I love a lot is *The Start-up of You* by Reid Hoffman, the LinkedIn founder. The mentors whom I've learned from have been authors. I read quite a bit.

I also have the advantage that, because we serve so many customers who are CEOs, is that I learn from seeing people succeed. I see certain traits in them. So while I don't do a formal mentorship, I work with this customer, and they seem to get it. They seem to understand things. My mental model is to look at them to ask what they doing that seems to be different than other people and why. How do they handle adversity?

I wish I would've had a formal mentor. My mentors were when I was younger in my life: managers or bosses who guided me in a good direction. But learning from your clients probably helps you learn from their mistakes, and you might not make them. We learn from our mistakes too.

Mistakes are super important. This weekend, I was talking to my wife about it because I've got children in college and high school, and now I want them to make some mistakes. I want them to make a series of small mistakes, so they can learn from them and avoid the more significant errors. I've made lots of mistakes, and those are the things that stick in my mind more than anything else: the pain of mistakes and recovering from them and learning. I attribute that to management. The true metal of doing something right is how you handle adversity. Anybody can manage the good times. But how do you manage it in those tough times?

I mentor my children. Of course, you mentor your children as much as they let you. I think they need secondary sources of mentoring. A lot of times, they're not going to take your advice for it because you're a parent.

But I'm active in that process at work a couple of ways. In my role, I have more information about the business than anybody. My job as a CEO is to break barriers down for people to get their job done. I share insights with them, such as the big picture, and I explain why a decision is made. When people are involved in a project, and if they understand why we're doing it, what the impact is, then they have a greater understanding. It also increases their business knowledge because people sometimes are good at one specific thing. We have people who are technical and customer service oriented, but they may not understand the business impact.

I think of mentoring more as working closely with employees. I never think about it as mentoring. I share information with them, which lets me see the *aha moment* when they say, "That makes a lot of sense." Then they go on and carry that understanding in their mind because nobody wants to be told to do something and not understand why. We hire smart people, so if you tell them what's going on, they typically will embrace that.

Everybody in the company works to make each other better. When you hire the right people, they will help mentor each other. I have to lead by example. I never thought of it before as mentoring, but more of enabling people with the information and helping them grow.

Some entrepreneurs come with some ideas in an area where they're strong. I'm in a technical field, and a lot of the entrepreneurs I've worked with come up with a technical idea—new semiconductor, a new molecule, a new whatever—to build the business, and they understand. They come in with a technical background, and they can do amazing things.

But they may not be strong in other areas like sales, marketing, HR, and finance. HR can typically evolve, and understanding basic-level finance is probably not too difficult. But for a typical entrepreneur to understand real marketing, such as understanding their market and how to market correctly, I don't know if that comes naturally to anybody unless they're coming from a marketing background.

Building a high-performance sales organization requires understanding all the metrics and how the sales process works. I've had to do it consistently. I think those are the areas that entrepreneurs I deal with and meet. That was the area that I had to learn the most. We built our company on relationships and referrals. But it wasn't until later in the company that we had to say, "Well, we should probably do marketing and understand how to make sales consistently."

My chief role besides culture and strategy is the sales and marketing in this company, and I'm a not a sales person. If we looked at the history of the company, we've grown pretty much 20 to 30 percent per year for the last twelve years. We've been on the *Inc.* 5,000 fastest-growing companies and the *Boston Business Journal*'s 50 fastest-growing companies in the state over the previous three years. So we're continuing to grow at a nice pace.

If I were to write a book, I would advise you to leverage your network. Constantly build it. All along, I've offered to help people, and I didn't think about it, but I've mentored people all along in my LinkedIn network, for people I know. It's good to help people when you don't need them, right?

Create those real relationships every day, and those same people will be there for you. People want to do business with people they like. Good people and honest people will recommend you and refer business to you. A lot of people wait until they need a network of people and then build it as they go along and build those relationships. It doesn't matter what you're doing. I think it'll be valuable to any entrepreneur.

I've been to some networking meetings where people are networking to network. For me, I want to build. I'm fascinated by what people do; I'm fascinated with helping people succeed. Anybody who asks me, I'll talk to anybody. Anybody who calls me and wants to chat about some insight, I'll take the call, and I would do it without any gain.

Helen Feber
Referential
Referentialinc.com

I formerly worked for Hewlett Packard, where I had several different roles but ended up as a product manager. One of the most significant issues we had when launching a product was not having enough customers for journalists to interview about the new offering. I voiced, "Somebody needs to start a reference program!" After I'd left to pursue a career in consulting, I got a call back from HP asking, "Would you be willing to help us start an advocacy program?"

And I agreed.

In 1994, to begin with, it was only me, but over time, both the HP program and my consulting business grew considerably from there. Over the decades, we've kept our consulting business laser-focused on customer advocacy and developing programs for clients of all sizes. I love the advocacy space. I enjoy talking to my client's customers to figure out what they're looking for in terms of engaging an advocacy program. Many people want to highlight themselves to enhance their careers, and sometimes they want to get their company positive public exposure too, so it can be a real win-win.

As Referential has grown, we've developed mentoring as a 360-degree activity. Any of our staff can expect to be mentored—not only by peers and management but also by subordinates and clients. Depending on any particular set of actions, priorities, or projects going on, there's always a different pool of talent available to help provide that mentoring. In addition, at a more formal level, we perform account reviews where it tends to be slightly more client and management-level mentoring of our staff.

Each day, there's a constant exchange of ideas taking place among our team. We've created that environment both in terms of the in-office setting and the online tools available to make it easy for staff—no matter where they are located—to have access to thought-leadership ideas and knowledge sharing. Mentoring is part of our culture. It doesn't have to be a one-on-one relationship; everyone is available to mentor others as they need.

For our business, a pivotal moment was when Fred Reichheld brought the whole net promoter score concept to market and released a book called *The Ultimate Question: Driving Good Profits and True Growth* (2006). I had the privilege of attending one of Fred's presentations, and he signed my copy. It was lovely because it was the first time that anybody had been brave enough to put a reasonably simple concept into the market to assess the happiness of customers. He managed to break it down to something straightforward and has a one-question test for it. I appreciated that because it created a paradigm shift around how we could work with our clients to improve their scores.

As I think about the biggest mistake we have made along the way, it was that we should have created the knowledge-sharing environment sooner than we did. When I look at where we are today and the phenomenal growth I see in my staff, I wish we'd done it faster.

Day in day out, I'm continually mentoring and being mentored by my staff. We're a consultancy, so we're mentoring our clients as well. But it's more than being a subject matter expert. For me, it's about business management, mentoring on how to be a consultant. I mentor our clients on how to consult because they're going to have to do the same with their management. They often don't have that skill set, even within large companies. We help them and mentor them to empower them and give them context. It's a holistic approach to mentoring. I believe you should never stop doing it!

I think about how the market has changed: millennials are now in decision-making positions within companies, and how they work with online information is different than former generations. In many situations, our millennial employees are mentoring more mature staff on the new style of doing things. I appreciate their input because there are always innovative new ideas that we can then bring to our clients, and I'm always open to being schooled.

Look at how the sales cycle has turned on its head from the old days. Today, somebody has a business issue, and one of the first steps they take is to reach out to their network of friends, colleagues, and peers and ask, "Has anybody seen this, and how did you solve it?"

It's all being done over social media. When a proposed solution surfaces, they talk to their colleagues, "Well, who's using this to solve this problem?" Someone will answer, "Oh, I am." Then they talk to one another.

In the meantime, the vendor of the solution has no clue that it has a prospective customer until way down the buyer's journey when a lot of advocate conversations have already happened. Eventually, the vendor gets approached when someone says, "Here's an RFP." But they're oblivious to the customer advocates in their installed base that have facilitated this engagement.

I think the dawning realization that any of your customers can get tapped at any time through social media means you've got to keep your customer base happy in a different way than you used to. You used to have a few key customers who you wined and dined and kept smiling, and you trotted them out as references. Well, those days are long gone. I appreciate the way my staff keeps me up to date with the latest apps and where the conversations are taking place. Often, it's in areas I would never have thought of looking. So we are constantly learning from one another.

We work a lot in the high-tech space and have our headquarters in Silicon Valley. The biggest issue I see among entrepreneurs is having them actively listen to their customers or users—not appear to listen—and reflect on what they've heard. So often, it's a person with a bright idea who has a gadget with lots of acronyms associated with it. It's good stuff, but they don't listen to how to position it. They're in the market in terms of the business problem their app or gadget solves, but I see a lot of good ideas start to die quickly because the person with the idea isn't listening or reflecting on what is being said by users to understand how to attractively position it.

The other challenge I see is getting entrepreneurs to understand when and where they need help and when to bring in the right skill set. The general attitude tends to be, "I can do it all." Well, no, they may be a bright person who knows how to program or how to design chips, but they don't know everything. The right skills are needed in each role early on to get over the initial significant hurdles to get a company launched, and that's where I see failure taking place.

To be a successful entrepreneur, you have to have that vision, but you have to be willing to take the input, adapt, and add. That's what it takes to be successful because if you develop tunnel vision, that's where things go adrift. You have to play to people's strengths. You'll get people coming into your organization, and you might've hired them into one role when, in fact, they're talented in another position. Have the courage to allow them to try another role, and see how that success plays out.

I believe in leading by example: be the person your staff aspires to be. Within our focus area, I don't want to ask somebody to do something I would never dream of doing. When I assign a task or project, I've always experienced it first, and I have that knowledge of what it takes to complete it. Some of the things are "grunt" work, and every company has those aspects, but it's not that I haven't done it. Leading from the front enables me to give guidance, and maybe it's such a tedious job I might recommend, "You have to break it down and do it for fifteen minutes, and then do something else. Come back and do another fifteen minutes, and keep chugging through it so that you don't get totally burnt out."

There are different ways you can guide, but I think by tackling each type of task within my field and having had that exposure and experience myself, especially in a young growing company, it helps significantly.

Finally, my guidance would be to understand what success means to you. For us, it isn't the dollars—don't get me wrong, it's lovely when our revenue goes up—but for me, it's about the people. I want my staff to feel like they're learning and able to share as they're growing as consultants. I want them to be empowered to elevate our clients. I don't want them to do just what's on the contract but to also help our clients as individuals. As managers of their programs, I want my staff to help our clients elevate their careers and advance their brand in the marketplace. That could mean writing a blog about them, suggesting a speaking slot, or putting them forward for awards.

Having that human-to-human connection makes a remarkable difference, and it will help you through bad times when things aren't going so well. The client's going to be loyal to you, and it will help you as an individual to grow and be able to mentor and be mentored.

Dan Malven
4490 Ventures
4490ventures.com

My firm is called 4490 Ventures, an institutionally backed venture capital firm that invests primarily in Series A–stage software-based businesses. We invest broadly across the software spectrum but focus on a particular stage of the company: the first institutional capital companies raising $5 to $10 million. We look for businesses that are generally disrupting existing industries through not new products but products that enable new business models.

One of our most exciting investments has been for a company called Level Ex. I'm on the board of that one. The easy way to think about it is we make video games for doctors. Now, unpacking that a bit, we create super-realistic, clinically accurate mobile experiences for doctors to train them, educate them on new drugs and devices and procedures. It's not for medical school students or doctors in the early stages of their careers; it's for experienced doctors when there are new drugs or devices that they need to understand better, and we've created a good way for them to do that.

We do it by specialty, so we have different apps. For example, 40 percent of all neurosurgeons in the country are registered users, and I believe that 30 percent of all general surgeons are registered users. We have 20 percent of just one year old. We release these apps into the app stores, and the doctors are consuming them voraciously and telling their colleagues about them. So that's been an exciting thing to watch.

I learned the venture business from a man who mentored me early in my career, and I've brought a lot of those lessons to what I do. He's an individual named Fred Wilson at Union Square Ventures. I'd never been in the venture business before, but I shadowed him, and we worked closely together for many years. I mostly learned by watching, then I would ask, "Why did you do that this way? Why was that?"

So 80 to 90 percent of our mentoring relationship was me watching. Then we'd take 10 percent of our time, and I'd asked some questions, and Fred would unpack why he was doing the things he was doing as a venture investor. So I took those lessons with me, and I use them every single day.

I was a technical founder before I got into the business. I founded two software companies, and I was writing code in both. I described it as writing code by night and raising money by the day. So it was a great experience understanding at a deep level of software-based innovations. Then, at the same time, understanding the implementation of those innovations into commercial activities.

At our firm, we are a flat partnership, a partnership of peers. So we don't have junior folks rising through the ranks to mentor. Our mentorship is about the CEOs, the executive teams, that we invest in, and with whom we sit on the boards. We spend a lot of our time with those portfolio company teams. A lot of our job is mentoring and offering advice for those founders.

I learn from works of fiction, and it's been valuable to me because it goes back to the Shakespearean drama of the core emotions of greed, avarice, and love. I often deal with the human emotions of the CEO and the founders, and I'm not what's called a control investor, meaning I don't take a control position. I don't have more than 51 percent of ownership. We're minority investors, so we have to influence without having control. We have to get inside the psyches of the people we're trying to change. Whether it's books or movies, high-quality fiction is illuminating to witness how people think and how to read their emotions. So that's probably been more of it for me than reading business books.

The venture business is like Major League Baseball. If you're a career 300 hitter, you're in the Hall of Fame. You have a lot of lawsuits in the venture business; it's the way it works. If you don't, then you're not taking enough risks for the significant outcomes. Well, I invested in a company where, on paper, all those acquisitions should have fit together well. But the human component of those integrations did not work.

We had prominent personalities, founders who were suddenly coming together, and they all had their unique points of view. The risk of those integrations not working is something that I discounted, and I lost my money.

I took that learning, and now I think more intentionally before I invest in something that has that dynamic or when I think of allowing companies wherein I'm on the board to do acquisitions that look good on paper but may fail because of the human dynamic.

Learning how to manage human egos is continuous learning. You can never understand it too well. I spent a lot of time thinking about that quote by Maya Angelou, "I've learned that people will forget what you said, people will forget what you did, but people will never forget how you made them feel."

I spend a lot of time thinking, "If I say this, is that CEO is going to feel inadequate? Are they going to feel bad?" No matter what I say, or even no matter what they say, how were they feeling at that moment? I do my best to navigate that and shape where I want the outcomes to be. I spend much time thinking about what's going on behind the scenes in terms of their ego. They might not even be aware.

I mentor to a large extent. A good anecdote would be talking to a founder about loosening the reins a little bit, even though they got to where they did by controlling. It's one thing for a business to get from zero to fifty employees. Generally, a founder can have a lot of direct influence over all the parts of the company until they get to about fifty employees. But once you get above that number, it becomes layers, and they have to influence through layers, which becomes a lot more complicated. They have to loosen up and learn how to delegate.

The former CEO of Twitter, Dick Costolo, is a friend of mine, and he told me to watch what good politicians do. He said that politicians have to influence and inspire through multiple layers because they're talking to so many people at once. So they have to make their message digestible through different layers of people.

I had to explain that to the CEO I was working with and advise him to develop that skill set. If he wanted the business to grow, it would only do so if he could learn to delegate. I don't like the term "giving up control" because that has a negative connotation. "Influencing through other means" was how I described it to this CEO, and that resonated with him, and he started changing the way he influenced the course of his organization.

It's hard to generalize where entrepreneurs need the most help because they come in all shapes and sizes. One piece of advice I have is to be more self-aware and more accurate to who you are and what your skill sets are and then surround yourself with people that augment it. Don't try and be too many things. Teams exist to fill in the gaps, so be self-aware of your shortcomings, and then work together to create an organization that fills them. Many entrepreneurs are not wired that way, so that takes some influence to get them to that place.

If I were to write a book, I'd advise people to focus on solving a genuinely unique problem, and by the nature of the problem, your solution gets more and not less valuable over time. A unique solution is a scarce resource. Just as in any physical system, the other resources flow to where the limited supply is found. So if you solve that one particular thing with a way to do it that increases in value over time, you'll attract the people, capital, and other components needed to fill out a complete solution.

Melissa Gonzalez
Lion'esque Group
Lionesquegroup.com

A pop-up is a short-term retail experience; it's an opportunity for brands and retailers to make a human connection with consumers and their customers. At our last count, last year, we had created about 150 experiences, but we have been doing it a while. I did my first pop-up with a brand in September 2009, so we're almost at a decade here and have vast experience in pop-up retail.

We do about one a month, but there are quarters where we do multiple per month, so it's been diverse over the years. In the beginning, we did it with a lot of emerging brands. Shopify was becoming a thing, so many of them didn't have e-commerce, and now you're seeing it becoming a mainstream opportunity for brands and retailers. We've done it for a decade across sectors, working not only with apparel and accessories, but also with mattresses, luggage, and cheese. So it's been an exciting time.

I have favorite experiences for different reasons. We recently did one at the end of the last quarter the previous year. That was interesting to me because it was a little bit different for us, and there wasn't necessarily a retail component. We did a pop-up dinner with Amazon Prime Video to gain awareness around the season two premiere of *The Marvelous Mrs. Maisel* show. We created a 1950s version of the iconic Carnegie Deli that used to exist in New York City. So that was just a fun activation from the creative side, creating an authentic environment and immersing people in storytelling.

The first thing we do is dive into what our clients are looking to achieve. Who's their customer? What is their journey like today? What's the story we're telling in the space? What's the right location to do that? What's the footprint we need to do that? We dive into an ideation phase before anything, and some have more figured out than others when they approach us, but that's how it starts. We try to understand as much as we can and do a deep dive with them and then create a program.

It's been a journey, and we've taken our twists and turns over the ten years—evolving as retail has evolved. I didn't leave Wall Street saying, "I want to do pop-ups." I left Wall Street knowing I wanted to do something more creative. Wall Street had given me a solid foundation in having business acumen.

When working on a trading desk, you're problem-solving, matching markets, or digesting information as quickly as possible all the time. That experience gave me a good foundation. I had an affinity for retail stocks and technology stocks, which is relevant in what I do today in understanding what makes a company work, what moves the needle for them, what becomes a challenge for them and what hits their margins, and things like that.

That has given me a unique perspective and built a creative team around me. Although I am creative, I also produced indie films and hosted a TV show while I was working on Wall Street. Bringing in a design team and project managers who understand retail have been marrying the two, and over the ten years, making sure that I'm learning as much as I can, we're staying nimble, and we're adjusting as the world does. Over the past five years, it's happened at such a rapid growth rate.

I work hard to make sure we're understanding technology and understanding how that technology is shaping consumers, their expectations, and needs and how retailers have to listen and be mindful of that and keep in mind when designing and masterminding an in-store experience.

I make sure I take my pauses to read and go to trade shows and conferences and make sure I'm always learning as much as I can to be at the forefront of the conversation so we can bring that to our clients. But it's been a learning curve over the past ten years too. I'm always working on these: How I scale the company? How do we have the right team in place to provide the resources that we need to our clients? What are those needs?

We have three buckets of clients. We have fast-growing digital natives, and for the most part, they don't have in-house store teams. They're digital natives, and they know e-commerce very well, so we serve as an adjunct retail department that currently doesn't exist.

When we work with our second bucket, which are those mass brands that may have had stores but are looking to rethink or elevate the physical experience, it's a different conversation. We're working closely with an existing store team, and we have to synergize with them as possible, in helping with some of those pain points.

The third bucket is real estate, and that's been an interesting change over these ten years. When we first started, we would be hitting the phones and begging landlords and real estate developers to allow us to do short-term retail, and now it's become table stakes for many of them, understanding they have to have platforms for it. We're currently serving as advisors to many of those developers, and thinking, What's the right footprint to short-term retail? What does it mean to create a turnkey program? Where should they invest? How do they attract brands? It's been an exciting evolution over the ten years.

I recommend attending conferences. Shoptalk is a great conference, as they've become the conference to go to for thought leadership quickly, so Shoptalk is always on my list. Go with a game plan, because it's a robust conference where you can do a lot in the few days you're there. If you're looking at retail tech, I still like NRF in January. RetailX has now combined GlobalShop, RetailTouchPoints, RFID Journal, and IRCE all at the same time, in Chicago in June, so that's a big one.

I also think it's essential to think worldly. There's a lot of innovation happening in the retail world outside of the US, so I'll be going to the World Retail Summit in May. Find an opportunity at least once a year to do something global, so you can see what's happening in other parts of the world. It is insightful.

I like books, I like magazines, and I like podcasts. So on the book side, I like *Thank You for Being Late* by Thomas Friedman. It's an interesting story about how an opportunity came up because somebody showed up late, and it gave this person a chance to sit and think of an idea. I think the more important message is that we're always running as fast as we can as founders to do the next thing, and sometimes we believe to be busy means being successful. But sometimes it's when you carve out those moments of quiet that the best ideas come out.

On the podcast side, I recommend *How I Built This*, which has a lot of great stories of founders and how they created their paths and the challenges that they've had, and they have great conversations in that aspect. Then I always keep up with *Forbes* and *Inc.*, and in the retail world also with *design:retail* magazine, *VMSD*, *Women's Wear Daily*, of course, *Glossy, Digiday*. They're all helpful publications.

There are mistakes, and there are experiments. On the experimental side, when I first started the company, I thought we were dealing with emerging brands, and none of them had proper e-commerce because it was ten years ago. Shopify wasn't as robust as it is today, and I don't even know if Square existed. My first experiment was I thought I was going to scale by creating an e-commerce marketplace, and I did that for about eighteen months and quickly realized that it was not my core competency, and I like to be in front of people.

Physical retail is what excited me, and e-commerce is a whole other animal. I burnt through that cash and then shut the company down. I was still emotionally connected to it, and it was so painful for me to realize it didn't work, but sometimes, that's the smartest thing you can do. Understand that if something doesn't work—and it sometimes has nothing to do with you, your skillset, or your ability—it's just that it wasn't the right fit. I experienced that learning, but on the other side, it has made me such a better consultant. In that period, I learned a lot about e-commerce and the challenges. If we're going to create successful store experiences, we need to understand how the online world works.

Sometimes, I think a mistake is when you say yes to everything, and I think, in the beginning, it's what you do, and learning to edit. Some of that has been helpful by becoming a mom and picking my time and bandwidth; I'm more protective of my time since I've had my daughter. You do things to be supportive of others, but other times, you have to choose: do I do this, or do I go home and have some family time?

That life balance has been a good check for me, but in the beginning, I said yes to so many things, and sometimes I did things because they seemed to be free, but nothing is free. They might not cost you any dollars, but they cost time, and time is money, and it can be a distraction. That's been one of my biggest learnings along the way.

The second has been being smarter about how I build a team. I've had some great team members along the way, but I was being smarter as a founder and understanding what's the team you need around you. Identify your strengths and, as the company evolves and grows, determine which skill sets you need around you. What compliments you?

In the beginning, I think I hired a lot of people who did the same thing, and so, we weren't as well-rounded as we could be. It took me a minute to lean back on my learnings from working on a trading desk where it's such an open-air environment. In the entrepreneurial world, everybody talks about this open-office environment by being so new and innovative, and that's precisely what trading desks have always been.

I came from that world, and when you're in that open, collaborative environment, you quickly learn how much culture matters. I didn't pick that up and bring that in-house as soon as I could have, because culture is everything, especially when you're a small company. But that's the only way you can make change happen; that's how you have internal synergy. People thrive off each other if it's an excellent cultural fit. So understanding that skill set and cultural fit is essential, and as we've continued to fine-tune that, I've seen changes happen with how we operate as a team.

I've been a mentor for XRC Labs, which is a retail tech accelerator program, and I can't say I'm involved with them daily, but I have been a mentor. I find it interesting, and they learn from you.

Megan Berry, the founder of REVEAL, was a company I was a mentor to, and they're in the pop-up world but in a different way—by having a pop-up kiosk. Having had the opportunity to work with her and help her shape her offering based on what I've seen in the market was exciting. I root for her, and when I see her win awards, I'm happy I was able to be a sounding board for her.

Sometimes, when you're a founder and a mom, you only have so much bandwidth, but I try. Sometimes I'm an advisor in a one-off capacity, and we get phone calls through people who are trying to get into this market. Not necessarily in a competitive way to me, but maybe they're trying to figure out how to attack it from a real estate or brand side. I was an advisor to the founding team of Storefront for two years, advising them how to think of markets and what's the most important thing to focus on for growth.

I was also a mentor and advisor for a company called FotoFwd (now called M-ND Media), and they created a technology company and were among the early ones of capturing photos for designated hashtags. We've integrated them into our pop-ups when it made sense. I have more examples than I thought, but I do try to do it when I can, and I think that"s how the world goes round.

There are plenty of people who have been kind enough to be a sounding board for me—taking the time to sit with me and help me think through things. Some more consistently, some on a one-off basis. It's important to give back when you can and when it makes sense.

I get two buckets of entrepreneurs seeking advice. I get the entrepreneurial side, "I've left my corporate job, and I want to build a brand, and how do I do that?"

I always say, "I don't know that I've been the master of building my brand. I built a company," but I give a lot of advice about staying focused and creating a filter, as that's advice I received early on that I'm always trying to make sure I revisit.

Creating a filter is so important when you start a business, and by a filter, by establishing that, then you help yourself make better choices. A filter could mean, "as a company, and I expand, do I want to expand geographically? Do I want to expand vertically? What does my perfect customer look like?" Even if it's B2B or B2C, I think, on the B2C side, people go through that practice, "I'm catering to female shoppers, aged twenty to forty." But on the B2B side, I think sometimes a lot of people forget to do the same thing and ask what an ideal customer is to them.

Make sure you have the right filter. Sometimes you're going to close a deal because of the dollar amount; sometimes you might close a deal because it's strategic. And what does strategic mean?

How is that going to help you grow? When you're lucky, you get a client that checks both boxes. Then, as you think of growth, do you want to be on the East Coast? Do you want to be national? Do you want to be global? I give a lot of advice on that filtering side because I think it's so crucial in the beginning. Be open-minded and flexible, and make sure you're going back every six to twelve months and evaluating that filter; it helps you inform a lot of those decisions that you make as a founder.

If I were to write another book, I would write about retail 2030, like where we're going to be in the next decade. But if I were to write one on the entrepreneurial side, I don't know if I would write so much a "how to do" book, but I would probably in the first few chapters, share my learning. I would also tap and incorporate interviews with some people I've admired, and I've seen them grow their businesses successfully.

I think we're so seduced by thinking growth means we raised money, and that's not always the case. So I would want to dive into those different scenarios—of when raising money makes sense and when it doesn't. I would discuss the advantages of growing it on your own. When does a merger make sense? And walk the readers through those scenarios because I think that, as founders, that's such a tricky area to understand.

Tedde Van Gelderen
Akendi
Akendi.com

One of the main things that define us is having the belief that what you do is going to work out and learning that stuff doesn't happen in the way that you want. Things will take time. They will not always go well. You have to fail a lot. Deep down, we must know that we will figure it out eventually.

It will never be only failures; there will always be some successes. You might have five things that fail, then six elements will succeed—it will never be a hundred-percent failure. Know that you're going to build upon those successes and that the failure rate will go down. You will get more often one in five to one in three, and you will have periods where it's even higher and better than that. Ultimately, if you make more good decisions than bad, you will end up in a better place if you persevere. I find again and again that whenever you do this thing, people drop off too soon and don't continue. They don't keep going, and that is the significant distinguishing factor between people who get there and people who don't.

I haven't had mentors other than myself, and that's not because I don't think there are good mentors out there. There are tons of good mentors out there, but my business is so specific and unique. I believe many companies are like that—so specific that it's hard to be coached in a way that's going to get you there quicker or more effectively.

Ultimately, it is you. You're the one making the decisions. You're the one that's going to get there. The coach will cheer you on and give you general pointers that are no doubt useful, but I've never relied—neither heavily nor lightly—on them. I relied on myself to make the decisions to get to where I am now.

One thing that happened to work well with my business was the use of my website. I am always surprised by how little companies rely on their website as a source of leads, sales, and presenting themselves. It's ironic because I think whenever you ask anybody about needs that they have—whether it's a new car, a service, a thing that they're looking for—about 99.99 percent of the time, what do they do? They go online to look for it.

When it comes to businesses, I'm surprised by the answers I receive from entrepreneurs when I ask, "How do you get your sales?" They give various responses such as their network, the people they know, and the quality of their work. I hardly ever hear them say, "It's because we have a good website." I explain to them three things. Do you do the service I'm seeking? Do you have the product I'm seeking? Have you done this before? Can I trust you? Are you a company that can deliver?

When you combine all those elements, the website is an ideal vehicle to answer those questions. In my business, it's been one of the critical pieces I got right early on and led to where I am now. My website is so well equipped to answer the questions. I got my first client through my website, not because I knew somebody, or I was networking.

Businesspeople say that their business is different. I go back to my first questions. How do you find out about your competitors? How do you find out about other people that do what you do? It's always the same answers: we go to their website. You search. Okay, if you find other people that way, why wouldn't you be found yourself?

This is something that went right for me from the early stages. I've done this business now three times in total. Every single time, it always started with an excellent website.

I'm not officially a mentor, but I am part of groups with people like me who have small businesses or run businesses, and we regularly talk to each other. I'm a mentor for other people, but they're also mentors for me, which I find to be a powerful thing because they're going to be good at parts of their businesses. I can tell them about my website experience, for example, and they will tell me about their HR experience. I find those peer group meetings to be super powerful in coaching because they're not overall coaching things. They don't coach you on all aspects of your business. We all have our expertise, and we all have our good and bad sides. I love to talk to people about certain aspects of their business that they're good at and take nuggets.

In these peer groups, by far, the most often discussed topic is HR, which is a challenge in any business. Apart from what I just talked about the website and services, which is the core offering that you have?

The biggest problem is to keep a healthy team. How do you keep a healthy team together? How do you grow a healthy team? How do you create a good culture? The topic that comes up most often when we share stories is what we do in bad situations. We have to deal with some cases where there's a conflict or something doesn't work well. Also, how do you maintain that? Especially when you grow from three people to eight to twenty to thirty, dynamics change. We talk a lot about the differences that happen at each point and what it means for our businesses.

My business is smaller; we have fifteen people right now. At some point, a couple of years ago, it was twenty-five. What I find is that a lot of people make an excuse for a small business to say, "We can't compete with the bigger companies in terms of the HR, and the benefits or the culture that they have around mentoring and helping people." I always found that concerning to hear because I believe that any business size can have mature coaching or support in the company. It's the people; the more experienced people in the company have to play that role. There is no excuse to say we're too small for that.

I think you have to treat yourself seriously and maturely and put the same practices in place as big companies. We can have the same things in place, and they don't always necessarily mean more money. We don't have to go on fancy retreats or have all these prominent speakers come in or do something fancy. You can do much more personal things led by senior people in the company to create that culture where you get the same support you would get in a bigger company.

We talked about this fallacy that we can't compete with bigger companies. Well, I think you can. You should think about it as if you're a big company and find suitable ways around the money aspect of significant investments because ultimately, the senior people know. They worked in these places. They've seen all the good practices and all the good things and the good tactics that are happening. Don't think that you're small and can't do it. Say you're small and you're going to do it differently but reach the same goals.

I wrote a book called *Experience Thinking* in 2018. It's about my domain, the field where I work. It's customer experience, user experience, and helping companies, which is what my company does—building products and services that are easier to use that people better understand, and that are more effective. The book was an outlet to capture a lot of the ideas I've had over the years that I've talked to our clients about but never formally captured.

The goal audience for the book is not practitioners, because they should already know most of what's in the book. It's for people that buy services like ours. We want to make things easier. That's great, but how do you do this? What are the key questions you ask yourself? How do I buy this if I do buy this from another company? What are the things I should be thinking about and watch for, and what's the process that they would go through? That's what I find often is lacking, and the understanding is low in a lot of our clients.

I wrote the book in a way as a guide to tell people; this is what the space is about. This is what you should care about. This is the process of how to go through this because for customer experience, design, and user experience design, there are some models out there, but they're not as widely accepted and shared as I hoped they would be. I see the book as a way to say, "Please look at the experience first," and that's what *Experience Thinking* is about. It's when you think about the experience and what you need to do to deliver that. The book helps create that guide to structure the process of getting there.

It's also an outlet to mentor readers. When you read the book, you will have questions. You will have understandings. I get the awareness now. I get how this works, but then what do I do? What we found is that we typically coach people in three distinct ways.

One way is to help them do it themselves. Part of our business is also doing training. We found that's not always answering the question for them because they get trained, but the field is so new and so unexplored for them that they find it hard to do it themselves.

A second version of coaching that we often do is a derivative of that. Yes, we train you, but we're also going to be there when you try it out. We're going to work with you as you try out these new techniques and these new processes we just learned and taught you. That's the second form of coaching.

Sometimes, our clients are so scared that they say, well, "I don't want to start doing that yet. Can you show me?" In the process of showing it and letting them peek over our shoulders, they learn a lot about the field.

That combination of these three things of training them, coaching them, and having them do it themselves while they watch us work well in most cases where we feel we can make a difference.

Another book that I find that I don't see enough written about is *The Next Step Up*. This space that I'm in—the user-experience, customer-experience base—is rapidly growing. There are a lot of people who stepped into it, or they learned about it, then they think it's cool, and they start to work in it. There's an emergence now of a lot of teams growing within companies that do this work.

What I find is that there's such a diversity of people that walk into this space that there's not enough time spent on good structures of managing teams in this space. I would love to write another book about how to manage a team with this user-experience expertise or CX expertise. Drawing from my own experience, of course, but also talking to other people about the different circumstances that you get into, whether it's a big organization with a large structure or a small tech startup that needs to get by on a shoestring. There are different dynamics and cultures. I'd love to write a book about the management of those teams.

BOOKS

Many of us turn to books for mentoring, as you have done! Books are natural mentors, and we often seek the consult of books for specific instruction and answers to our questions. We have found that entrepreneurs, business leaders, and CEOS are usually avid readers.

Much information on just about any topic one can imagine can be found among the vast offerings of books that can help you learn something new. Whether you are seeking a more productive way to run your company or instruction on how to scale your organization, you can be certain mentoring is available on the printed page.

Our next group of leaders recommends the books they found to be critical to their successes.

Cameron Herold
COO Alliance
Cooalliance.com

I've always believed in what I call R&D, which stands for "rip off and duplicate." I try to find people who are already doing something in a significant way and see how I can take the best of what they're doing and bring it into my business.

As an example, I've been recently thinking about my books and how they're marketing tools, and I met with a friend at a group called the Genius Network. I'm in my fifth year with the Genius Network now. The founder, Joe Polish, is my daily accountability partner.

One of the members, Paul Collagen, has significant expertise around podcasting. When I checked his book and saw how much his book was bringing people back to his website and into his sales funnels, I realized it was a tremendous marketing tool (his book was still a fantastic resource).

I'm looking to take pieces of that and weave them into all five of my books, so every time each of my books goes to next reprint, I'll be weaving in more of the marketing, so that's the way that mentoring has worked by joining Mastermind groups and investing in myself.

As I said, I'm a member of the Genius Network. I've done seven years of strategic coaching. I've been to three Baby Bathwater events. I go to the main TED conference every year, and I've gone to five Mastermind Talks event. I've very invested in being around mentors so that I'm not the smartest person in the room, and that's how mentoring has grown my business.

My coaching is a core part of my business revenue. I coach seventeen CEOs, globally, plus their executive teams. When I'm teaching, I tend to get ideas for my own business. It either reinforces things that I know I should be doing or, as I'm working with someone on their business, I get insights into my own company.

For example, I was coaching Joe Polish from the Genius Network and working with him on some of his operational ideas. It struck me that everyone was marketing to entrepreneurs when it's the second-in-command that needs to learn how to grow their company. In that meeting, I realized I shouldn't be teaching Joe how to run his company; I should be showing his team how to build a company. I started the *Second in Command* podcast because of that meeting, and I also started the COO Alliance—because of that meeting.

From coaching and mentoring others, I learned a couple of significant business areas for myself to add. I think the mentor often gets value from learning. I get a lot of inspiration and energy when I coach someone, and they take the ideas and do something with it. It feels great. It feeds me. It shows me I have a lot of value in my work—that I'm not a drone pushing buttons. It's like when you get a great comment on one of my books, or I get someone who comments on my podcast; it feels good because I know they're using something, so that energy feeds me to do more.

I'd say that all my clients implement my advice because they're paying me $80,000 a year for three hours a month of coaching. So they're not doing it without wanting the ideas, but I don't try to be irritating to be correct; I don't push them to do it unless it feels right. Let's say during a ninety-minute coaching meeting, they come out with fifteen ideas. They might put ten of them in place, and they might take some of the other five ideas and merge them with their own. They take my idea and their idea, and it becomes what they will go with. I think all my coaching clients want to learn, and they're paying for that.

The one big mistake that always sticks out for me was back in 2006. I was the second-in-command, the chief operating officer, for a company called the 1-800-GOT-JUNK? We had taken the company from $2 million to around $100 million that year.

I'd been the COO. We'd gone from fourteen employees to three hundred employees, and we almost lost the company because, financially, the CEO and I did not know how to leverage our balance sheet. We didn't know how to go to the banks and get financing, and we kept spending the money we had as cash on growing the business, which works fine when you're a small entrepreneurial company. But when we needed to borrow more money to drive growth even further, the banks didn't want to loan to us. We'd spent the $5 million that we had in cash, and we thought it was great as we had no debt, and we had been profitable every year. We were the number 2 company in Canada to work on profitable growth, and we spent all our money on renovations. Then we needed to borrow money to get us through the next couple of months.

The bank said no because we didn't have any cash. We said we spent it.

They said, "Well, you shouldn't have. If you'd come to us with five million in the bank, we would have loaned you five million, but now that you spent the five, we won't loan you anything."

We said, "That's stupid."

And they said, "You don't understand finance."

What we realized was that we did not understand finance, but more importantly, neither of us had been listening to our VP of finance who was telling us to go slower, to get bank financing in place, that we were reckless, and that we were growing too fast.

We opened thirteen corporate locations, and he was telling us to be careful, and we kept saying, "No, it's okay. We have this cash." We didn't listen to him, and the significant learning was that if you're going to have people on your team, listen to them or hire people that you will hear. We needed to find a way to listen to the more quiet, analytical, amiable people when we were such dominant, expressive people.

Our VP of finance was telling us to slow down, but we kept saying, "Oh, don't worry about it. We're fine." We steamrolled over him until, suddenly, we had this new CFO come in, and she rang the fire alarm and said, "Holy s——, we're running out of cash." And we had to borrow $400,000 from Brian's mom to meet payroll.

Now we turned the company around, and we were fine, but that was a massive lesson for us. If you're going to have people in your company, you're hiring them because you want them to be a part of the team, so your job is to now listen to them.

Cash is like your oxygen. When you're four years old, and your mom or dad throw a penny into the swimming pool, and you dive down to get it, then come up gasping for air, you're not going to die. When you're twenty-five, and you go scuba diving for the first time, get down to eighty feet and get sick, but you probably won't die. When you're thirty-five, and you go scuba diving and get down to over a hundred feet and run out of oxygen, you will die.

As your company gets bigger, you can't go back to the bank of Mom or your bank account or mortgage your house. The zeros get too big. Friends-and-family funding is a smart way to grow because you don't have to pay interest on it, and you don't have to deal with audited financials as long as you know you're growing. We had no credit lines. We never gave up any equity.

We were profitable every single year for six years. We never went to Mom until suddenly, there was nowhere else to go. That's scary, but I think about a lot of entrepreneurs, and I think their parents and families should only give the money if the model is going to work. I think a lot of people have bad business models, and I think the key is to make sure they're working on a business model that will generate cash.

I have a bunch of mentors. I'm involved in four Mastermind groups right now, where I actively participate as a member. I'm going to War Room; I'm going to Genius Network next month. I'm going to the TED Conference in April, and I just came back from Abundance 360. I'm always around other CEOs because I try not to be the smartest person in the room. I think that would be probably the core of where I'm getting my mentoring right now—those Mastermind groups.

I think books and podcasts are powerful. I listen to a lot of audiobooks. I tell people think about your business and what you're working on over the next twelve months, then find books related to your work. Don't read the next business book that's trendy, because it might not have anything to do with what you're working on. Drive your learning toward what you're focusing on building. If you're hiring a bunch of people this year, read lots of books related to hiring, interviewing, and selecting people. If you're building out a board of advisors, read books about the board of advisors. If you're working on your sales funnels, learn everything about sales funnels.

The best book on hiring right now is *Who* by Brad and Geoff Smart. One of my favorite books recently is called *The Hard Thing About Hard Things* by Ben Horowitz. It's all related to the leadership lessons of building your company, onboarding people, wartime leadership building a business, and fast growth. Those would be probably my two strongest book recommendations.

Most of my coaching clients have about fifty employees when I start coaching them. They tend to be in the $5–10 million range when I start working with them, and I only work with high-growth companies. My criteria are that they have to be young, fun, entrepreneurial, high by role, high growth, pre-public, and then I obsess around the people side of the business first.

I look at alignment with the vision, getting all the right people into the company, getting rid of all the cultural cancers and nonperformers, building out a high-functioning team, and then building a company into a bit of a cult. The goal is for the company to become a magnet for exceptional talent, working on employee engagement (first), customer engagement (second), then profitability (third), and that's what scales. We tend to work on everything related to operations, execution, and culture.

The core of what I coach is probably in my first book, which is called *Double Double*, but another book of mine is *The Miracle Morning for Entrepreneurs,* which has some substantial tactical take-home value. Hal Elrod and I co-authored that together about eighteen months ago.

I think that most entrepreneurs and most people lack focus. They wake up in the morning, and they're busy being busy. They work on the urgent versus the critical few. They're working hard but not necessarily with any direction in mind. As an example, I woke up this morning, and I committed my top three goals. My accountability partner, Joe Polish, and I set our top three goals with each other, so I mapped out today my top three goals for the day, and that drives us both forward. So I know what Joe's three goals are for today, and he knows mine. Everything else will get done, but at least I'm going to focus on those.

I work with companies to help them get focused on their core values, core purpose, core demographics, understanding who they're marketing to, getting their teams to focus, making sure people have their top threes for the quarter, the month, and the week. It's an all-around focus.

If you have a light, and you disperse light, it can light up a room, but if you focus light, if you concentrate light, it becomes a laser, and it can cut through steel. How do we focus? We only have three resources, people, time, and money. How do we focus our time? How do we focus our people, and how do we focus our money to get us the highest ROI?

One of the ways you focus your people is to ask the following: What are the company's goals for the year? What are each of the business areas and goals for the quarter that will drive the company's goals for the year? What are each of the individual's goals for the quarter that will make their business area goals happen? What is each of the individual's goals for the month and the week that will make their business areas goals happen? And then a sign-off process to make sure that people know what people are working on, and they're working on the critical few things.

Business is so extraordinarily simple, but people overcomplicate it, and they also get sucked into the minutiae. Most people woke up this morning and started working on their email. They didn't start with their morning success habits. They didn't start by studying their top three goals for the day or by working on the critical few things. They got busy. They're busy and working hard, but it's like a fly trying to get out of a window. You keep banging your head on the window, but if you turn your head, there's a door that's open right here, where you can fly out.

The morning savers are the core part of the book. They start with S for silence, and it's showing up first thing in the morning, even before you get out of bed with a minute of silence to ease into the morning. Then it's actualization, so it's you, having an affirmation story, having your morning statement, the one statement that you make every day until it's become ingrained. My one affirmation statement for this year is that I'm grateful for everything in my life, and I say it every day, and I write it down every day in my gratitude journal. Then I have my visualization, which is listening to, or rereading part of, a book, or just all my vivid vision. I have my business vivid vision and my personal vivid vision.

Then it's exercise. I don't like exercising in the mornings, but it does kick-start your day. I do some burpees, or a seven-minute workout first thing in the morning, to get the blood flowing and the energy going. Then it's R for reading, even if it's five minutes of reading, not reading the newspaper or emails, but grabbing a book and spending five minutes reading in the morning. The last is scribbling, which is your writing. That's when I write in my journal, or my gratitude journal, in the morning. Those are the morning savers.

Then I have a list of a bunch of other habits as well where I have a pocket of probiotics and vitamins, so I take all my vitamins. I start every morning with a glass of lemon juice, I have a Palo Santo smudge that I like, and I smudge my whole body in the morning. I finish every shower with a cold shower first thing in the morning as well. Then I eat some protein to kick-start my brain first thing in the morning. Protein shake, or some cold cuts, or something like egg white to get my brain going.

My vivid vision for the COO Alliance is we're launching this network of *Second in Command*, so it's called the City Forums, the COO Alliance City Forums, where we will have groups of *Second in*

Commands meeting every two months in thirty cities all over North America over the next two years. The goal is to grow that locally into a network of *Second in Commands* globally, so that's what I'm focusing on building. The reason is that there are so many groups for entrepreneurs to learn and network from, but there was nowhere for the second-in-command to go.

I describe all aspects of my company, the marketing, sales, advertising as well as what my members and employees are saying. I describe it three years from now so that everyone can see what I can see. It's not a one-sentence statement but a four-page description of my company three years in the future. That' gets powerful when you describe it in that level of detail.

My personal vivid vision is the same. I'm doing a rewrite right now of my personal vivid vision, and I committed to the COO Alliance to have it done by the end of February. I have it right in front of me, so I'm working on it today, but it'll cover areas like my mantras and affirmations, my health improvements, my improvements as a dad, my improvements as a partner, my daily routine, fun activities, travel, people whom I'm grateful for and want to spend more time with, my habits, sex, books that I want to read, technology to learn, and fitness goals.

I'm going to incorporate all those. I'll describe all those things, and then I'll share it with the people closest to me so that they're clear on what I'm building myself into over the next three years.

Most entrepreneurs need help in core leadership skills, such as coaching, delegation, time management, problem-solving, interviewing, productive meetings, classroom teaching, email management—all the soft situational leadership and all the soft skills leadership that most managers and leaders never get any training in. They make it up, and they're winging it, and I think if they would get the training around those soft skills, they could scale the company.

Some of it is available online, in books, and some of it is them being aware that they want to grow. I think people don't wake up in the morning thinking about who they want to become as a leader, who they want to grow as a person, and what they want their company to become. They keep trying to work harder, so it's leaning out into the future and describing themselves as a leader and saying, "This is the leader I want to be. What do I need to learn to get there?" If they would describe themselves as a leader they want to be, they'd realize there's a gap. There are things they need to learn along that path.

All those are available. There are great books on leadership, such as *The One Minute Manager*, and it's fantastic. There are great books on time management and videos available for free. The key is to think about how you want to get better at these things, then devour that content, then do it. Most people don't do this stuff. They say, "Oh, it's too hard, or I'm too busy." Then they go back to being a fly banging their head against the wall.

I have five books out now. My first book was *Double Double*. My second one is *Meetings Suck*, which every employee at every company needs to read. It's not only about how to run meetings but also how to show up and participate in meetings and know which meetings you need to build a successful company. Later, I co-authored the *Miracle Morning for Entrepreneurs*. I launched *VividVision* last year, and this year, my book called *Free PR* came out with one of my former coaching clients, Adrian. It's about how to leverage and generate free publicity to grow your brand and to grow your company.

I'm planning another book about the highs and lows of CEOs and why most entrepreneurs are bipolar, why we ride this roller coaster and how to leverage each of those stages of the roller coaster because we can't get off it. We're on it forever. It's how to understand and leverage those roller-coaster stages and how to teach your employees and partners about the process.

One of the things that I've worked hard on with my books is making sure that every single person at every speaking event I do gets a copy of my book. That's been powerful for me as well to make sure that my clients and everyone in the audience can benefit from my information.

Avetis Antaplyan
Hireclout
Hireclout.com

There are three facets of mentoring that I believe in.

First, I mentor a lot of startup companies at USC, UCLA, and Cal State Northridge. I help them learn a little bit about the business.

Second, there is also mentorship within our company as we do a lot of coaching and mentoring of our staff versus management.

As our people evolve, we ask them to mentor new employees in our company, even if these folks are not on their team. Everybody here works as part of a pod of four or five, and they have their own leads and managers. But beyond that, we like our folks to have mentors outside of that group.

On the third level, we utilize a lot of mentors for our company. For example, we recently took on EOS, which is a prominent consulting and coaching organization that has helped us revamp and structure our organization. We went from startup energy all the time, where everything was done on the fly, to a more established process with procedures, accountability, charts, scorecards, and things like that.

We've utilized folks who are knowledgeable and influential in our industry to mentor us. We have people come in to speak to our folks here. I'm on the board of a company, and the owner of that company is a very brilliant young woman. I've asked her to mentor some of the women in my company so they can look up to someone outside of our industry, a woman who has succeeded in a big way.

It was a significant change when we shifted from that startup atmosphere to a more structured one, and we're still going through it now. The folks in the company were used to a particular way of doing things. When we started changing it and providing more structure and expected more from them, there was a little bit of bucking the system or getting frustrated because there are so many systems to keep them accountable. However, what they've learned pretty quickly is that with accountability, there is now more freedom.

There are no random managers coming up to them asking, "What you are up to?" "What are you working on?" We already know what they're working on. We meet once a week, report on what we've done, and talk about the issues we've had and the challenges we're facing, and we resolve these issues.

So yes, we are still transitioning, and it's a lot of work as it takes you away from your core jobs and responsibilities. But eventually, as you create the systems and processes, it frees you up to be more productive, more efficient, work less than before, and get better results.

Everybody's been great and flexible with the change. I've had folks who have shown some stress or frustration, but overall, everybody's been pleased with it. There was one individual whom I think had she stayed on, she would've had a little more frustration with the systems, but she isn't here to see them. Love them or hate them at this point.

I'll give you several examples of my mentorship.

Cal State Northridge has an excellent entrepreneurship program within its business program, and they incubate startups within this program. They asked me to be part of a group of judges for the competition. However, I was out of the country at the time, so I couldn't do it. Instead, they asked if I would coach the startups. They were surprised when I said I would be happy to, and it was a terrific experience.

I found a lot of skill gaps and knowledge gaps between what they think is going to be a scalable, strong business that could be monetized and the actual reality. I saw a lot of gaps in what the university teaches and what the real world teaches. We met several times, and they showed me their business plan and product, and I poked holes, and they improved it each time. The contestants went from, I think, sixty or seventy down to twenty, and then down to the top five. They didn't receive first, second, or third place, but I think they learned a lot in the process.

The other example of mentorship was that I speak at USC's International MBA program. Again, before they can start their companies, I ask them, "What are some industries that are hot? What are some sectors that you could potentially take part in?" I recommend that a lot of them do entrepreneurship programs—to almost be an entrepreneur before you become an entrepreneur—so they can learn a lot about business. You don't have to go work for a corporate *Fortune* 500 company and be another number. But what you can do is work for an established startup company and move the needle and do a lot of different things and learn and see if it's for you.

Many folks don't realize the sacrifices they have to make to make it as a startup company. They think it's fun. They see these billion-dollar exits. They see the glamour behind it. They don't realize how much work is needed and how many sacrifices they have to make to succeed. They don't always like it, by the way.

Mentoring has been something I've been doing for a while, and I enjoy it. It's one of those things that takes a lot of time, a lot of effort, and you can't half-ass it. The way I think is you either do it right or don't do it at all. When I do something, I'm going to make sure it's done with nothing to gain. I go all-in as if it were my company, and I'm an official advisor and board member on their companies. I enjoy it as I get to see the appreciation, learning, and progress they make throughout that process. Even if it's a two, three, or four-month stretch, I see how much they learn during that time frame. It's my way of giving back, not cutting a check, which is easy. Instead, it's part of the early, difficult stages of a potential company.

Honestly, sometimes I recommend that they don't start a company. Sometimes I don't see a way to monetize it. Again, it's not always the best thing to do. You want to encourage always, but sometimes you have to say, "I encourage you. I think you're great, but this is not a great business long term."

I haven't had a ton of set mentors, someone I continuously go to. However, my partner, Jeff Mitchell, who's a sharp guy with thirty-five years in the business, doesn't necessarily have the overall business mindset. Still, he's one of the most patient, smart, creative people I've ever worked with. He taught me to ask early on in my career what I was trying to accomplish. When you get upset, and you want to make that difficult call, what do you want to accomplish? What are you trying to do? Is yelling at this person going to help you in the long run? So he was almost a pseudo-mentor for me throughout the years.

Even as a young person in debt, there was a time when I became frustrated, and I would say I can't do this. He would say, "Your credit is vital at this age. Stick it out. You'll be fine." I look back and go, "Wow, what a great decision." And I've done the same for him in a different light. But yes, he's been one of my most excellent mentors.

I read one book a week. One of my favorite books I read recently was *Radical Candor* by Kim Scott, which discusses the concept of giving feedback to anyone in your life, specifically, employees by managing up, sideways, and down. She advises using radical candor in a way where you build the relationships so you don't come off as a bully but demonstrate that you care about them.

Another one of my favorite books was *Who: The Method for Hiring* by Geoff Smart and Randy Street, which is about the process of hiring great people and only A players, which is always easier said than done.

I've read many, many books, as there are so many great books out there. I read a book called *Rocket Fuel: The One Essential Combination That Will Get You More of What You Want from Your Business* by Gino Wickman and Mark C. Winters, which is about the visionary and the integrators parts. My partner and I had our challenges communicating because I am a hundred-miles-an-hour, pedal-to-the-metal-at-all-times type. He's a little more conservative. So understanding our differences and appreciating it and utilizing it was life-changing to realize that's a normal thing.

We've all made lots of mistakes. One of the biggest mistakes we've made as a company was settling for average talent. Because at the time of the decision to hire the person, we all knew, let's say, that person was not a star. We all knew they were not A players, but for some reason, we went ahead with the hire. At the moment, we didn't have any more energy to keep looking. We felt the person could do the job well enough. We knew we had to grow, as we have so much business, so if we didn't hire this person, we were going to lose out. What ends up happening is you settle for average or at best solid B-minus C players. It's incredible how much time we spend with C players: 80 percent of our time is spent trying to fix C players instead of working on A players.

If someone's an A player, and you give them the time, energy, skills, and tactics, you know they can be incredible for your company. But we spent too much time training and trying to change our B players. If I were to go back, I would do what I'm doing now. I have twelve open positions, but I absolutely refuse to settle. As a company, we refuse to settle. I'd rather have an empty seat than an average employee, to be honest with you.

Sometimes we have to get out of our own way. Most entrepreneurs started their companies because they're passionate; they love the product, love the service, and have the drive. What ends up happening is we control everything—not in a micromanagement way at all but more of "I got this because I could do it better. Don't break my babies." So you end up wearing twelve or thirteen different hats. And no matter how fast you run, no matter how long you run, you're going to drop the ball.

There's no way someone could have eight seats and truly be accountable to doing 100 percent of the job. There's no way. We're not superheroes; we're human beings. I think the biggest issue is finding the best people, not settling for average, and then trusting them and letting go and delegating and making sure you hire the right people.

Once you do, you trust them to get the job done. The most common mistake for entrepreneurs is that we either settle for average and good enough for now and end up doing more of the same thing, and all they are is the support staff, or hire the best and let go and let people do what they have to do.

I would say come up with core values in which your entire organization believes. I don't mean cliché things we want to be or things we were in the past or things we read in the book. Close your eyes, and think about the best people in your company or around your company. Figure out which traits make them great. Create those core values, whatever they are, sink into them when it comes to hiring, firing, promoting, and stick to it. Do not settle. Find the best people. Stick to it. Make sure they're growing. Think of them first when you're making decisions, and the rest will fall into place.

Figure out who you are as an organization. Don't play to other people's strengths. If your competition is doing something in a low-quality way, and they're doing better than you, don't follow their procedure. You got to figure out who you are. If that's who you are, then that's fine; do it better than them. But if you are not that, you're a quality-based, relationship-based business, stick to that, and only hire people who agree with that model.

Sometimes open-minded entrepreneurs without huge egos know to hire good people to help. When you're open to all their ideas, you're continually rowing—everybody on the boat is rowing in a different direction. What you end up doing looks like growth, but you're doing a lot of spinning in the ocean and not getting anywhere.

But if you have your vision, you take in ideas and know where to go with them.

Jim Bellas
Diplomatic Language Services
Dlsdc.com

In my experience, mentorship works best when it's an organic, integral process. It's more than relying on finding somebody and engaging them to mentor you or for you to do that for someone else. Instead, the general concept is to understand that mentoring is a relationship in which somebody with more experience or more knowledge helps somebody who has less.

With that premise, mentoring, therefore, begins with onboarding in a systematized way, making sure that somebody is given the attention and instructions appropriate for their exact stage. So if you are onboarding someone who's experienced, you're going to treat them differently than someone brand-new, first or second job out of college, or the first time that they've encountered the work that they're now going to do for you.

The process of bringing somebody on board is mastering the art of delegation as much as it's the art of mentorship. The progression is the following: directing, coaching, supporting, and then delegation. Moving from step to the next and never dropping back more than one level for corrective action. Someone who knows nothing about what they're doing needs to be highly directed. Once they know where the bathroom is, where their desk is, how to get in and out of the building, and work the levers of the company, then they're put into a position of being coached for specific skills and practices.

Then from being coached, they're supported, because now that they've gotten most of the talents, they need to be regularly acknowledged. Then, ultimately, when they're fully self-actualized, that's when you arrive at the level of delegation. At any point, they could be a mentor for the person that's directly behind them in terms of that process of coming onboard.

Foundational to all this is creating an environment where truth telling, trust, and respect are the fundamentals. If you can't tell the truth about, "I don't know what I'm doing," then you're doomed to be stuck in that particular position. As an example, when I first acquired this company, I sensed a residual deal of fear from the previous management.

To address this case, I published an article for everybody which read, "The only mistake you can make is not to tell the boss you made a mistake. And if you don't make *that* mistake, you're doing fine. And if you don't know that you made a mistake, and you find out about it later, the only mistake you can make is to delay admitting that you didn't see that you'd made a mistake." The whole goal of that was to present me with problems I could solve before it was too late.

So we created an environment where nobody gets punished for telling the truth, but instead, they get rewarded for it, and that then builds an environment of trust. On the other side is the permission to know that if you're not making mistakes, you're probably not doing enough or stretching enough, because nobody goes through life with a 100 percent batting average. Recognizing that you're going to strike out regularly means that you should be respected for having made an effort, and you should be trusted for having told the truth.

I've not had a super-positive experience with mentoring. When I was growing a company that I had successfully grown to a certain level, I then wanted to leapfrog to another level, so I reached out. I engaged this chap who had succeeded at a much higher level than myself, and we hit it off. Our values appeared to be the same. He liked me, and I liked him. I was certainly impressed by all he had done. He made introductions for me to people that I wouldn't have had access to, and all that was helpful. Where I failed in that mentoring was that I began deferring, increasingly, to him, as so many different issues came up.

My gut would say, "No, this is the wrong decision," but I would nonetheless defer to him. So there's a seductive side to mentorship, where it enables you to do things you couldn't do otherwise, but it also puts you in the position of second-guessing yourself and not trusting your best instincts. That's the dark side of mentorship.

Now, that having been said, having a connection that can get you entry to places that can get you information or experiences you wouldn't otherwise have had is valuable. But I would caution anyone that it's complicated. Subsuming my instincts, experiences, and capabilities to a mentor may have been probably the biggest mistake I made.

Another thing I had to learn several times was that I was not going to be able to do everything all the time. I had the good fortune to recognize early on that the core of an entrepreneur is not the lonely guy with his hair blowing back on the top of the mountain. He's the guy at the bottom of the hill trying to climb it and find the people that he can attach himself to on ropes so that we can pull each other up.

For example, I was good at marketing and sales, and I attached myself to someone good at the product, and I was fortunate enough to attract somebody good at finance. I was the guy who frequently got all the attention, but without them, no way could I have succeeded the way we did. That pattern repeated itself throughout my life. You hear a lot about Steve Jobs, but what you don't hear about are the finance and product people that made the difference for him to create what he did and achieve what he did.

Mentoring myself through reading has been the key. The foundational books that helped me are authored by Napoleon Hill and Dale Carnegie, and then more recently—and still probably the best book out there—is Stephen Covey's *The 7 Habits of Highly Effective People*, which is a constant reread for me. By reread, I mean picking a particular chapter and work on that specific aspect.

A transformational book for me was *What Got You Here Won't Get You There* by Marshall Goldsmith, which is a genius book. Goldsmith consults with million-dollar employees who are failing at their next position, and the board is about to fire them. They bring him in to go through examining the process of the thing that got them to that CEO position was not the thing that was going to make them successful in that CEO position. It's a remarkable read to go through that process.

Most recently, for me, is Brené Brown's *The Transformative Power of Vulnerability*, and her more recent book, *Daring Greatly*. Her whole premise is that the things that make us courageous are when we address the places where we're vulnerable and are willing to be vulnerable with ourselves and with others as well. It's a remarkable book. She's got some great TED Talks for those who want to listen to the core message. It's worth checking out Brené Brown.

Despite my jaundiced view of outside mentors, I have to say that I found mentors in my partners and coworkers, the ones who appreciated my strengths and brought their strengths. The two of us working together created a mentorship for me to appreciate the things that they did exceptionally well, which I struggled with, and them appreciating what I did well, which they wouldn't have even wanted to take on.

One from my early years was my partner, Ed Brandt, who gave me the courage to go out and do it on my own, as opposed to continuing to work for someone else. Ed's belief in me and my trust in him helped us form a partnership that lasted for over twenty-five years. It led to a business that started as a mom-and-pop and grew into a company that attracted venture capital financing. I never would've done that had he not been my mentor—for not only finance, but also for the core values of a business, the respect of people, and the commitment to trust and respect that is the foundation of a relationship.

As I went through the struggles of starting up a business and all the fear that can come with that, his confidence in me and my trust in him created a mutual mentorship for each of us.

In later years, it was relinquishing control of the day-to-day operations to someone who was a much better operator than I was, which then set me free be the creator I could be.

Jim Helwig was a mentor for me, as a general manager that came on and successfully ran the company in a much more methodical, predictable, organized way, and still with the same core values that we both held. He set me free to then do the creation, marketing, and leadership, where I'm naturally good at, as opposed to making the trains run precisely on time, which he did so well. Correspondingly, my trust in him enabled him to thrive.

I've served as a mentor in the parent-child relationship, and I guess the easiest way to describe it is to be the change that you want to see and to walk the talk and do the things that you say. In a parent-child relationship, that happens continuously by pointing with our feet rather than our fingers.

At work, I wanted to create an environment where the employees can recognize their strengths, and for the culture of the company to focus on their strengths, and for the performance review system to not be centered around finding the areas of weakness and saying, "So you're good at these six things. Let's now concentrate on this one where you're no good."

Instead, I wanted to recognize when they're not excelling in a particular area, to figure out how you can diminish that portion of the job and reassign it to other people, and then focus on the one, two, or three things that they are good at doing.

The other important aspect is delegating and putting employees in a position to be able to operate at the level at which they have achieved already—and encouraging everybody to be a multiplier of other people.

A formative book for me was Liz Wiseman's *Multipliers*, and it dovetails well with the whole strength-finders-based culture. You operate in ways of asking questions as opposed to giving instructions, looking for ways to augment somebody as opposed to competing with them, and setting up relationships where it's about the team winning as opposed to one particular person being a star. Again, for me, mentorship is achieved through the organic process of creating an environment.

I was on a retreat with my son—he's president of the company now—and he was expressing this frustration of seeing what he wanted to get done and not being able to get there and sometimes wanting to give up.

I said, "You must know that that's a feeling that you have whenever you take on anything. You'll begin to ask, 'Why am I here seven, eight, nine, ten days in a row, fourteen hours a day, when I should be spending time with my significant other, or my children, or taking some time for myself?'"

You have to remember that regardless of any negation that happens as a result of failures or mistakes, you've created something that you wanted to have. You created a better world by doing your part to create a world that you have some influence over, to be the world that you'd want to live in, to treat people the way you want to be treated.

The people that you employ, the livelihoods that you create, and the personal growth that you see happen in other people are what kept me going in those times where it was exhausting or when it didn't feel like I had succeeded in any particular way. It was a reminder of that overall good that's created as a result of my efforts and as a result of my ability to attract other people that want to achieve the same goal.

The genius of YPO is in a hidden aspect of it, which is the forum, a group of six or ten equal members of that same organization, who are noncompetitive. They have achieved some level of success to be a member of YPO. It requires having been the leader of an organization before the age of forty that achieved a particular volume of revenue and employed a certain number of people. So they've done something in their lives.

They're now in a room with you in a 100 percent confidential, nonjudgmental way. It's transformational in that you're not there to prove you're better than anybody else. You're there to have your personal board of advisors help you see what you're trying to get done, what you're trying to express, what you're struggling with, and process it in a way that you can't do in a company. When you're the head of a company, you create a cascading fear in your employees if you're starting to explore things at a level that addresses your core fears.

In that environment, I can present on my business, family, and myself. It's a fully integrated approach to being able to understand what's keeping you from getting what you want and what is it that you need to do. It's less about advice giving and more about experience sharing. When it's working, somebody else in that room has had the experience you've had and can ask questions and share the experiences they've had. It's been a fundamental, core source of strength for me to be able to take my greatest fears to that group and come away with having addressed not only the problem but also the underlying emotions that went along with it.

It's a personal board of advisors. It's somewhere that you can go and process and explain what you're trying to get done. YPO is also terrific on the education, and the organization itself is equal parts of networking and education, and a social aspect to it. So it's a holistic approach.

Probably the best experience I've had in any business organization has been with YPO. Getting involved in the leadership at the local chapter level, where you have a chance to get things done without having authority over anybody, has been a transformational experience as well. Doing it through the negotiation of common purpose, and aligning people around wanting to make an excellent experience for a year, either with education or with overall leadership of the organization. Now that was a terrific experience as well.

The area that most entrepreneurs need mentoring would be fundamental. I think the sooner somebody figures out that they're not the be-all and end-all of what's going to happen, that they need to surround themselves with people that are going to augment them, the better. Recognize that you're not Hercules, you are part of a team. I suppose in the common vernacular it would be the group of superheroes as opposed to the superhero—you're not Superman, you're part of the Avengers.

The second thing is to understand that everything takes longer than you say it will and recognize that stamina is not to be undervalued. Grit and stamina are the pieces that will carry you through the fact that you thought it was going to take three months, and it's now three years later, and you still haven't done it. But there's an optimism bias that causes us or enables us to do something, but it also puts us into positions we didn't foresee all the things and all the unintended consequences that were about to happen.

I think it's important to remember the core reason that you're doing what you're doing—for me, it was to make the world better—doesn't go away, and that's a goal worth persisting at. Sometimes a specific thing you're trying to get done isn't done. But if it fits in the environment of creating a better place to work, a better place to shop, a better product for the world, or a better service, that in that small way of fixing your part of the human body by fixing your cell of it, that's worth achieving.

Creating the environment that you'd want to work in, that you'd want your kids to work in, that you'd want your best friends to be in is worth doing.

Jeff Eisenberg
EVR Advertising
Evradvertising.com

Mentoring is close to my heart because it involves so many things that are important to me. One, I suppose anyone who's in business needs to succeed, and I find that my best chance of succeeding is by having effective team members and growing. The way you grow team members is to mentor them, as, without that proper nutrition and watering, they won't grow. So it's a win-win.

The other half of it is that I genuinely enjoy helping people grow. Hopefully, it's with my business, but I learned a long time ago that you get what you give. True leaders have the heart of a servant. If I am here to serve them what they need and want, then I will be the recipient of all they have to give. I'm shocked that not everyone gets that or doesn't have the energy or time to help others.

I've been a student of leadership over the years. I love reading about it and collecting meaningful quotes. At the core of it all is the difference between transformational and transactional leadership. I live to be transformational. I do not like spending my time on transactions. I'm always thinking, "How will the next interaction with this person, especially regarding this particular topic, be at the next level?" I'm always thinking, and I will invest more time in that particular conversation or interaction if I see a chance for uplifting someone. I prefer to spend more time and get some growth out of it. I've never been one to say it's easier to do it myself: I'm the ultimate delegator.

My degree as an undergrad is in economics, and I have a graduate degree in sports management. When I was in college, I was thinking about what I wanted to do. I've always been a sports fan. I have always played and loved sports. So I took a class in the economics of sports as a junior, and it occurred to me like, "Wow, people do this for a living?" This was back before the proliferation of sports management grad programs.

I looked into it and found two grad schools that offered a sports management degree, UMass and Ohio University. Today, they're the preeminent grad schools in the field because they were the first, and they're still around. When I got out, I was hired by the Philadelphia Phillies. I went on to spend thirty years in professional sports with the Philadelphia Phillies, Milwaukee Brewers, Buffalo Sabres, and the LA Kings.

Ten years ago, after I had launched and run a new AHL team in a new arena in New Hampshire for the Kings, I found the growth path was slowing. Since I like building things, I decided it would be best to look for another opportunity. We had an incredible run with that team. I was very connected with the area and liked it very much. So I bought an ad agency in town and stayed here in Manchester, New Hampshire. That's what I've been doing for the last decade.

When I bought this ad agency at the age of fifty-three, people asked, "What are you doing?" But I just wasn't done yet and definitely had (at least) another run left in me. I wanted something I could grow. It's been awesome, and I'm thrilled I did it. I'm sixty-three now and feel that's still young.

Mentoring is a significant thread through everything we do at our ad agency. Since I bought the business, we've quadrupled in net revenue and are on the way to more, and our staff has, of course, grown as well. We had eight people when I bought it, and now we're over twenty.

We have a high standard for who works here in terms of the quality of work we get, and mentoring is the basis of growing effective employees, the operative word being *growing*. The people who stay here—and we're half millennial here, at least—are the ones who enjoy growing in a collaborative environment. I don't typecast any age demo into any behavior; everyone has their own personality and orientation toward work.

But younger people are especially thinking about their future career, and they want to learn. Professional growth becomes a mechanism to grow skill sets and productivity as well as a retention mechanism because people feel valued, and they're growing. The first level of teaching them mentoring and leadership is, "I've done a good job, and now I have people working for me. How do I get them to do a good job?"

I, of course, can't be involved in everything, so how do I get people to be effective? Ronald Reagan said, "Trust yet verify," when he was dealing with the Russians back in the Cold War, and that is a saying of mine too. I'm not a micromanager, but you have to earn that independence. Once you've earned it, and once you've proven that you're a good thinker, and you're reliable, and you're accurate, then go. Do it.

But when you're mentoring, you have to have checks and balances. You have to check in and make them earn their stripes. That's not micromanaging; that's monitoring their progress and helping them think strategically. And that takes time and investment. So that's the first level.

I have people who've been with me for a while and now have to teach their people how to do it. So now I'm going layers deep. I'm a small organization, but I'm now I'm teaching people how to mentor. These are the stages of mentoring. It's part and parcel and the fundamental core value of the way we run our business in terms of internal-facing core values. Mentoring is at the core of our employee training, strategy, and retention plan.

Two mentors that I have had stood out. One is David Montgomery, the former president and part owner of the Philadelphia Phillies. I started there right out of grad school at twenty-four, and he was only a director at the time in 1980. One year after I was hired, the team was sold, and he was promoted to VP, and I went right along with him.

I worked with him for the first nine years of my career. I learned so much from him about how to work and how to communicate. I learned integrity, work ethic, and emotional intelligence. I revered him, and he let me grow. I've always had an entrepreneurial streak, and he let me be an "intrapreneur," as I took over, of all things, the computer operations back then and applied it to the business. He had started the process—way ahead of his time. He told me he didn't have time for it anymore, so I took it.

I applied the computer to everything we did at the Philadelphia Phillies, which got me into marketing, ticket sales, accounting, and even baseball operations. We were getting proficient at ticketing, and he let me sell our services to the Philadelphia Eagles, the Philadelphia 76ers, and Temple University.

I made a study on how to communicate with David. For example, he was a voracious reader. I know that he used to go on business trips, and I would watch him walk out of the stadium—which was our office—with this enormous briefcase that made him look like one of those lawyers going into a weeklong trial. Trying to nail him down in person wasn't always easy, so I got very good at communicating my thoughts in written form. I learned that if I wrote something, he would read it and respond.

I also learned to be aggressive. His assistant used to say, "Look out, Jeff's coming, look out," when she would see me coming down the hall. I knew that was endearing to him, or at least I convinced myself that it was. I know he wanted me to be that way, but he had fun with it, so I learned to remain proactive and hopefully not too pushy.

Now, I always tell people who work for me, "Learn your boss's idiosyncrasies, their thought processes, how they consume information, and play to that." It's only logical.

My second great mentor was Wendy Selig-Prieb. Wendy was my boss at the Milwaukee Brewers. She's the daughter of Bud Selig, who was the longtime owner of the Brewers. When I got to Milwaukee in 1991, Bud Selig, who had brought baseball to Milwaukee and was then-president, was becoming the commissioner of Major League Baseball.

By the time I got rolling there, he was a full-time commissioner, so Wendy took over as president of the Milwaukee Brewers. I've never been more aligned business-wise with anybody in my life. We thought so similarly, and she would always challenge me. That opened opportunities and there were very few impediments to our communication and business processes.

If I laid out a good, defensible argument, Wendy would go with you. She'd demand sound, logical reasoning, but you could sell her that way, and since I was able to make progress by aligning with her strategic train of thought, we accomplished a lot. I was there for four years, and when I got recruited to go to the Buffalo Sabres as the VP of sales and marketing, it was a tough decision to leave.

A book that comes to mind that has had a profound impact on me is *The Accidental Creative* by Todd Henry. He happens to have a history as a creative director for an ad agency, so it does apply directly to creatives of this type, and it applies more broadly to the creative mind. We need to be creative in everything we do, and it's a remarkable book for pointing out many things we can do to make ourselves more creatively productive every day.

I'm picking this right out of the air, and it might seem illogical to people, but it wasn't to me. I always made effective use of time management. I'd say, "I don't know if I'm going to be able to finish this, but I'll spend an hour on it," and I would find that that got me going. It broke through any procrastination I might have, then I ended up getting more done in that hour than I thought I would.

However, Todd Henry speaks more to "energy management." This certainly involves time management, but it also means looking at your calendar and making sure that your energy is spent well and that you have energy remaining to expend on the right things at the right time. Sometimes we can't avoid overbooking a day, but try to space things out. If there's going to be a meeting where you're going to need to think hard, put another one that's easier next to it.

This all falls under something he calls "whole life planning." It comes naturally to a lot of people, and it does to me too. When he talks about it, he basically codifies it and raises the awareness of it. We all look at our days, but we need to look at our week, two weeks, month, and even our quarter. What are you going to tackle during the time period you are looking at? What will make the biggest difference? What bandwidth do you have time-wise and energy-wise?

The whole premise of the book is how we become creative on demand. Something comes up, and it requires you to respond quickly. How do you respond creatively "on demand?" It's all about preparation.

There's another book that is a little bit more workbook-like called *Traction* by Gino Wickman. It's more prosaic and functional. It presents a framework for all the things we know about building and running a business. It gives you a rather formal framework within which to operate. We're religious "tractioneers" here at the agency with a leadership group that meets under this format every week.

Traction breaks down how you look at your business and focuses on what you're going to accomplish this quarter. Every week, you revisit and ask, "Where are we?" Its many fundamental exercises and processes combine into a great guide for how to think and plan your business.

For example, it gives you ways to evaluate your employees. It suggests a "GWC" evaluation approach—get it, want it, capacity. If they don't have positives in all three of those, they might not be the right person in the right seat.

Moneyball by Michael Lewis is another book that comes to mind. It's a book about baseball and how Billy Beane, the general manager of the Oakland A's, revolutionized how baseball rosters are built through quantifiable statistics.

He broke the mold of the old scouts. The old baseball guys would come in and say, "Ah, you don't need that data. I know talent when I see it." The book reveals how Beane proved them wrong by using data analytics to build very successful teams on a limited budget. I see a broad statement that the book makes about the broader business world in terms of how we quantify our production. I'm not saying there are not qualitative factors involved too, but it influenced me (and others) regarding the way we look at our business and how we build the "rosters" in our office.

I believe that entrepreneurs should make it a core practice of theirs to be a student of leadership and to truly explore what it takes to be transformational. If you're going to grow your company, you're not going to do it by remaining active in everything. You will eventually have to let people go do their thing with independence, and when this happens, you need to know how to help them be successful. It doesn't always happen on its own.

Here's one I love. People will say, "I hire good people, and I let them work." To me, that is so naïve. There are fundamental values of leadership that people must focus on. I have found that collecting good quotes and thoughts on leadership helps me focus on important fundamentals. For example, "Be abundant." That isn't something most entrepreneurs probably think about when they walk in the door. Be abundant. But your people thirst to work directly with you, at least periodically. They want time with you, they want to talk with you, and they want to hear what you're thinking and see your vision.

I like to interact with people anyway. That's what fuels me. I'll often just get up and walk around and ask people what they're doing. They thrive on it. So be abundant, be there, be a presence.

Another core leadership axiom for me is, "Be an agent of change." I have a saying, "If it ain't broke, break it." I happen to work in an industry that is well suited for this because we're undergoing a tsunami of change practically every day in the advertising business. This is the best thing that could happen to us because it allows us to help people. It creates opportunities.

I've taken ten of these "leadership axioms" and presented them not only to my leaders but to others as well. A while back, a buddy of mine at Northwestern Mutual asked me to come over and talk to their leadership group. After I met with them, I realized, "Hey, dummy, you haven't done that for your people." So now this has become a regular routine at my office.

It's not about doing one thing 100 percent better; it's about doing one hundred things 1 percent better. We need to instill in our people that there are no silver bullets. It's hard work. It's rolling up your sleeves. If you do one thing 1 percent better, and the next week, you focus on another one thing, soon they're all going to amount to something, and good is going things will happen.

It all starts by getting the right people in the right seats. Don't be afraid to let someone go if they aren't a good match for your business. Free them to go and do something they can be great at. Don't compromise on your standards! Find those who want to share your bar of excellence.

Then make it your job to learn what's important to your people. Know what makes them tick and what motivates them. Explore how you can develop your leadership and the leadership of those around you so that you feed an ecosystem built around what's important to people.

Angela Hurt
Veracity
Veracityit.com

If it weren't for mentoring, this company would not exist. The pre-launch of the business came from a mentor of mine that I spoke with at length about my vision and things I wanted to do. The mentor helped shape the company by pushing me in the direction to make it happen.

Another unique way I've been involved with mentoring is when I worked through an organization called the Women's Business Center here in Kansas City. It's a nonprofit that connects entrepreneurs—particularly female entrepreneurs—to mentors depending on what they're looking for. I've used the organization for situational mentoring, as they connect you to people who have different skill sets that you can avail—be it legal advice, HR advice, or different things of that nature.

Early in my business, that was key to our success because startups tend not to have as much money to spend on professional services, and that was important for the growth of our organization.

I had more of a formal mentor when I sought out somebody that I wanted to mentor me. I loved how they grew their business, and that they had a similar model, and offered a different service, which I thought was in line to pair for a great mentor-mentee relationship. I knew his head of HR, so I asked her for his help, and she was very surprised that he said no. His point was busy with a lot of internal mentoring.

But probably six months later, she reached out to me and said, "Doug called me into his office and asked if you were still interested in mentoring." Since I was, our first lunch was so satisfying.

He said, "I know I told you no because we have this internal mentoring program, and I thought I was doing my deed by doing that, but then I realized that we all need mentors in different places."

He continued, "I was going through purchasing a big piece of land that was very expensive. I thought at that moment that I had five people I could reach out to, and I knew they had been there and done that, and I could learn from them."

For whatever reason, he realized the value that he could add to somebody like myself. He felt compelled to say yes, six months later. It was a great thing for me. One of the things he always talked to me about was pursuing wealth for business and the impact that can make. That was key for me. He exited his business and is now focusing on family stuff, so I'm not as in touch with him anymore.

Over my thirteen years of being in business, I've met a lot of other people who have mentored me. One of my learnings is that specific mentors can get you to a particular place and, while they still have valid input, sometimes the change in perspective from other people is critical. I haven't seen my original mentor in years, but "m pretty sure if I called him, he'd probably help me out if I got into a bind. But now I'm part of other organizations that serve that purpose for me currently.

Some of my biggest mentors are people who didn't know they were my mentors. I watched them as there were people that I never wanted to be. Big sales and leadership were one of my biggest lessons, as watching how that unfolded gave me this guiding light. They were examples of how I wanted to be and how I never wanted to be. I was in several of those situations, and I grew immensely.

Also, there have been many books that I've read. One of my absolute favorite business books is *Getting Naked: A Business Fable About Shedding the Three Fears That Sabotage Client Loyalty* by Patrick Lencioni. It's about authenticity and vulnerability in business while being in front of customers and being vulnerable. It's a book I recommend to everybody.

I'm part of a mentoring program, and the first year of that program, we met every Saturday with not just our mentees but the entire group that was in that. We would have different book discussions, and *Getting Naked* is a book I introduced to the group. My perspective on mentoring is that if the mentor can't be vulnerable to the mentee or protege, they're never going to be vulnerable back to you. I think this book was vital in showing people how you can build relationships through vulnerability. I believe that I'm through my two-year program, and they're on their third or fourth class. I found out last week that they're still using that book as part of the program.

In our business, we have an informal program. We had a pretty small organization, about 150 people, and we're about ready to start a program that's more of a buddy system. We're in IT consulting, and when we hire people, a lot of those folks never work inside of our office space. They are on our client's side delivering products or delivering services.

We're going to start a program so that when somebody new comes on, they'll get a buddy in the company. They'll be a mentor in the company as they can explain how to navigate what it's like to be an employee at Veracity. We'll look for those who want to be involved with the organization as a whole and knows how to deliver on the client side. We have employees who roll from project to project and those who have full-on bench time. The people who stay plugged in and connected to the organization are known by top management when a project comes up.

The Steve Mesler mentoring program is through the Mid-America Gay and Lesbian Chamber, which is one formal program I do.

The other formal program I do is HEMP (Helzberg Entrepreneurial Mentoring Program), and Barnett Helzberg himself started that. It began in Barnett's basement with people like the Kauffmans and Henry Block, and folks like that who decided they were going to give back to our community by helping new entrepreneurs. It's been a cool three-year program. The exciting part of this is that the mentees pay $5,000 a year to be part of the program. Mentors like myself volunteer, but it does pay for a lot of different programming that they do, so it's slightly different.

Outside of those organizations, I do informal mentoring. I struggle to say no to anybody. If somebody reaches out to me in the community and asks, "Hey, would you have a cup of coffee? I'm thinking about starting my business, or I have a business, and I'm trying to grow it." I say yes nearly every time. I genuinely believe it's part of my purpose to give back to our community in that way. I love it; it's meaningful to me. Half the time, I point them in the direction to somebody else.

Early entrepreneurs, if they don't come from a finance background, need to understand how to read financial statements. Many people overlook that part. You start a business, get a copy of QuickBooks or whatever it might be, and start keeping your books because you can't afford to pay somebody else to do it. But you're running it like a checkbook. It's money in and money out; it's not accounting. When you do that, you don't get it.

Early on, I would look at our statement and look at the bottom dollar, and that's all I would do. It wasn't for years later that I realized the power in seeing month over month or comparing year to year. That was big for me. At the Women's Business Center, we had an instructor who understood accounting so well and explained seeing where your cost of goods sold are versus operational expenses and separating those two. I think that people undervalue that when you first start your company because you don't realize its importance.

I didn't start the company to sell it, but I do like the book *Built to Sell* because it talks a lot about to structure your financials. Not because you want to sell the company, but to structure your financials so you can understand your costs of goods sold and your gross margins. Keeping that separated early on is vital.

I'm mentoring a company right now that has been in business for over ten years, and we're still having talks about the importance and value of setting up financials correctly.

There have been a few things that I've learned, and one is understanding your value. Like why did I start the company with a vision that I have? And as the company grows, where am I going to make the most significant impact for the organization?

Everybody says this, so it's such a cliché, but hiring people smarter than you and people that balance what you're good at and what you're not good at is critical. I think that's huge. I have a tendency when I hire salespeople. I want to hire salespeople like me because I know how I operate, and I also know that there's nothing in me that's ever going to make a cold call. For me to find somebody that has that mentality is key for us.

My old COO drove me crazy in the way that she thought and the way she did things because she's very detailed and overly organized. I fly by the seat of my pants, so I knew how much I needed her; that was my other lesson.

I once was in front of David G. Thomson, who wrote a book called *Blueprint to a Billion: 7 Essentials to Achieve Exponential Growth*. He lived here in Kansas City, and he was at a workshop where he made this comment about the seven habits of highly successful businesses. He discussed what it takes to get to $1 billion, and one of them was you have to have an inside and an outside. You cannot grow and prosper being both. I looked at myself at that moment. I was miserable and knew we were stuck because I was trying to be the outside face of the company and sell. I wasn't having fun, and I was overstretched.

That's when I ended up hiring my next employee, my CLO. I texted her and said, "Linda, I need an inside. I need somebody to be my inside while I'm on the outside so we can grow." I'd worked with Linda at my first job in Kansas City, and she was never going to leave where she was. I think I struck her at the right moment because she said, "Let's go have dinner."

Somehow, I miraculously got her to come on board with us after only being a business for three years, and it fundamentally changed us. We doubled our revenue that first year. We were able to double in revenue again the second year. It was because I was able to get back and focus on what I was good at, and she focused on what she was good at. That's the key.

If you're an entrepreneur/owner, you've got to be comfortable selling all the time. I see this in companies and organizations that are startup tech companies, and they're creating software. As they're trying to raise capital and do different things, they end up being this engineer. They're not comfortable doing the pitches. They're not comfortable going out to sell the product. Maybe you started and created something amazing, and either you need to take some classes and get ready to sell and present, or at some point, you need to know what your role might be in the company and having to outside hire a CEO.

I've thought in the past that we might get to a place where I'd have to hire a CEO. I think I've grown through that because of mentoring. I don't want to restrict our growth because of my abilities. For me, it goes back to vulnerability and authenticity. I look in the mirror and ask, "Can I do this? Will I be okay with the honest answer that comes back?" If I can't, I don't know if I'm capable of taking us to the next level. I think people have to be honest with themselves about where they are. I think it's hard for a founder to do that at times.

I came from a small town of six hundred people. I remember growing up, reading books, and attending a personal finance class, wondering, "What did I want to do?" I would see a job that paid $30,000 a year and think that I could do that. I was so limited in my mindset because of where I was from and what was expected of me. Sometimes I forget how truly amazing and extraordinary it is what I've achieved. I forget to celebrate the success because I keep wondering why I haven't done more rather than think, "Wow, look what I've done."

I talked to a speaking coach because she wants me to do some speaking engagements. She believes I have a story to tell. I went back home for Career Day. I've been out of school for twenty-some years, and my teacher is still there, Mr. Tolliver. He was probably in his early twenties when I met him, right out of college, and we thought he was old.

After one of the sessions, he came up to me and said, "This is something you should be doing. No offense to your parents or anything else, but growing up, did you ever think that you were set up for success? Did you think that this is where you would be? Do you feel like you had the support to get here?"

I said, "No, I didn't."

He said, "This is amazing, and you can inspire so many of these kids who have no clue that this could be their path, too." Not just these kids in these small places, but also other women.

A friend of mine was the CEO of a large company here in town and one of my mentors. I told him, "I think we're as big as I want to be."

He said, "Why? Why are you limiting yourself?"

I said, "Because this is comfortable, and I make more money than I've ever needed to make."

"Angie, what if you could teach? What if somebody was watching you, and you did something so amazing, even more amazing than what you're doing? What would that do for other people who are minorities or in some class of being discriminated against?"

When talking to people like him, I feel this tremendous responsibility, which is why when somebody asks me out for coffee to learn what they can do in their business, I agree, even if they're starting a company to compete against me.

David Spaulding
The Spaulding Group
Spauldinggrp.com

One unique way our company has been affected by or improved upon by mentoring was through our company president.

Patrick Fowler joined our company twenty-one years ago right out of college, and after he got his degree, I think he planned to work in the food service industry. My wife suggested that I consider him. He was a friend of my son growing up, so he came in, and it wasn't much of an interview, because I already knew him and his family.

I explained what I was looking to do, and he decided to join us. Since he had no experience, he joined at an entry-level. Over the years, he's grown considerably, and he's been our president for seven or eight years. He became head of operations a little bit more than ten years ago and was given the title of CO, and now he's our president. Patrick plays a significant role in the company, so I think it's reflective of him learning from me. I never think of myself as a mentor. I don't consciously think of doing that, but apparently, I do.

I have read several books that have mentored me, and one is by a fellow named Nido Qubein. I think he's president of a college in North Carolina. I was exposed to some of his materials about thirty years ago, and this was through Nightingale Conant. I've been a big fan for a long time of listening to materials; I started doing it more than thirty years ago and still do.

Nido had various programs, and I found them helpful for somebody in my business. We're now in our twenty-ninth year, and Nido had some great ideas, so I reached out to him at that time. He was kind enough to respond, and some of his thinking played a role.

When you start your own business, you are exposed to many challenges, and I found that motivational or inspirational books like

Norman Vincent Peale's *The Power of Positive Thinking* were helpful too. So it's not the thing that necessarily you say, "Okay, here's something that I can implement in my business," but a spirit of trying to be objective and positive. Likewise, Napoleon Hill's *Think and Grow Rich* is a book that often gets cited because it's quite good about how we want to think about the things we want to accomplish.

There's a marketing guru out of California named Jay Abraham, whom I was exposed to about twenty-eight years ago through the motivational speaker Tony Robbins. Over the years, I and some of my senior folks have attended some of his programs, read lots of his materials, and listened to various things. We've implemented a lot of his ideas.

Another example is Micheal Gerber, who wrote *The E Myth*. I think he's spot-on, as many people start businesses, as he puts it, with an entrepreneur technician who doesn't have any grounding in the other parts of running a business. They may know the technical side of getting the task done, but there's so much more to running and growing a business. Though I thought I knew all that, it's still refreshing to hear him talking about it because you end up picking up some good ideas.

One of my mistakes is not listening to my thinking about things. I go along with what my senior folks will recommend, even though in my gut I think it's wrong. I'll give a quick example, as I spent a little time in politics.

I was the mayor of my hometown at one time. We were interviewing somebody for police director, and my inner circle interviewed this fellow, and everybody raved about him, but I wasn't so sure. I questioned it, but they were so enthusiastic I agreed to go along with them. About four or five months later, I fired him; he wasn't what they thought he was going to be.

There have been other times where my internal thinking is swaying me to do something, but I get advice to go in a different direction, and on occasion, I've given in to that advice and ended up regretting it.

So I've learned to trust my instincts. That's one mistake from which I've learned. So even though I'll hear people out—and I always want to hear from people—if by the end I still feel a certain way, more often than not, I'll go that way.

I served as a mentor when I was involved in the government. I was still running my business while I was in politics. I spent about twenty-five hours a week as mayor, so I somehow managed to run a company. When I was elected, I said I was going to run the town like a business, and that ended up being effective. We cut taxes and introduced a lot of good programs and had a positive four years. I tried hard to educate my management team so that we would hold regular meetings, and I would buy books for them.

We'd sit down and read these books and talk. One woman, Leslie MacNeill, came to me from Rutgers, the NJ State university, and I hired her to be the director of one of my departments. She'd never been in management, and I think I served as a good example for her.

Even though I've been out of office since the end of 2003, we're still friends. I think she would comment that I proved to be a mentor for her. I think I've served in the capacity for the other directors as well because I set a pretty good example. I didn't consciously set out to do that, but it was the way I carried myself. I always try to educate people by giving them books and sitting down and talking. I do that within the company, including the management team, to educate and have people improve.

The area that I feel most entrepreneurs need mentoring in is around what Michael Gerber speaks about. The idea that most entrepreneurs go off on their own because they've developed a particular skill.

Say you've got a plumbing company, and I've been working for you for ten years. I'm licensed, and I see you making all the big bucks. I could do this, so why am I working for you? So I start a plumbing company, but I don't know anything about marketing, customer service, budgeting, cash-flow management, and selling. I don't know anything. But I do know how to put in a toilet. There's a heck of a lot more to running a business than the technical side.

When I started my business in 1990, I think I was smart enough to know that. I already had an MBA, so I had some education, but I knew there were a lot of things I didn't know. So when I started, there were many areas I focused on. I continued to rely on Nightingale Conant, reading various books on various topics. But I also read lots of books on all kinds of things, from consulting to marketing to sales, and that paid off well.

One reason we've grown so well over the years is that we're strong at marketing. Most entrepreneurs don't even think about that. I think too many entrepreneurs think they know a lot of people, and of course, they're going to refer them and hire them. But it's not that simple.

I've known many folks over the years who've gone off on their own, and while they may have excellent technical skills and are bright people, they don't have the other necessary skills. I think a perfect example of an ideal entrepreneur is Richard Branson. From a technical standpoint, he knows nothing about the companies he owns. He doesn't know how to fly a plane. But he knows how to create and run a business.

I wouldn't say entrepreneurs should not have any technical skills, because I have strong technical skills. I also have lots of other skills, and then there are things that I'm not so good at, like selling. I hired somebody to do that and hired somebody to be in charge of operations. But if somebody wants to be an entrepreneur, the first book they should read is Micheal Gerber's *The E Myth*, because that's a wake-up call that there's a lot more to being an entrepreneur than knowing the technical side of the business.

You should always be learning and then seeking out those who know an area better than you, like the salesperson or a marketing firm. If you're going to be successful, you have to continue to learn. You don't say, "Well, I've got my degree, so I'm all set. I don't need anything else."

Learning should be a lifetime exercise, so I regularly read lots of books, and I'm always listening. When I drive my car—and I put a lot of miles on my vehicles—most of the time, I'm listening to something educational or inspirational. I do not listen to the radio, and I rarely listen to music or the news. I'd rather use that time for education. The late Zig Ziglar spoke about automobile university and that you should take your time in your car to be educated. Read books. Many people aren't aware that our presidents, such as Bill Clinton and George W. Bush, are incessant readers. Bush reads over a hundred books a year.

I suspect that Clinton does the same thing, as he's always looking forward to learning. If you're running a business, you should always be looking for new ideas, and there are plenty of opportunities to do that. Recognize that if you want to have a successful business, you can't quit. Say, on day one, you're all by yourself and filling all the boxes and work charts, but over time you want to start filling those boxes in areas where you're less knowledgeable or less skilled. Those are the opportunities to bring somebody in whom you can rely upon.

If I were to write a book, it would be to put the technical side of business aside a little bit. Although I don't want to forget that because on the technical side, you always have to continue to learn, you always want to strive to be recognized as the best at whatever that skill is, whatever your technical area. But you need to focus on other things. The most significant opportunity is marketing, and I'll go back to the plumber example.

Do you see ads for plumbers now? No, you don't, because they don't market. They don't have any real concept of customer service. But let's say you have a plumber come in to install a water heater for you. It's an excellent opportunity for them to say something like, "On an annual basis, I would advise that we do some service to make sure that everything is working as it should. Okay?" As long as they're not trying to rip you off, and if they sincerely believe this would be beneficial, then why wouldn't they tell you this?

Doctors are another perfect example of people who have exceptional technical skills but tend to lack business skills. At your age, maybe you get a physical once every year or two. I never get a call from my doctor saying, "It's time to come in for your physical."

Never. So there have been times when it's been close to two years before I get a physical because I don't think about it.

How hard would it be for the doctor to set up a file in their schedule and say, "It's time for Spalding to get his annual physical"? He could have somebody give me a call or send an email and say, "It's coming up on a year. We think you should schedule your physical." Why wouldn't they do that? It's not only good for me—because if it's true that I should have a physical every year, well, if they're not making sure I do, then I'm at risk—but also good for them because when I walk in the door, they charge me a fee. Granted, my insurance company covers part of it, but they make money. But they don't think about that. They don't think about running a business. Perhaps they think, "I've got my MD and a certificate on the wall, so they're going to come to me because I'm a great doctor."

Well, they may be a great technician, but a terrible entrepreneur.

Anthony Mora
Mora Communications Inc.
Anthonymorapr.com

Mentoring has been a big thing for my company. Whereas I was mentored in business, I was never mentored in this specific business: I've learned it. I've had the company for twenty-nine years now. I was a journalist first and the editor of a couple of magazines, and then I went into PR. I knew some of the business because I had been mentored by my dad and worked for my older sister for a while, but those were in different areas.

I didn't have that luxury of learning from others, so I learned on my own as I went, and as I hired people, I saw how important that was. So mentoring was always a big part of working with the people who work for me. I generally hire people based more on their strengths than their experience and then work to show them how I work and what's worked for me.

I've had people who've gone on to work for other companies. Many of them have started their own companies, and that's been cool to watch where they've been able to take that experience and utilize it for their own success.

My business mentoring was done through members of my family where I worked for their business. But in PR and journalism, I was mentored in many ways by the media, by working as a journalist, learning what the journalists needed from their point of view. Then when I went to PR, I knew from the journalist's perspective and from the etiquette perspective what was needed and what was wanted.

I did a lot of self-mentoring. I read books, but I'm not a nonfiction reader. I also write plays and novels. That's one of the things that I had to learn in self-mentoring because when I started, there was that real sense of I had to do one or the other. I had to run a PR firm, or I could be a writer. It took years to figure out that line of thinking was completely wrong—I can do both.

I've written a novel, and I've had five plays produced. Now I'm finishing a new novel. I think if I hadn't allowed myself that freedom of trying to figure out who I am in this, I would have probably given the writing up.

A lot of that mentoring came from reading novels, including authors Dickens and Balzac. *The Great Gatsby* is a great novel about what not to do in business.

Most of my mentoring came from writers because a lot of their works showed me how they followed who they were. That was a big lesson it took me quite a while to learn. I was conflicted for a long time about the thought that I had to pick one or the other, then I realized I've got to follow who I am and then figure out how that works into business instead of figuring out what the business is and how I mold myself to fit that.

My first novel was called *Bang!: A Love Story*, and that was published about twenty years ago now. Then I adapted that as a play, and that played in LA and New York. I wrote five plays after that, which were all produced. Right now, I'm finishing a novel, and I'm in talks with publishers. So, hopefully, that novel will be out pretty soon.

I think the biggest mistake I've made hearkens back to what I was talking about. I was trying to figure out how people run PR firms. I would look at other people and try to mirror them. I didn't pay any attention to the fact that my personality was completely different. I was looking at extroverts who like to go to events and parties. I would rather stay at home and write than go to a party. That's who I am.

I had to learn that I'm effective for my clients by finding good stories. Our mantra is, "Effective PR is effective storytelling." So I don't get stuff placed by networking or glad-handing; I do it by coming up with good stories and giving them to the media. We try to work as an extension of their editorial staff, and that's where working as an editor gave me a great leg up on things because I was being pitched all the time, and I saw the mistake people usually make is they try to sell me. They use superlatives: "This is the best," "This is the greatest," "This is the newest."

I would turn off completely at that point, say thank you, and hang up, where if they came to me and said, "Here is a great story for your readers because…" If they had a compelling story, and even if it didn't work, I was going to listen to them next time. So when I went to the PR side, I remembered that. My biggest mistake was trying to fit myself in a mold of how I saw other people were working instead of figuring out who I am. What are my strengths? And how do I incorporate that into the business I'm working in? You can't force yourself to be somebody you're not, because even if it works, it's not going to work because you're not going to be happy in it.

I enjoy mentoring a lot because it's fun to watch people learn, particularly when they incorporate it into their lives. Much of it has been in the business, such as showing people how PR works and what PR isn't and focusing on effective PR, which is storytelling. Many people who work for me have been artists in different fields—writers, musicians, and filmmakers. When working with them, I show them how they can utilize the media for themselves. I share with them that the biggest lesson I had to learn is that it's not an either/or decision we have to make. If they want to stay true to their art, that doesn't mean they have to get rid of the business or live in a garage somewhere.

Sharing those ideas has been as big a part of the mentoring as the nuts and bolts of "This is how you launch a campaign. Here are the steps to do that. This is how you work with the media. This is how you work with your clients." All that's been important, but so are the life lessons of "You know how to do that. Now how do you live as you within your world?" Particularly, since that was something I struggled with for years, I've become a cheerleader on that front because it made all the difference when I shifted my mindset.

We represent a lot of filmmakers and writers, and I used to hide the fact that I wrote novels and plays when I would talk to clients, but now I don't. It's a big part of who I am, and this is a big part of what makes me work in PR—because in both cases, my job is storytelling. It's serving different masters, in a way, but without compelling stories on either side, it's not going to work. When I work with clients, I ask, "What is the story that tells your story?"

The area I feel that most entrepreneurs need mentoring in is the nuts and bolts: how a business works, the inner workings of a business. The other important part is how you land clients and how you do prospect. Those basic parts are important because it doesn't matter what else you do. If you don't pay attention to those, if you're successful, you'll only be so successful, and it's going to fall apart.

But apart from that, it's "Now that you know how to do that, what are your preconceived ideas that you have going into this business? What makes your stomach hurt when you think of it? How can you shift that?" Because a lot of those don't have to be there. A lot of those are taught to us by people who are dealing with those same issues and didn't resolve them, and that you have the opportunity and hopefully the freedom to make different choices so that you remain as yourself within the context of what you do.

It all goes back to finding that way to remain true to yourself, but not in a Pollyannaish way. Not "I'm going to be me no matter what." It's "How do I remain "me" within the context of this business and be successful in the business?" Instead of "How do I fit myself into the cookie cutter so I can do the business the way so-and-so is doing it?" It's "How do I find out who I am, then move that within the business and be successful as me?"

So you're true to yourself, but you're not true to yourself in that sense of "I'm not going to do anything that I don't want to do." No, it's how you stay true to you within that context so that you grow within it and you're more or less self-defining your own success as you go. That's where I think mentors are the most important. Instead of telling you, "Now do this. Now do this. Now do this," it's "This is how you get into it and learn for yourself and are able to grow within it."

It's about flexibility. It can't be "Do this" because that's how they did it. Some of that's going to work for you. *Mirroring* is a big term, but mirroring can also send you in a whole messy direction.

I wrote two nonfiction books on PR, *Spin to Win* and *Alchemy of Success*. But if I were to write another book, it would be advising entrepreneurs to learn the nuts and bolts. It's almost like writing. People try to write experimental stuff, and this remains true: don't break the rules until you've learned them.

It's the same thing in business. Learn the rules. Learn the basics. Then start to break them, not to break them but to bring yourself into it, because as you do that, you'll find there are huge amounts of room. There's much more room for you to grow because you'll start seeing different opportunities and different ways of doing things that you would have never imagined if you were going the cookie-cutter route of "This is how I have to approach things."

Try to look at it with new eyes. At the same time, realize that you're going to judge how successful it is by how successful it is. You need the income coming in. You need clients. You need the business to grow. So that's going to be a big meter to examine. But within that, you also need to be yourself, and you need to be happy within the business. It's not going to do you any good otherwise. Being a miserable success is not a success.

Experiment. Look at the parts of you that are in your other life, if it's the artistic part for example, and play with how to bring that into business. Because there may be other areas or other ways the business could grow that you'd never think of because we tend to split off. We keep this part of ourselves over here and this part of ourselves in our business life.

Well, what if you didn't? What if you let those other parts come into your business life? How would they change your business? What are the different ways it could grow? What are different arenas or different types of markets you could look at? What's a different way you could present it? It gets to be fun, and that'll keep you going if it's fun.

We're taught to compartmentalize. We work, we're miserable, we get off, and we play. Break that. Don't be miserable. Many of us were taught that if it's fun, you're doing something wrong. If you're not struggling and suffering, then you're not doing it right. I think some of that's beginning to loosen up. I hope so. But you don't have to look at it that way. Changing the mindset is huge, and then keeping in mind that changing the mindset in and of itself is not enough. Now you need to implement that successfully and find out how it works.

Much of this is getting yourself to the point where you can fly solo because you'll need to do so to a certain extent. You need to take over the controls. This is your plane. Where are you taking it? There's a scary aspect about that, but it's incredibly exhilarating and wonderfully freeing.

Sukhbir Dhillon
Addteq
Addteq.com

Our company has been affected by, or improved upon, by mentoring in a bunch of different ways. We were fortunate to get a lot of business, and our growth was doubling every year. We started with 11 percent growth in year 1 to 22 percent in year 2 to 45 percent in year 3. Everything was going well, and when everything goes well, you feel you know everything.

Somewhere around that time, we suddenly became a pretty flat organization. The company where we were getting our customers changed some algorithms about how the company is going to be ranked. That affected our business and immediately exposed that we were pretty light on the marketing side.

We were getting all this business growth without marketing and grew to a substantial size. When the other company changed their algorithms, I started scrambling. I started talking to different people, and they suggested three different books to read. I also joined a couple of various boards to understand what different companies go through and so forth.

What helped me was reading different books and focusing on particular problems. The majority of the mentoring came from books I discovered via the advice of other people such as, "If you're facing this problem, read this book on facing the problem and then read this other book." This process helped us grow to where we are now. We formed structures and groups and learned to make them more independent. Now we're at a point where we feel like we know many things, but we still don't know them.

We have plans to start mentor programs within the company. My first objective is to have the executive team globally mentored to a degree where they can further guide their teams. People will be encouraged to sign up for different mentorships, which can focus on different areas. For instance, we have a major support arm that wouldn't need to be mentored in how business teams work. The same thing applies to HR, R&D, and other departments.

My favorite book so far has been *Scaling Up: How a Few Companies Make It and Why the Rest Don't* by Verne Harnish. I use that book now and then as I go back and reread a chapter. Another book that I am reading is called *Surrounded by Idiots: The Four Types of Human Behavior and How to Effectively Communicate with Each in Business* by Thomas Erickson. That book is helpful for people who feel that they know everything, but the team always fails. It's beneficial to understand that not every human being thinks the same way. You need to be able to think from your team's perspective so you can explain things better.

Besides those, there were a couple of other books recommended by a mentor called *Microsoft Secrets: How the World's Most Powerful Software Company Creates Technology* by Ruth Milkman. The mentor explained to me that there were times where people at Microsoft were trying to come up with Microsoft Office, and it almost drove them to bankruptcy until they took a different approach.

Another book is called *Multipliers: How the Best Leaders Make Everyone Smarter* by Liz Wiseman. It's about individuals who may be high performing but do everything themselves. That can work in a five-person company, but when you scale to fifty people, that same high-performing person can become a bottleneck. That person can become a diminisher.

A particular person in my life who has been one of my most influential mentors is my close friend and business partner in Addtech. I've known him since I was seven years old, and I'm forty-two now. He looks at the world differently, which frustrates me, and may not frustrate him. He would provide guidance or tell me to speak to somebody. He may recommend a book for me to read. Then we go from personal advice to business advice to medical advice.

I would say failure is the mother of every success; understanding failure teaches a person so many things. Sometimes when we look at things and don't know why problems are happening. We didn't spend enough time to understand the problem. There were many such situations in my life. One of them I mentioned above was when the company changed its algorithm, and it affected us so much. If we hadn't taken the time to look at our shortcomings, we could have collapsed within a year.

Instead, we looked at where the problems were and tried to solve them. Two years down the line, we were past that worst phase. Our bottom line was red to begin, but after we emerged on the other side, our bottom line started showing 10 percent EBITDA (earnings before interest, tax, depreciation, and amortization).

That was one failure that taught me a lot. Before that, I had previous business with a risk-averse partner, whereas I was a risk-taker. I became risk-averse with him, and we started stagnating. We began as a staffing company to raise some money and then go into services. I stopped taking risks along with him, and it took me a couple of years and reading the Steve Jobs book to understand that I was not becoming the solution—I was becoming the problem.

That was the biggest eye-opener that caused me to shut down that staffing business and start a services business in 2013. Now we do services as well as products, and by mid next year, we will surpass the service revenue.

I have served as a mentor to others, depending on the individuals. I end up choosing people to mentor whom I feel are high performing the way they are structured internally. Even though they may be high-performing, their overall impact radius is small. I end up picking those individuals to mentor as my objective at all times is to make them make the people around them understand and know about the technology work process and to help them grow the impact radius for them. That's the biggest thing I look for as at one point faced the same problem, and I'm still overcoming it. I can give good advice on that to people. Other people may not be high performing but can become high performers. I usually stay away from advising them because I did not personally venture on that journey.

YPO has invited me, but I didn't get an opportunity to go there yet. I went to Vistage a couple of times. I have a couple of advisors who worked in bigger MNA firms, and they advise me from time to time. In another quarter or so, I may be looking at something in the New York area to join.

The area that most entrepreneurs need mentoring is probably the scale. When we come up with something, no matter how big or small it is, we usually think from our perspective. A single individual says they can do this alone; they can write this by themselves. It all starts with, "I am by myself."

Then you start hiring people. You may have your first hire after six months, or you may have your first hire on day 2. Even that's not a problem, but the moment you hit ten employees, the same guy who was so smart when he was alone is now struggling to communicate his ideas to other people. He must scale to twenty people and then shrink back and then scale the thirty people and shrink back, and about 97 percent of entrepreneurs go through that process.

Forbes reached out to me because we were ranked in Top 5,000 Fastest Growing Companies in the country in 2018. We probably appeared in that ranking three years in a row, but unfortunately, I wasn't aware. So I went to some event in New York, and after that, they reached out to me. We were showcased at a couple of events for our software, which helps visually impaired folks write software code.

We took it to another level there. When people are writing documentation, they can connect their Confluence, which is a documentation tool, to Alexa. You can talk to it, and it can create tickets, do project management for you as you speak to it. We wanted to take it to another level where you can write code by talking to it.

So we were showcased at a conference where there were six thousand people in attendance. *Forbes* might have seen that, and that's when they reached out to us. We talked about this, and I said that the title of my book would be *25 to 25* because there was a time when I only had twenty-five dollars left in my pocket.

I have already been thinking about writing a book for quite a while as *Forbes* contacted me. As an individual, you think about something; you should go ahead and do it. The max would take, and then a year out of your life before you decide, okay, it's not working out, I need to shut it down. Or it may work out, and you can be the next person on a big billboard. But that one step when you decide that, "Yes, I should do it," comes from that single individual at that point and maybe two or three other peers who may be putting peer pressure on you.

A lot of people who don't become entrepreneurs is because they never cross that threshold. Many companies don't even see daylight because the person thought the idea they had was not good enough.

The second step is once you have your company, you scale it, pass that one-year mark, and then you need a second level of mentorship to scale it forward.

In my case, I was debating for almost a year whether I should be starting a company or not. My wife (who at that point was my girlfriend), along with a couple of friends, challenged me after a couple of beers. They said, "You are just saying this, but why are you not doing it?"

A few years later, I saw that if that moment hadn't happened, nothing would have happened.

Todd Sager
Awe Turning
Awe-tuning.com

We design, manufacture, and distribute across the globe enthusiast automotive products under our own brand, AWE. I started this journey twenty-nine years ago in a 100-square-foot converted horse stable with no running water and a single incandescent light bulb. Now, in 2020, we're a fifty-person company with an 800 SKU catalog, operating out of our own 33,000-square-foot facility on a 4-acre campus in southeastern Pennsylvania, complete with lasers and robots.

While I haven't had a single long-term individual who has been a mentor to me over the years, I've been lucky enough to have crossed paths with many, many people from whom I have gained life-altering snippets of information. I've also read a lot of business books.

To learn how to run our business while simultaneously changing the business became critical during a recent scale-up we did. Even though we'd been around for twenty-four years at the time, and the business had gone through a lot of scale-ups during that period, the one we did in 2015 was multimillion-dollar huge, and it added a ton of people, processes, and equipment (and also a very large mortgage).

In previous times, we were able to adapt to our new scale organically, as it tended to happen in a more gradual manner. This time, the change was so great and so sudden that we realized we needed to formalize the adaptation approach. In retrospect, we had assumed that we'd adapt as we'd always had done in the past, but this time, we continually found ourselves still doing things the "old way" even though we had done major investment in resources that were supposed to be the "new way."

We already had processes established, which we followed day to day to create our designs, take orders, make products, and ship them. Our challenge was to learn how to take advantage of all our newly acquired resource opportunities while still serving our current customer needs (and also servicing the significant newly created debt that came with financing those new resources). To take full advantage of the new opportunities was no small feat; in the end, it was going to essentially require a fundamental reinvention of the business. It was like the old saying about changing the tires while the bus is moving; we were running the business while simultaneously trying to profoundly change the business.

I belong to a number of different executive peer groups, as a learning resource, so I decided to approach them for mentoring help with our "moving bus/tire problem." They introduced me to concepts that would first identify "key performance indicators" in our company and then, most importantly, establish a way to make the monitoring of these KPIs be impactful.

It was apparent that while people in our organization had the best intentions, and truly cared about the customers and the products we made for them, there wasn't a cultural foundation from where we could deploy and succeed with big change initiatives. I realized that unless we found a way to actually be successful with major process overhaul, we risked people in the company becoming immune to the potential of such initiatives, and for them to see new initiatives as just the next "flavor of the day."

Major change needed to have a high degree of success, or it was doomed to be ignored the next time it was attempted. So, before we could deploy a KPI system, we first had to establish a culture of accountability, where people took individual ownership of their roles in key initiatives.

When asking myself why to that point in the company's history we didn't have a culture of accountability and ownership, I explored the choices that had led us to that particular state of affairs. I discovered I tend to confuse *abdication* with *delegation*. As your business grows, you realize over time that you can't do everything yourself, but there can be confusion between abdication and delegation as you hire other team members. You think because you carefully interviewed, and then hired, that you have somebody in place doing the job you used to do.

But if you don't have key metrics by which to measure this new hire's performance, all you've done is abdicate that role you used to do to somebody else. When you hire a finance officer, you shouldn't just say, "You're hired to handle the finance needs of the company." You have to put metrics in place to ensure that the role is performing as intended. It can't be that the box has been checked off and the assumption made that this new person is the expert you hired, so, by default, they must know what they are doing. That's not true delegation.

True delegation requires that the entrepreneur have some understanding of every single aspect of the organization, even if they hire people smarter or more experienced than them to do the actual work. If you're hiring somebody to do the role, and you don't understand how it works, or a method by which to measure its success, you're setting yourself up for possible failure by not optimizing utilization of that resource. That person may be able to do what you want them to do, but if you don't understand how that fits in with the rest of the organization, because you don't fully know what that role is, you're underutilizing that opportunity. Know everybody's job, but don't do everybody's job.

In my research on culture overhaul, I read a book that really helped me understand the distinction between abdication and delegation. It's called *Extreme Ownership*, written by former US Navy SEALs Jocko Willink and Leif Babin. They drive home the difference between identifying "a task needing to be done" and the concept of having somebody actually own that task and executing it against a specific goal.

Given our challenges of fundamentally overhauling the business after the major scale-up, extreme accountability was something that needed to happen in our organization if we were going to move the needle in a meaningful way. Just identifying a long list of tasks isn't the same as actually executing those tasks quickly and efficiently.

Extreme Ownership was especially powerful to read because it's not a dry textbook but an entertaining and compelling read (honestly, when there are US Navy SEALs involved, how could it not be exciting?), which really helps in getting multiple people engaged and making the exercise generate actual results. To really illustrate the concept of extreme accountability, the book used combat-related scenarios, because when there are lives on the line, there's no room for getting it halfway done. That's what extreme accountability is about: high performance. *Extreme Ownership* made such a profound impression on me that I had my whole executive team read the book (the first of many we would read together).

Once we had our culture of accountability heading in the right direction, we deployed task-management systems, such as the one found in another excellent book: *The 12 Week Year*, by Brian Moran and Michael Lennington. By shrinking our time horizon down to quarterly as opposed to annually, we placed more urgency on actual completion.

Finally, we deployed the KPI system brought to me by my peer group, which instituted an even more timely accountability mechanism, a daily line walk through each department in the company to keep the KPIs live. We also broadcast our performance throughout the whole company so that everyone, not just senior management, was engaged. Most importantly, because the people were now mentally ready to rise to the challenge, results were swift and positive.

To make the results lasting, we deployed the lessons learned in another really powerful and engaging book, set as a novel, called *The Goal*, by Eliyahu Goldratt. The message of the *The Goal* is that you must first look at all the departments and steps in your entire company as links in one long chain, and the goal should be to ensure that business flows along this chain with as little restriction and delay as possible.

For example, don't focus only on how efficient your production floor can be and then forget about how inefficient your shipping department is, because no matter how quickly your production floor can make your product, your shipping department still has to get it out the door to your customer so you can get paid.

If you don't understand your process bottlenecks, and you're always looking at each department individually inside your one organization, you're missing the whole point. It doesn't matter how extremely efficient one part of your organization may be if the rest of the organization does not meet that same efficiency standard. You're going to run into roadblocks that are going to undo all the hard work you've done upstream or downstream of that one bottleneck.

The Goal is a story told about a single manufacturer, but the concept is about the whole enterprise cycle—from start to finish. It also gets your mind to stretch outside the walls of your organization. In our case, if we have a bottleneck with a distributor who sells our product, it certainly affects our company on the downstream by restricting the availability of our product to the end user. On the upstream, if we have a vendor that's not producing to quality or on time, we're not able to sustain the rest of the flow.

A lot of businesses make up for this inefficiency by buying more labor and materials and creating all these buffers in their world that are a substitute for efficiency. That gets expensive. It also gets messy because you have to put those people and stuff somewhere. Then you're buying more space, and now you're in the spiral of spending money to make money, which is something that always needs to be done, but ultimately, you want to spend less than you're making. I would describe *The Goal* as a book about manufacturing that absolutely also applies to all businesses in general.

On the topic of me providing mentorship to others: well, the enthusiast automotive industry has a relatively low barrier to entry, and like a lot of other trade-based industries, there are many people in it that start businesses because they have the craft skills, but they don't necessarily have the business skills. This is the core topic of another great book: *The E-Myth*, by Michael Gerber. I was introduced to that book many years ago while taking an accounting course offered by the Wharton School of Business, and they were wise to make it required reading. It really opened my eyes to how my approach to my own business was fundamentally backward. When I had decided to hang my own "open for business" sign, I, too, was one of those capable tradespeople who had simply assumed they could run a business.

On the flip side, since my own business story started in a hundred-square-foot garage, an extreme barebones startup, and progressed to today where it is one of the most recognizable brands in our industry, I've gained credibility as one who has "come up through the ranks," who turned a passion into a sustainable operation.

That credibility has allowed me to mentor others in our industry. When I can, I reach out to them, sometimes unsolicited, to say, "Hey, if you want to talk about this, or if you're looking for input on that, let's connect." I elicit dialogue with them by email, social media, and instant messenger. I do a lot of one-on-ones, where I ask them what they need, what's going on, and let them know that if they need help, I'm here to fill in some of the blanks or at least tell them about my mistakes and about how not to do it.

One of the main reasons I feel the obligation to others in my industry is because when I was early in the game and frustrated by many obstacles, I reached out to someone like my "today self" to see if he would be willing to teach me the ropes. One of the big names in our industry back in the 90s was New Dimensions, a large automotive enthusiast product e-commerce and installation facility near San Francisco, clear across the country from me. It was run by a guy named Tim Hildebrand, and he was really ahead of his time, doing those things in the '90s.

To his credit, Tim accepted my request to learn "from the master," and I flew out to his facility to spend a week immersing myself in his business. Technically, he opened his doors to a competitor (albeit a tiny one), and I've never forgotten that generosity he had extended to me (I tried to pay him back by unsuccessfully air-shipping a bushel of the sweetest Pennsylvania white corn I had ever tasted in my life, but that's a different story for another day).

When interacting with new business owners, offering the same mentorship as Tim did for me, I frequently come across a recurring topic, the concept of top-line revenue being, what I like to call, a "false profit." It's a common thing that many young entrepreneurs believe: their key performance metric is sales, sales, sales, sales, and sales, and they feel that obtaining sales cures all ills.

With our own company, we learned the hard way how rapid growth can be very costly, on top of what was already a very cash-flow-intensive type of business, and therefore, we really had to learn how to focus on our bottom line, to know how to make sense of the quantitative profit needs of the business (not just the big revenue goals), and also to deal with the timing needs of profit (cash flow). So, unfortunately, I find myself uniquely qualified to speak about all the pain that can happen when you focus too much on top-line revenue.

Many new entrepreneurs see profit as the reason they're in business: to put cash in their own pockets. It may not be the only reason, but it's absolutely one of the main reasons that entrepreneurs want to start their own businesses. So when the cash comes, it tends to get siphoned into the pocket of the entrepreneur instead of staying in the company, or worse, it can be used solely to keep the lights on, neither supporting the personal lifestyle of the business owner nor creating healthy growth opportunities.

What a lot of entrepreneurs struggle to grasp is that cash reserves are a critical business tool, like a piece of equipment, along with the other resources they need to run the business. Cash is one of those resources, and many don't understand that while it's still in the company's bank account and not yet in the business owner's pocket, it's not simply there to pay the bills.

Cash reserves, typically referred to as "working capital," should be established to allow the entrepreneur the ability to operate in a mentally healthy manner. If there aren't those cash reserves, the entrepreneur can constantly be in a hand-to-mouth scenario and can end up being stressed while trying to make payroll, pay vendors, pay rent, and pay all the other claims on the cash. They constantly will be walking a tightrope with no safety net if the unforeseen happens (and it always does). The constant state of stress will inevitably lead the entrepreneur to work from an overly conservative mindset; they won't make big moves or experiment with new concepts. The lack of a cash safety net will keep them from taking steps to grow their own business.

By earmarking cash that needs to stay inside the business as reserves, any shortfall in cash needed to support the business owner's lifestyle will be revealed, which then will speak to the true profit margin that the company must achieve in order to operate in a healthy manner, to serve both needs. To realize that cash must be left in the bank is a sophisticated evolutionary step for the new small business owner, a bottom-up approach, and to actually structure the business to do so, while also supporting their personal lives, takes discipline.

Creating a profit margin that generates sufficient cash reserves inside the company while simultaneously enabling a healthy and enjoyable lifestyle for all stakeholders is perhaps what I'd like to write about in my own book someday.

REVERSE MENTORING

While interviewing the seventy leaders included in *Supreme Leadership Mentors*, we learned quite a bit. Specifically, we found again and again that the single most common trait of a great leader is knowing to accept mentoring wherever it is. In this next section, you'll meet mentors who welcome learning from the younger generation—their employees, interns, and mentees.

The saying "You can't teach an old dog new tricks" has no place in this next section. This group of leaders made themselves available to the upcoming generations and the knowledge they brought to the industry. Enjoy this next group of top businesspeople discuss how they remain relevant, educated, and in the know by learning from their mentees.

Paroon Chadha
Passageways
Passageways.com

In the world we live in, there are many opportunities around us where people get into running a business or build products at a young age early in their career. Then there's the second aspect of when you're learning so much stuff, there's a chance to pay it forward, and we've done a significant amount of work on that side of the table as well.

For my MBA at Purdue, our finance professor, Professor Sullivan, asked us to talk to a credit union in town. At this credit union were me and another gentleman I met at Purdue, Chris, who was an undergrad. We made a sales pitch to Purdue Fed for a product we were tinkering around with called OnSemble, so it still exists. Purdue Fed made a seed investment and became our first customer.

It was a long shot that we connected, but we met some wonderful people at Purdue Fed, and they made an investment of $100,000 in our business, which we returned to them more than fifty times. Fifty-times return was done before we finally had to buy them back, and they are no longer an owner in the company. We were expanding internationally as a company, and a credit union is not meant to be investors in companies that take on those risks.

Because of that, I came into contact with Bill Connors and Bob Falk, the two CEOs at Purdue Fed. Passageways was a two-person team, and then we grew from two to more than a hundred people across different countries. These two men were generous in giving me advice. Because they were first Bill and then Bob as the CEO, both had seen us in a formative period of our lives. They gave me and Chris great advice and then gave us open mentorship. I remember once Bill said, "Paroon, my goal has always been to train you to have a conversation with me, even when I'm not there."

I said, "How do you figure that?"

He said, "Well, I'm going to retire, and I'm going to move, and I'm not going to be in Lafayette, Indiana, anymore, but at the same time, all the conversations that we have between now and the next two, three years, I'm going to ask you what you think I will tell you to do."

That's what he did every single time. He not only gave us solutions but also gave us solutions by forcing us to think like a CEO. When you start, nobody knows how to think like a CEO, and that his advice was worth its weight in gold. He also took us to various conferences and dinners with other CEOs and exposed us to many things that came in handy later in my life.

This experience impacted us because there's a need to be not only an operator but also a leader in terms of building a team, strategizing, and raising money. To do all those things, you need you to be more than a CEO, but truly a leader.

Bob is similar in the way he guided us after Bill left. Bob is still in town, and I still meet with him frequently. Gail, who was the chief operating officer, joined Passageways toward the end of her career. She is retired now in this town as well.

All three taught me that as a leader, one has to be generous. The generosity gene is almost the most critical gene to have as a leader. You have to be generous to people when they do well and when they don't have their best moments, and in just the way you think about the future. Sometimes you make-believe in your mind in terms of how people may get there, because the impossible is done with the team lead, especially in the tech world.

We've seen that happen time and time again here at Passageways. They trained me to be thinking like that, and that is different from where I came from. Growing up in India, I think people are much more cutthroat, and you get the credit for what you deserve, which is a different culture. You can't get credit for what you've not achieved, and in the US, whereas on the other side, where sometimes you get trophies just for showing up.

Somewhere in there, when you get to the real business world, how do you calibrate that framework and come across as somebody who is thoughtful while you're also encouraging? I think that that was a big part of what I learned from these two guys, and their teaching continues to pay the bills.

I took it upon myself to make mentorship a substantial part of my work life and became a Big Brother here in the local community. As part of the Big Brother Big Sister program, I got a chance to partner up with a kid by the name of Alvin, for five and a half years, before he graduated and ended up at Purdue. You can do a little bit of this at the community level, because some organizations may have a structure, and some may not, but that should not stop you from starting your journey to be a mentor.

I encourage people on my team to get involved with the Big Brother Big Sister program, and there are several of us who are involved with the local chapter in Lafayette. Now I'm on the board of Big Brothers of Greater Lafayette, and it's rewarding to see that program grow. They have a day every year when we bring in all the littles and let them walk through the organization. The littles get to meet with different people, see how people are working. I've had several instances of people attending a business meeting as a young person just starting their career. They need some real-world experience, so all that is in the category of taking some personal initiative to be able to mentor people around you.

There's a significant benefit to mentoring that comes about, even for you. In my field, in the tech space, you have to work with young people. A lot of the people on the engineering teams, especially, are in their early twenties. To understand where they live and how they think, I knew my best shot was to see that through the eyes of a seventeen, eighteen, nineteen-year-old, and that's what I got to see by working with my little, Alvin.

I didn't plan it that way, but it was easy for me to relate to my engineering team, just because I had spent a lot of time with Alvin. So the benefits of mentoring include not only the feel-good aspect that it brings about—and indeed it's what makes this world go round—but sometimes these serendipitous benefits that you may accrue over some time.

Mentoring always goes both ways; it's rarely a one-way street. I want to encourage everyone to think about that in your journey, because this is one of the things that people don't talk about, and when you start to talk about it with somebody, you'll always hear some fun stories.

Now, as a company, we have certainly continued to take on the initiative to help people and mentor people. Lafayette, Indiana, is the hometown of Purdue University, so there are probably about half a dozen different speaking engagements that I do every year on Purdue's campus. I share with people at the entrepreneurship center and at the business school for people who are considering a career that is at the intersection of technology, business, and entrepreneurship. Many interactions have allowed me to share some of the insights I've gathered and the ways to utilize time well while at school.

I feel like this is one of the most amazing aspects of my journey. Certainly, the US does this better than anybody else in the whole world, where university campuses just give you a fantastic opportunity not only to find yourself but also find business partners and mentors. Being aware of the fact that you are on campus and this is the one time in your life where you are probably sitting with fifty to eighty people who are all hoping to start a business is a unique time in your life. You're also sitting with people who could be your life partner, too, whether a business partner or spouse.

Being on a university campus is just amazing. I found my life partner during my undergrad in India when we were both in the same engineering school. Then I found my business partner when I was doing my master's here at Purdue.

When I speak, I tell them, "Look, right now, you're a blank slate, and that's a great place to be." I do a fair amount of that, and I have encouraged my team to do a fair amount of that as well. Between our team, we are the largest technology company here, so we get a fair share of chances to share our experiences. We do more than a dozen or so speaking opportunities at Purdue and around here in town as well.

I think there are several such opportunities all around you, especially when you're in school or the early part of your career. I think one has to send out the signals to stay open and indulge in it, and the benefits will be there right away. If you never had a mentor in your life, I would encourage you to try it, even if you don't find a lot of success in the first go around. Try it a time or two, and you'll be sold on it just like I am.

One of the challenges that people continuously run into is deciding which book to read and which book or podcast to listen to. I don't intend to add to the confusion there, but certainly what I would advise is to take a step back and think about your framework and how you assimilate information when you read or when you listen to podcasts or books.

One of the confusions I had early in my life was trying to read a lot of books, and I've changed that a little bit. I'm always reading books in search of those eight or ten books that I'm going to read every year. So I may read a book, on an average, maybe every two or three weeks, but if I don't like it, I'd probably read it, and then it'll be a casual read. I'll flip through it, read maybe three or four chapters if I don't think it's for me.

But if I find a good book, I'll add it to my collection of books that I'll read every year. I feel like this is a significant difference that has come about over the years for me.

I credit a gentleman by the name of Naval. He blogs and writes, and he does a podcast as well to help me to figure this out. He's an entrepreneur who started AngelList. Now I read these same beneficial books again and again.

Recently, I came across a book that is super helpful: Ray Dalio's *Principles*. Ray Dalio also has a lot of free audio and video on the web, if you want to sample it. I think it's amazing because it has great principles on how to live your life and to run your business. That's what the book is all about.

Then I have some books that I read just because they are formative to my work. *Eating the Big Fish* is a book that allows you to plan on how to outdo your competition, which is one that I have to read every year, and it's amazing how every year I get different things out of it. I also encourage people to read *Crossing the Chasm* by Geoffrey Moore, which is a book that helps you understand how the market behaves when you come up with a new product and the innovation cycles and the product life cycles. That's another book that I read every year.

When you run a business which is backed by venture, you have a pretty significant leadership team and accomplished people around you, and you will certainly feel the need to have a lot of people go through CEO coaches, and there are various avenues.

I'm a member of YPO, which is a professional organization that creates a safe space for all CEOs. It's a membership organization, where you pair up with eight or ten other CEOs and meet monthly to discuss your challenges. I make use of all those advantages that today's environment provides. There are board of directors and accomplished people who have been through similar cycles time and time again. But for me, I have a super close friend, somebody I grew up with and admire a lot for the way he thinks. His name is Sanjeet.

Sanjeet is based in Singapore, and he's been in C-level positions. He was the chief marketing officer for about twenty-five or thirty countries in the Citibank world. Now he works at another insurance company out of Singapore, doing Asia, Pacific, and Europe. He has mentored me on a personal level. We are about the same age; we went to the same high school.

In everybody's life, there are going to be challenges. We struggled to have a baby, my wife and me, and Sanjeet was a fantastic mentor through that journey. I still go back to him when big questions show up, such as who should I take the investment from, should we go to a different country, how to expand, or how should I think about X or Y.

If you run into a challenge in values, if you get conflicted somewhere, you need an inner sanctum of people around where you can have the safety of not being judged, but to be able to share things and let them objectively tell you what they think. Sanjeet has been that one person consistently for me for the last two decades.

I think the inner sanctum has to be created where there is a complete sanctuary from judgment. That's what it comes down. Where you can say, "Hey, look, I want to do this, but at some level, I'm conflicted because it doesn't go well and on this value plane or doesn't fit well. Or I'm worried about what people may think." Somebody needs to walk you through certain situations like this, as it gives you a way to be thoughtful about those situations that aren't acting on instincts and more of just a spur of the moment.

I feel like working with people fresh out of school is a fantastic place to be. I am a big believer in reverse mentoring. This summer, I have two interns working here, and they are both going to graduate soon, so they have another year left at school. Likely, I'll continue to work with them, and I'm sharing not just project work and just what they're supposed to do for this summer, but I'm also sharing with them what does it feel like to be doing what I am doing right now. Where we have offices in different countries, there's a business plan, a board, and an aggressive growth path.

These are young people, but they are high-caliber people, and I've known them for three years, through various introductions, and I wanted them to get an early look into what this looks like. These are just the two whom I'm working with right now, but certainly, I think there are about half a dozen businesses I've invested in, and I regularly get a chance to work with the founders and the CEO of those companies, talking about what challenges they are running into, often over a round of golf, or maybe just catching up over some cold beverages.

But I certainly make it a point to share my perspective when people are going through their journeys. If you're an entrepreneur, you're somebody who wants to run a business in a small town like Lafayette, Indiana, or somebody who's trying to be innovating in the secure collaboration space. One should seek out mentors who have a good experience in what you want to do. I think those are the areas that stand out in my book, and I'm happy to work with people who are inclined toward one of these suites.

The challenges that entrepreneurship brings about are unique. You don't go find that out anywhere else. You don't learn it at school.

Talking about emotional resilience, one has to have that to be a good entrepreneur. It's rare to find people who succeed in what they set out to do just exactly the way they put it down in the business plan. So this is a roller coaster, and that's the word most commonly used to describe an entrepreneurial journey. I feel that emotional resilience is something that has to be built. It's exactly like going to the gym and exercising your biceps or your triceps; you have to develop those muscles to make them bigger. It doesn't just happen. Your IQ is important, but I think your emotional quotient is far more critical.

Most entrepreneurs are going to overlook this particular aspect of it and then realize that when it came to initial customers, initial employees, or initial investors, lots of pushbacks and rejections happen. That rejection is standard. That reaction is how it's supposed to be because you're doing something that has never been done before. Most people don't get it; they just push back because they've never seen it, and they don't believe that you can pull it off.

Yet entrepreneurs can routinely make the impossible happen these days, so it's become such an amazing ecosystem. If I think about people who do well outside of the entrepreneurship ecosystem and people who do well here, the most significant difference is the emotional resilience that people have who end up taking entrepreneurship.

I think in a five, ten, fifteen, twenty-year cycle, you would end up creating a reflection of who you are—the organization takes on your personality. You have to be conscious of how you behave in these situations and how you grow a team around you. The culture of the organization is going to reflect who you are.

In the stories about some of the famous entrepreneurs, such as Steve Jobs not being polished in certain areas, there's much embellishment that happens in those stories.

The fact is that each of these guys and gals have to be amazing emotionally; that's the only way to change the world because that journey is not going to be a smooth ride. So that's the area where I focus on the most: physical health, mental health, the ability to create a sense of trust around you, and all that requires you to be conscious about it. These things just don't happen naturally.

I think for entrepreneurship to be done well, you need to learn how to succeed and play the game the right way. As you that, you shorten your learning curve. One has to be conscious of what skills you develop in your life, and I think everybody's making those choices every day, and I just want to make sure that people understand.

The single most significant thing that I feel one has to understand is that entrepreneurship is a multi-varied journey. Multiple variables will be thrown at you, and you have to be able to handle all of those well by developing the important skills, which may differ a little from each other. I would say reading a lot, writing a lot, being good at logic, math, and arithmetic are skills that are easy to understand, and they should be your focus.

Once you've done this, there are a couple of the things that become important, which you need to learn, and I think one of those things is being good at sales or being good at persuading people. I would say that's the critical focus that one should have in mind, simply because as an entrepreneur, you have to sell your product.

Customer development is undoubtedly a big part of it. Still, then, you have to raise money, you have to recruit the board of directors and the right employees and develop the right leadership for the team, and you have to convince the partners to come to join your business. There are so many different aspects of sales. People just call it sales, and *sales* is a bastardized word, but it comes down to being persuasive in so many different directions that it's got to be one of the foundations of where you become good.

People are shy about it, but if you're good at reading, writing, and logic, being persuasive is going to come naturally to you, because you have to piece all that together.

Sometimes reading a lot gives you ways to think about the same problem, and you get exposed to a lot of ways to tackle a challenge. Writing helps you formulate your thoughts. Logic allows you to see the right options like the ones that you should favor. All those three come together when being persuasive. You see it flow when you are talking about it, whether it's recruiting a new VP of sale, a new round of investors, or whatever the business may throw at you. I feel like that's not understood by most people when they are thinking about this career.

Between emotional resilience and the essential skills that make you a good entrepreneur, I think that's where I would focus.

Kent Kelley
Meeting the Challenge, Inc.
Mtcaccessibility.com

Our company lives and dies by mentoring. We're a small company, so we interact with all our staff, and it's the key to our success. The growth and development of meeting the challenge depend on mentoring because we're a company that consults with the highest level of knowledge and expertise on disability rights laws. So if our staff doesn't understand that concept when they go out and do their field assessments and other tasks, then they don't know what the company is all about.

Every person hired here starts at an entry-level position, so that allows the staff to gain an understanding of how our company operates successfully from that interaction. It reaches from the bottom to the top of our company, and we also have an open-door policy, where every staff member has access to me and all the other senior staff levels when they get hired. Through a structured mentoring program based on supervision, training, and mentoring by our senior staff members, new hires can ensure that they acquire the skills and knowledge necessary to rise in the ranks of our company. We have twenty-six members and I don't sleep even with only twenty-six members; I can't imagine trying to mentor half a million members.

We have both a structured mentoring program and an informal mentoring program. My office door is always open, and I would like to think that every one of my staff members would take a bullet for me. They have access, and I think that's the way we built the organization. Our business model is a team approach. Even though there is a hierarchy of employees, they all have access to every one of us. We have kind of a bullpen, where there are two senior knowledge leaders that can not only overhear what the other consultants are talking about on the phone but can also provide real-time help and knowledge for whatever question they may have.

The bullpen is augmented by my open-door policy, where they can always come in (and they do, frequently, like every five minutes) and ask questions about contracts or methods of assessment, technology, or whatever. We have a wide-open policy of collaboration, and there's free décor. That's why I made that comment earlier that I hope they would take a bullet for me. That's because we have developed such a strong mentoring program that we all kind of find ourselves as family members in this organization.

I've always had a saying that if you don't share my enthusiasm, then—it's from the Steve Jobs movie—I won't say the words. But if you don't share my enthusiasm, then you don't belong here. If our enthusiasm inspires them, then we hope they're compelled to either talk to the knowledge leaders, their subdivision, or even come to me personally and say, "Hey, I've got an idea."

Then we routinely respond, "Well, that's a great idea. Let's move forward with it."

We do disability rights consulting, and you must have the mentality that we're doing something that's going to benefit the communities and the clients that we serve. We built a successful team that's committed to that philosophy. That creates enthusiasm because they've all had experiences with family members and other people with disabilities. They know that what they do benefits the communities. It's not just working for a paycheck; it's an activity that improves our communities.

When we first started this process of our consulting group about ten years ago, we had no structure. We were an entrepreneurial company, and we wanted to get the message out and provide knowledge and value to our clients. So we didn't have a formal mentoring program. Our business model was you hire a field technician, then they hold the end of the tape and help measure, and hopefully, they would be inspired. But we realized that lack of a structure created employees that weren't necessarily committed to our goal, which is creating a more accessible world for everyone.

We decided instead to build a team of people who are completely committed. If they were to realize what the greater good of the company was, we had to mentor them. So we created an educational program around the disability rights laws and also engaged them in every process of our deliverables to our clients. They were included in staff evaluations, participated in company decisions, everything. Now they were not only the persons that held the tape, but they were also interacting with our clients on a high-level basis.

Our clients include city council members, mayors, and county commissioners. The employees had to learn to interact with them. They couldn't just be people that were out there in the field doing the grunt work for our company. The mentoring we provided them not only gave them the knowledge but also the ability to communicate with high-level officials.

I made a hundred big mistakes growing our company. I was hired by the founders of the company ten years ago to develop a consulting division, and since I'm a business strategist, I thought I knew everything I needed to know. I made so many mistakes mostly because I came from a varied background where I had some personal experience with people with disabilities, but I didn't know the law. So I made a lot of mistakes.

The business model with which I started was a big stick versus carrot. I didn't realize that what they needed—what my clients and my potential clients needed—was information on how to solve their challenges with compliance with the ADA. I tried to shove it down their throat. That didn't work. So then we developed training to educate them, and then they chose our company to help them consult with their projects.

The founders of our company left their high-paying jobs to start this little company, and they decided that they had knowledge that could be of value that would be outside their grant with the ADA centers that they received from the Department of Education. So they hired me to start this consulting division. They expected maybe $100,000 in revenue a year from that, and we have far surpassed that.

The knowledge that we have to offer to our state and local governments, our restaurants, hospitality, and how we can help the people in our communities is precious.

The founders had a tremendous mentorial impact on me. First, I came from a varied background. I was vice-president of commercial lending for a bank. I had been a commercial real estate broker and a construction company manager. So when I came to this company, it was outside of my realm of experience, except that I was close to a person with a disability. And I had to live on a day-to-day basis with how inaccessible our community was for persons with disabilities. The best part of that mentoring was they not only instilled the regulatory knowledge that I needed to succeed but also gave me the ability to make mistakes and then create successes out of those.

The Balanced Scorecard is one of my favorite books. We have to report (and I dislike that) to the board. So the book gives me the coaching to create infographics that allow my board to understand that I'm kicking butt. I recently started to read *The Ten-Minute Trainer* by Sharon Bowman because training is a big part of our business. We do that pro bono and also for fees.

Communication is the critical element I feel people should seek to improve. Many entrepreneurs have great ideas. They believe they are going to build influential companies, but if the leaders can't communicate with the people they work with, then their success is going to be challenged. I believe that communication is what allowed me to be successful with this company. If you have a shut door or if you're living in an ivory tower, you have no chance of success. You have to talk to your people every day, every single person in your organization.

Fortunately, my organization is small, but as an entrepreneur, if you can't speak to your people, they won't succeed. I had one of my largest clients call me when I was traveling for work, and they said, "We want to fire you."

I said, "Wow, that would ruin my company. Why is that?"

And they said, "Because you haven't communicated."

So I made a commitment to them. I had kind of relinquished that authority to communicate with other people, and I committed to them to not only give my staff to be on board with them every week and interact with them. That's resulted in another million dollars' worth of revenue from that organization because we made that commitment to communicate.

I work with a lot of young people, and they don't know how to communicate. They can send you a text message or post on social media. (Hopefully, they don't tag me.) We hire entry-level people who are in their twenties. I have to hire the right person for my team. I don't care if they can communicate or not in the beginning, but they have to fit into my team.

It's a team that's committed to hard work, travel, and knowledge of the regulations. If they want to move up, they can do that through constant communication with me and their supervisors. I encourage them to learn and grow from the people around them and eventually learn to communicate with their clients, which are very high level. If they follow our lead, they can learn to communicate well.

Mentorship is happening all the time in our company. We take it very seriously and have created a daily environment of constant mentoring that also has formal mentoring and training sessions designed to move employees forward and generate passion for their work. I found that if you're always positive and encouraging and give compliments and recognition, they perform better.

I want all the people who work around me to develop their strengths, beliefs, and personal attributes. Be enthusiastic! It's contagious. Like I said, if you don't share my enthusiasm, you don't belong here.

Finally, this is the most important thing: I learn from my people. So there's always something new to learn, and I learned that from my people. But be willing to learn, and I encourage my staff to learn in every way they can.

Matthew Kornau
Kaleidoscope® Innovation
Kascope.com

We have a diverse workforce of engineers, designers, software developers, and UX people that range in age, professions, and diversity. We pair experienced people in the workforce with some of the younger folks, and I think there's a nice mix of interaction from what drives the older folks in their career versus the younger ones. Also, with that diverse workforce, we pair them on projects together, so the experienced people can learn from the younger folks who bring new ideas to the table while getting the experience from the older folks.

In the ophthalmology space, we have some professionals with years of experience in the corporate industry. Some are doctors, and in terms of the training, we were able to field to additional offices by bringing the training levels up. I think it helps people to see their roles and how their work impacts others around them; it brings everybody's skill sets up together.

I have probably about ten former customers working for me today. I saw how they conducted themselves in industry, whether it was Ford Motor Company or Johnson & Johnson. When they were looking for a different career choice in a smaller entrepreneurial type company, I was quick to bring them on because I learned so much in terms of dealing with them over the years directly.

Probably the best book that taught me from mistakes that I've made along the last thirty years at Kaleidoscope is *The 4 Disciplines of Execution: Achieving Your Wildly Important Goals* by Chris McChesney, Jim Huling, and Sean Covey, and that's defining what the wildly important goals of the company are.

In the beginning, I set up a lot of diverse goals, and I think if you get more than one or two wildly important goals from the book and get everybody articulated around informing their goals underneath to meet the two main goals, you're more successful.

Several things define a wildly important goal. It has to be measurable. It has to be articulated so everybody can understand it, and it has to have a defined timeline to have success. Your goals have to be defined, but they have to be limited. You can set other goals down the road as you complete those goals and business changes over time. You have to be flexible, but if you have ten wildly important goals, your rate of success is going to be minimal, and you probably won't succeed at any of them. Your attention will be too diffuse, not focused enough.

We learn through our mistakes. Culture is vital to our company and our growth, and I brought some folks in to the company who didn't necessarily match the culture of the company. That can be debilitating for the rest of the crew, and I've learned that you have to weed those folks out quickly to maintain the company's culture and growth. I've learned to screen for those more undesirable elements in the hiring process. I've brought in three recruiters that are in line, and they've been with me for a while, so recruits are screened pretty heavily these days.

We have a pretty open environment and an open-door policy, but we have monthly lunches with the CEO where we bring in five different members each month and sit down together. We have a group of people who elicit feedback and then pick five employees each month. They can ask any questions they want in terms of growth, not only from a professional standpoint, but also from a personal standpoint, as I think it's important to recognize both of those things. I've learned a lot from them. I've got probably as much goodwill and understanding and new lines of thoughts as I was passing it along to them.

Then we have one-on-ones for onboarding, and whenever we bring in a new employee, I sit with them for an hour. So does everybody else in the company, so as they're onboarded, they get to know everybody. We also have external opportunities and encourage people to ride and participate in conferences. We have lunch & learns where people bring in maybe not something exactly related to work, but an interest of theirs, to bring them on and get feedback from the crowd, so there's plenty of mentoring opportunities within the company. I think, in today's work environment, the line between work and personal is more blurred than ever.

Over my thirty years in business, I've had numerous employees that, in talking with them, felt they had to look for new horizons when recognizing their ambitions about where they wanted to go. I've had many leave for corporate positions because they came to the company right out of school, and being in a consultancy, it's a different atmosphere. I think it's essential for them to get that type of experience, and I've had a number of them come back after getting that corporate experience too.

If somebody has an ambition outside Kaleidoscope, I encourage them to go for it. Usually, it means more business for Kaleidoscope because they've left on good terms, and I think most of the people know that they can come in, as it's an open environment. If it's not right for you for whatever reason, personal or relocation, or whatever, I encourage them to be open and honest, and I'll do the same with them.

We have people who have left that have gone to corporate, then they've gone back to school to get their PhD at MIT. They're in positions where they're a lot more successful than I am, and hopefully, they learn some things here that helped them along their way.

The area that most entrepreneurs need mentoring in would be in leading a company that does innovative products and experience. Entrepreneurs need to create new business environments and be flexible in terms of the growth of the company. They need to listen to their employees, as they have ambitions and needs, and I've had many employees bring in ideas that I never thought would interest us. That's how we grew from being a design consultancy with industrial designers to adding biomechanical engineers.

From a business perspective, teaching employees what the business is about and being open with the finances and understanding how a company runs give them a deep appreciation of what the business is. I think they respect our openness and truth. Talking about whether you're having a good month or a bad month and why you're doing it makes a stronger employee and a stronger company.

I feel it's essential to embrace the "other's first" approach. Try to work harder than anybody else. Lead by example. Provide your customers and employees with the best quality of work you can offer and be a servant first, whether it's to the employees, the team, the customers, or whatever end-user may be. I would think that would be the biggest thing I would include if I were to write a book.

Mar Ricketts
GuildWorks
Guildworks.com

The most interesting way mentoring has affected or improved our company has been through our clientele. Being a specialty design engineering application/installation company, we work on large projects with many different architecture firms. As we become a part of the project and design, we end up working more closely with the architect and developing a stronger relationship than we would with other types of contractors. Those relationships become friends and colleagues, and they teach us a lot because architects are, in many ways, the business runners of the world.

Architects design buildings and spaces that change the faces of the cities and places where we live. Understanding how to lead that development and pull real estate developers and investors into a vision is the gift of certain people in that trade. We learn many things by working with architects, such as how they approach clients and develop the spaces for their grand visions. This experience has taught me to do the same thing when I reach out to other architects or clients who contact us directly.

I hold this broad vision of how architecture and the built environment inform everything that comes into contact with the design. As a result, architecture can act as a container for our experience and a metaphor for life.

I've had a lot of standard mentoring. Still, customer relationships—specifically with architects—have been the most exciting mentors because they're unique and quite different than the conventional mentor-mentee relationship. Much mutual inspiration happens in the course of our projects, as they'll have an idea that bounces back and forth between us, and soon we've developed something that we would not have otherwise considered. We have quite a creative team at GuildWorks, but I don't think we would have reached as far as we have without that dynamic collaboration with our clients. It stretches the boundaries and what is possible with the design for both parties.

Being a design-build company that pushes boundaries, we find it a mistake to underestimate the scope of what it takes to get something done. Everyone I talk to vastly underestimates the time frame. A project might seem easy and that it can be done quickly, but all these things take more resources and time than you can anticipate. It's hard to estimate correctly, and the mistake of not knowing what it's going to take to complete a project can be a significant challenge.

I've felt the impact of that mistake and learned to multiply my first evaluations to get closer to that target. We've made some big mistakes where we've lost money on projects because large projects take so much more time to finish. But we're committed to the end, so we do what it takes to successfully finish the job, even if it costs us.

I've had many business mentorships in recent years about operating a more extensive and growing business entity. When I asked myself what's the route of mentorship that's meant the most to me, I realized it was a mixture of three books and three people dating back to my years in architectural and engineering college.

Buckminster Fuller and the books he wrote influenced me, as one of my professors and another colleague were his students. I received this secondhand information from Buckminster Fuller as well as firsthand from his books. He treated his life as an experiment to see how he could benefit humanity. He didn't do very well as a businessman, but he did have brilliant ideas about transforming reality.

Reading his books, I gained many beliefs from his scientific approach—how he did his problem-solving and how he thought and looked to the base roots of issues. He thought about things in an entirely different way than most people, and his teachings deeply influenced me, particularly his ideas about innovation.

I learned to innovate more and consider the root of the innovation. What's the origin of the design? How can we change that design problem? And what can we do that hasn't been done before? This is nothing new. Society has been doing it all along with other great innovators. I felt free to innovate and push boundaries because of the great lessons and wisdom in Fuller's books and mentorship.

I've had several different mentors in the business community, including my current mentor from the school of business at Portland State University. They've all made an impact on me, and I'm not sure any particular one has had a more significant effect than the other. I keep reading and picking up different things and getting several mentorships along the way, and each has added a little piece to the puzzle of figuring out how to better manage the business.

When I mentor, I tend to see the opportunity for success with youth rather than people with a resume. I think many companies only hire from the resume, and yes, that's part of building a strong team. Still, I'm always looking to the fit of the individual and understanding their drive, passion, and innate abilities and offer the right environment and opportunity.

I like to help people who are fresh out of college or starting a career; helping them go along that road to develop this career makes sense to me. There's often a catch-22 for new graduates, where they're expected to have the experience to get a job, but they can't get that experience without having a job. I try to offer that experience and opportunity so they can overcome this hurdle.

For instance, why are the youngest people brilliant programmers? Not that I'm in the programming business, but this same sort of thing happens in design. Recently, we brought someone in from the business school to change a lot of the spreadsheets that help us run and estimate the business. He was brilliant doing some things that we had paid other expert consultants to do at a much higher dollar rate, yet they weren't able to creatively solve the way he did.

There's something in the young spirit that doesn't have the wisdom that we carry after years, and it can lead to more mistakes or not comprehending the scope of work. But there's something that comes with that kind of drive, inspiration, and freshness that isn't well-formed, and that can mean a new solution.

A number of our hires have grown successful businesses of their own after working with us for years—from specialized rigging to design, fabrication, and construction trades. In some cases, we're lucky to have ongoing relationships with them.

When I've noticed the potential in someone and was fortunate to have them on staff and see those results, that feels like success! So the way I carry it forward is to provide that opportunity for others. Giving those opportunities to people and learning from them as you mentor them is a great way to be. Being a mentor always teaches you more too; there's a dual road there that's a give-and-take.

I fit in with the business folks who are part of the makers-and-builders movement. These people are technicians and highly specialized at what they do. They're innovating new things and starting their businesses, but they don't necessarily know what it means to run a business. This group needs mentoring in basic business. Certainly, when I started, I didn't know how to start a business. An architectural education doesn't include a business side, which is challenging when so much of architecture is about business.

Amongst all the other peers in my network, when I see someone up and coming, I'll meet with them and get to know them. I'm curious when they're builders and fabricators about how much background in business they have. So I start mentoring them and introducing them to different methods I've found. I teach them how to grow their business because I certainly needed it and wished it had come when I'd been in their shoes.

If that advice and experience sharing had come to me earlier, I would have accelerated the process. Our company has been around for twenty-five years, but I feel like we're in this springboard of an emerging business the way I envisioned it when I first started. It's just taken twenty-five years to get here. I now enjoy helping others go through the steps with a little more ease and knowledge by pointing them in helpful directions.

My success goes back to my time reading Fuller, pushing boundaries and inventing new things. The success of GuildWorks has been the willingness to stay the course as a design-based company with innovative thinking and not veer off our path.

Many times, we've wondered about entering the product market. Yes, we could be more successful financially, but that's not what the GuildWorks brand is about.

GuildWorks is about being an innovative design thinking company that pushes the boundaries of the built world. We stay true to that, as hard as it seems sometimes. Now I'm seeing the success from staying committed to our brand because of the interest coming from around the world. People find us, and like that we are different than our competitors. We hold to that and don't let that get distilled through the process of running the business.

We're currently engaged in writing a book to give to architects. It's about design principles and what's possible with fabric architecture and "Architecture of the Air," as we call it. Fabric structures are an age-old form of building that dates back to tipis and Bedouin tents, but now it's enjoying a renaissance as a new style of building with modern materials and science behind the forms. It's not widely adopted into traditional architecture yet, and we want architects to see fabric as a primary building material, just like brick and stone.

This reference book will demonstrate how architects can journey into thinking about this more as a design process. Not all architecture needs to be hard and linear. When you look at the human form, we're curved, flexible, and soft. We strive to create architecture that responds to the human form and reimagine and reinvent spaces that strengthen the connection between people and the places they inhabit.

In this way, we develop a mutually beneficial collaboration where we give them some mentorship tools to think about design, and then they come to us with more exciting design possibilities that we can bring into reality.

Tom O'regan
Madison Logic
Madisonlogic.com

Madison Logic is a New York-based marketing technology organization that helps fast-growing businesses accelerate their growth and convert their best prospects faster. We help B2B organizations convert their best accounts more quickly through a platform that integrates with CRM and marketing automation and allows organizations to identify the companies and market for solutions our clients sell to.

We do what's called comprehensive account-based marketing, which is identifying the right organizations, engaging them through account-based marketing demand generation and display advertising, and yielding a significant return on investment.

The traditional mentoring that I experienced in the early parts of my career involved looking up to an executive who ran a similar business. I gained insights and knowledge from someone who's gone through challenges, failed, but ultimately succeeded. That type of mentoring was successful, but where I've seen the most impact is here at Madison Logic, where we do something called reverse mentoring.

We enable entry-level Madison Logic employees to find a mentor among the executive team, myself included. They can figure out our path to success and learn about the challenges we overcame in achieving our goals. One incredibly valuable aspect of this for me is that we then get to understand the path of people who have joined our organization within the year.

These entry-level employees are trying to figure out how to set their career paths to achieve success. What I found most interesting is how they perceive communication by myself and the executive team. We get to learn how they interpret decisions we make, and we gain an understanding of how everything we do as an executive team and an organization impacts the employees.

This has enabled me to gain a greater understanding of how the things we do impact everybody in the organization. Now that I understand that, we've altered our communication style, put in place a chief people officer, and created a culture team. We've become more transparent, opened new channels of communication, and increased the frequency of internal messages so that people in the organization not only know what we've done but also why we've made certain decisions and changes. I have seen that people in the organization now have better engagement. We're retaining more people. They understand some of the challenges that we face, but they feel good about the communication and direct feedback.

I've imparted this wisdom and experience to a lot of my CEO friends, and they've incorporated these techniques successfully at their firms. The information they're getting and the direct, honest feedback they get from people within the organization that they wouldn't otherwise hear from their executive team or peers are incredibly valuable.

This year, we've implemented objectives and key results, or OKRs. There's been a lot of talk about the benefits of OKRs vs. MBOs, or management by objective, which is less measurable. I recently read *Measure What Matters* by John Doerr, a famous venture capitalist at Kleiner Perkins. He writes about the impact that OKRs had on a fledgling Google and describes how he invested in the business early on. The executives and founders at Google implemented OKRs to manage the most specific metrics driving that business. Now there are thousands of organizations adhering to this OKR process.

Implementing OKRs at Madison Logic was a transparent process with the board, our private equity firm, and everybody at the business in the loop. Everyone at Madison Logic, myself included, has to develop and articulate their specific and personal OKRs. This way, everyone in the company knew what we were striving for and aligned their objectives to the company objectives. It's been a significant evolution, moving from more general themes and strategies to "Here's what we want to do. Everyone knows what this means for the business when we achieve these objectives, and here's how we are going to measure them every single month." We're very transparent about that.

The more traditional mentor style is you look up to someone that is more successful. Maybe they make more money, or they work in a bigger firm, and you want to figure out how they got there. That type of mentoring had been successful for me, but the opposite is equally as effective. I never knew that engaging in mentorship with someone who hasn't yet gotten to the pinnacle of their career would help me more than some of these successful executives, especially now that I've been a CEO for some years. I value the mentoring I get from the reverse mentees I have here at Madison Logic. It's rewarding to serve as a mentor to them, answer their questions, and help them figure out how to get what they want.

I hosted a breakfast two weeks ago to welcome our intern class of 2019. We had many people come in, and I told them that although they may not understand what career path they want, they can dip their toe in the waters.

I said, "Every one of you has some wants. You know where you're at, you know where you've come from, you know what you want. You must ask yourself what you're going to sacrifice to get what you want." This has had a lasting impact on the intern class. I was having lunch with my mentee today, and she began asking more about this. She told me that she had never thought about her career and her life in that way. It's changed the way she's looking at what her next role will be and what her career path could evolve into. That's something I get to do in my mentoring that's valuable; I get to see how little pieces of wisdom are making people think differently and shaping their lives.

I think that most entrepreneurs need mentoring regarding growth. Entrepreneurs need a peer group and mentors to give them support, confirmation, and validation around scale. When business scales, things break down. It gets hard to maintain high levels of growth consistently without changing and augmenting the organization. Learning from people who have gone through substantial growth phases and have scaled organizations is helpful. You're going to find out what they would've done differently, and maybe you can get some feedback around what you can do in your own situation.

I'm in the YPO, Young Professionals Organization, a group of twenty-five thousand local CEOs. The reason I joined the YPO is to be able to speak with a leadership group that is all CEOs. Whether it's multibillion-dollar companies or multimillion-dollar businesses, they're all at different levels of growth. We get to learn from them where they failed and what they failed to do. We learn how they've been able to change their organization, their leadership team, and the structure in order to put processes in place that will enable consistent growth. This is definitely an area I see entrepreneurs have a keen interest in, and it's significant.

I asked our intern class to think about where they are, how they grew up, where they want to get to, and what they want to sacrifice. If I wrote a book, it would be around what successful individuals wanted to do, what they were striving for, and what they knew they needed to sacrifice to get there. There are many aspirational individuals today who not only want to work at the best companies but also want to start and run the best companies.

Maybe they want the McLaren or the Lamborghini, or they want to be like Gary Vaynerchuk and fly around in private jets. They want to get into the 1 percent. The reality is 99 percent of people don't make the sacrifices needed to become successful, run a business, and get there. They won't put in the time, and they won't do the things that are consistent with what this level of success requires, including maybe not seeing your family as much, missing certain events, or not spending much time with friends. The book would be focused on how getting what you want involves sacrificing in some specific areas of your life, and that these sacrifices enable you to get what you want. At the end of the day, no one can have everything.

Janice Tippett
Millennium Marketing Solutions
Mm4solutions.com

I look at everybody as a mentor. I've realized, after twenty-nine years in business, that I can mentor every single one of my employees or even business associates by sharing my knowledge. When looking for a mentor, I have a lot of peer groups, specifically industry peer groups, that are excellent resources for finding a mentor. I'm a member of a women's presence organization. I'm a member of the advisory board. I look at all my interactions in these groups not in the role as an official mentor but as an opportunity to give and receive lots of little mentorship moments. I look for lessons everywhere I can.

When I was looking at the questions and read, "Who do I ask to mentor me?" I couldn't pinpoint it to one person. I sat back, looked around, then said, "Everyone and everything." I watched my father get up every day and go to work, I looked at responsibility and work ethic, and I examined every single one of my peers or customers. I learn wherever I can. Years ago, when I first started my business, I think as an entrepreneur I got in the business because I thought, "I know better, I'm independent, and I'm gonna make my own way."

Slowly, as you start to have some success, you learn even more about yourself. My sister joined me about seven years after I started my business. She came aboard as a business partner, and she's nine years older than me and had worked more than twenty years in the government. So she brought a different background to the business, where I had started at age twenty-one.

She said to me one day when I was getting frustrated with the employees, "Janice, your job is to lead, guide, and inspire." I took that to heart, so now with my employees, I try to say in every interaction, "How can I learn from them? How can I inspire them? How can I guide them?" I don't want to be their boss. If I need to roll up my sleeves and sit side by side with them to get a project done, I will do it. Then I lead by example. That is how I can guide them and inspire them.

On the other hand, I also don't have one specific person that has to come to me and said, "Will you mentor me?" I look at all my employees with the mindset, "How can I mentor them?" It's wonderful when you can get these little diamonds, and I have one right now who's amazingly smart and has the right amount of drive personally and professionally. It's fun to be able to lead her and guide her and inspire her. I help her figure out what her goals in life and her career are. That's been a cool experience. That's a long answer to a short question.

You could say that we have an informal mentoring program at my company. It's not intentional, but it happens. My directors, my leaders—we all have the same mindset. What books should we read? What can we attend? How can we inspire the ones around us? What blogs are they reading? What podcasts are they listening to? My leaders and I know that we're only as good as the people we attract to our team to surround ourselves. We also mentor our customers. Owning a marketing agency gives us opportunities to communicate with a lot of different types of customers and customers' employees. We believe in mentoring them. We do a lot of webwork and a lot of design and printing and strategy and promo. Every job is custom, and so the person we're dealing with on the other side may not be in a position where they're knowledgeable, so we believe in mentoring our customers.

When you run a business, it's not only about your customers and employees. It's also about having good relationships with your vendors and even mentoring them with knowledge. They help my business in turn because I resell products and resell services. They help me be better. I guess it's everywhere I go. I'm always asking, "Who can I learn from and how can I help somebody else learn?"

I walk around my building every morning, and I engage with every single employee. I have about thirty-five employees, and it takes some time, but I check in with each of them. It might be a simple hello, or I might ask something about what's going on in their personal life. "How did your daughter's recital go last night?" as an example. Then I check in about business items. What tools are they learning? Where are they on a project? Is there any help that they need? I find out if I need to get a peer to help them with something or a vendor to come in and explain some stuff. I want to find out which roadblocks they might be experiencing and how I can help them. Or maybe I can get one of the other leaders to help.

We also have formal meetings and strategy sessions. They're like think tanks, and we do them about once a month. Everyone brings in their knowledge, and we all can share. Nobody's the only expert—we're all experts—and we're all encouraged to bring something that we have learned and might be of interest.

For my personal experience with mentorship, I have to go back again to the peer groups. The women's presence organization contains women that are presidents or senior executives of corporations that are in the same price range in their geographic area. We are noncompeting and geographically located, so we can meet every month and share challenges. We also share successes and resources. As an owner of a business, it can be lonely, so you need that support. Your friends and family don't understand the challenges you're going through. But the peer group—they do. So you can call them up and mentor each other through those challenges.

If I had to pick one book that has influenced me, I would choose the good old *E-Myth Revisited*. I think many people get into business because they think, "I can do it better." Then you realize you're at capacity. Now that I'm at capacity, how do I scale? How do I survive? How do I keep growing?

You gotta delegate.

However, I guess mentally I also have had to get to the point where even though I enjoy them, I admire them, and they're good people, even though I'm leading and trying to inspire them, it might not be the right fit.

The best thing I can do for them as a leader and a mentor is to help them by making that decision for them. They need to move on and find a better fit. I'm not the answer for everybody, so I sometimes need to set them free to find that better job opportunity. My big mistake was not realizing that and trying to put a square peg into a round hole. That's hard from an interpersonal perspective. It's uncomfortable. Hopefully, then, they do go out and find a better opportunity and they look back and say, "Okay, that was the push I needed."

The little diamonds you have in your business are a different story. The way we mentor them involves taking the extra time to make sure they understand the thought process behind what we're doing. Instead of just working with them on the project, I spend one-on-one time and give them the background of why we're doing something so that they can understand the bigger picture. If they need extra tools, I find out what those extra tools are and give them extra access to other leaders.

You're grooming them to move up someday. One important piece of that requires that you understand what their goals are—not just career goals, but also personal goals. I feel like in today's world that we don't encourage people enough to actually set personal goals. I feel like anytime you can help instill an understanding of setting personal goals, that's probably one of the best things you can do.

In a company like us with certain diamonds, certain rock stars, we might not have a position where they can go any further. If they feel comfortable through sharing personal goals, they can then hopefully work on a transition plan together if it is time for them to move on. It is worth building strong relationships with them even though they sometimes leave because hopefully, your paths will stay connected somehow. You can't burn bridges with the way social media is today. If it's a positive relationship, and every conversation is a mentor-mentee one—coaching, leading, guiding, and inspiring—you then make their long-term goals part of the conversation. If they decide to leave, can you help them with your connections? Likewise, with their connections, can they go out and find a possible replacement for their position while you help them?

That's how I wish things will be with each employee that chooses to move on.

It takes money to invest in a business. In my business, a lot of people come to us and say, "Hey, I'm starting this X business, and I need marketing. I need a logo. I need a website. I need this." Then they say, "I don't have a lot of money…but once I start making money, then I'll come back and pay you more." It seems silly, but that's how people think. I always say it's like opening a retail store but not putting "Open" on your sign or a sign above the door. If you're not marketing, nobody is gonna know what your business is.

In 1990 when I started my business, I got a $10,000 loan from a friend's husband who ran a CPA firm. It was $10,000 at 17 percent interest, and I was twenty-one years old, and at that time, all I could buy was the original Macintosh computer. It had five fonts. So we had five fonts on one computer and a 300 dpi printer that was the size of a bus and weighed as much as a bus.

That's what I started with, but that's a lot of money to a twenty-one-year-old. In my first year in business, I made $14,000. That's all I made. I think a lot of people try and get into business with no startup capital, no understanding of the importance of marketing, and no understanding of how to reinvest cash back into their business. It goes back to personal goals. One of mine was someday to own my own building. I was fortunate enough to accomplish that about fourteen years ago. I was able to purchase my own building.

Goals aren't enough by themselves. I wanted X, but then what was the plan? You need personal and professional goals, and then you make the plan. I wanted a business where I wasn't responsible for generating every dollar that I made at the end of the year. When I started my business, it was me alone at first. Then for the next couple of years, it was me and two other designers. I was making good money, but every dollar I made I had to generate myself. I was basically a solopreneur, but I wanted to have a business that generated money with or without me. So then I needed a plan. What did that look like, and how did that get established? Which people did I need? What services? How much capital?

Then I purchased a printing company, and that took me to the next level. It was a small little print shop, and I purchased that for $400,000. I had to put a fair amount down, but the former owner financed it. You are searching for opportunities and then going after those when you find them.

Recently, we've been getting a lot of website jobs where clients have gone with a less-expensive provider, and that provider has delivered them a website. It's a functioning website. There are pictures and content, but when you look at the website, there's no clear statement about the company. The marketing part of the website is missing. It needs to quickly tell the visitor, "This is who the company is, this is what we do, this is who we serve, and here is how to contact us or here's the call to action I want you to take."

The technical side of building a site is a minor piece of the process. The most important is the story behind the company. Does the website tell the story?

To be an entrepreneur, you must learn marketing, and there's a lot of marketing tools. You can do it yourself, but I would never have owned my own building if I didn't partner with a banker and an accountant. I decided and told them, "I want a building." I worked with my banker, my accountant, an attorney, and a broker for a long time before everything came together. It was about a three-year process. You have to find the right partners. They will help you. Hiring quality professionals will make you money. In a way, they are mentoring you as they work with you.

Mentoring shows up in so many forms.

CONCLUSION

We sincerely hope you have enjoyed your access to 1,750 years of business leadership experience.

What—how does that work out?

(Our criteria for finding entrepreneurs to interview for our book was that they have 25 years' worth of experience leading a company—and 70 X 25 equals 1,750 years!)

That's a lot of mentoring knowledge!

In sharing their views and personal experiences around finding mentorship when it was needed, our leaders have proven that mentorship is readily available anywhere and everywhere.

We hope our leaders have encouraged you to look around and consider the many avenues to finding mentors for yourself. Perhaps your family members can teach you what to do—or even not what to do. (Learning from the mistakes of others is just as helpful as learning what to do.)

Look around your community, and see which organizations you can join—those that include business leaders. Meeting folks in your community can put you in a natural position to meet their networks and contacts and grow your scope of influence.

Within your places of employment, if you don't have a structured mentorship program in place, consider which of your coworkers might have the time and interest to mentor you. As we've learned from the leaders in this book, mentors are on every level: higher-ups, lateral coworkers, and even younger mentees.

Your contacts within your company can easily lead you straight to your clients. What can you learn from those you are in business to serve? We've learned that you don't have to be in the same industry as mentorship crosses barriers and is often applicable across the board.

Everyone has something to teach, and everyone has something to learn.

Are you more the type to find mentorship elsewhere? Our leaders have shared how individual books have been instrumental in their journeys. Don't have time to read? Consider listening to podcasts and audiobooks.

We've learned from this fantastic group of 70 entrepreneurs and leaders how mentorship has been crucial to developing their paths to success. Whether you find mentorship among family, community, coworkers, clients, books, or even your mentees, all aspects of mentorship will be priceless for your entrepreneurial journey.

ARE YOU A LEADER WITHOUT A BOOK?

Nothing increases your authority and visibility as powerfully as a book.

It's a cash-generating asset that funnels in clients for your business and allows you to tell your story the way you want it to be told.

At Leaders Press (a *Wall Street Journal* bestselling press), we've developed a process that allows you to get your book out without you ever having to write a word.

It's featured in *Entrepreneur* magazine and all our books produced this way are bestsellers!

Discover how you can quickly and painlessly get your book out and put together an extra revenue stream!

Download your free copy of *Outsource Your Book* at www.leaderspress.com now!

Download it for free at www.leaderspress.com

ABOUT THE AUTHOR:

ALINKA RUTKOWSKA is a USA Today best-selling author, a Wall Street Journal best-selling author and a top 100 Amazon best-selling author in business and money. She's sold more than 100,000 copies of her books and her book creation process has been showcased in Entrepreneur magazine.

She's the CEO of Leaders Press, and has launched all its titles to best-seller status. She's the founder of LibraryBub, which connects independent authors with around 10,000 librarians. She's a sought after lecturer and has been voted top 5 speaker and named most creative book marketer at the Bestseller Summit Online.

She's been featured on ABC, NBC, CBS, Fox Business, Writer's Digest, Alliance of Independence Authors, International Book Publishers' Association and many more.

LEADERS PRESS (www.leaderspress.com) is a USA Today and Wall Street Journal best-selling press, which creates books for entrepreneurs from scratch and launches them to best-seller with a 100% success rate.

It has landed its releases on bookshelves together with Nobel Prize winners and World Economic Forums speakers.

The Leaders Press team has worked with top business leaders such as Po Chung (the co- founder of DHL International), Mark Nureddine (the CEO of Bull Outdoor Products) and Chris Catranis (the founder of Babylon Telecommunications).

Their mission is to help 1,000 entrepreneurs share their wisdom with the world by 2030.

INDEX

A

Ameet Shah	20
Alexander Kutyrev	26
Adam Phillips	73
Alan Barlis	267
Avetis Antaplyan	318
Angela Hurt	340
Anthony Mora	353

B

Bryon Beilman	279

C

Catherine and Leo Zupan	29
Chris McCurry	114
Cory Capoccia	166
Cameron Herold	309

D

Don Zerivitz	109
David Merrell	144
David Dangle	201
Dan Malven	289
David Spaulding	347

E

Erik Kaeyer	60
Erick McCallum	87
Ernest Freeland	221

G

Gordon Gronkowski	216

H

Hans Keirstead	3
Helen Feber	284

I

Ian Kaiser	43

J

Jonathan Rubinsztein	36
Joel Butterly	49
Justin Bakes	70
John Aronson	94
Joe Dinoffer	126
Jacopo Bracco	152
Joshua Hebert	174
Jim Bellas	324
Jeff Eisenberg	332
Janice Tippett	403

K

Kevin Wilkins	55
Katie Fleming	122
Kathy Stack	207
Kevin Duncan	229
Kevin Collins	245
Kent Kelley	385

L

Lynne Waymon	140
Lauren Asghari	209
Lawrence Farrar	225

M

Maryann Donovan	81
Mary Feury	103
Mark Moses	148
Michael Heinrich	156
Michael Allen	231
Melissa Gonzalez	293
Matthew Kornau	390
Mar Ricketts	394

O

Ofer Hubar	162

P

Paroon Chadha	375

T

Teresa Carew	15
Tyson McDowell	191
Tom Hillman	271
Tedde Van Gelderen	300
Todd Sager	364
Tom O'regan	399

R

Rob Lobreglio	130
Rochelle Kopp	134
Rob Hoyt	239

S

Sherry Orel	180
Scott Swartz	250
Steve Mersky	256
Steve Spain	263
Sukhbir Dhillon	359

www.ingramcontent.com/pod-product-compliance
Lightning Source LLC
Chambersburg PA
CBHW031558110426
42742CB00036B/132